POLITICS AND GOVERNMENT

POLITICS

AND

GOVERNMENT

A BRIEF INTRODUCTION

ALEX N. DRAGNICH
Vanderbilt University

JOHN T. DORSEY, JR.
Vanderbilt University

TAKETSUGU TSURUTANI
Washington State University

CHATHAM HOUSE PUBLISHERS, INC.
Chatham, New Jersey

POLITICS AND GOVERNMENT
A Brief Introduction

CHATHAM HOUSE PUBLISHERS, INC.
Post Office Box One
Chatham, New Jersey 07928-0001

PUBLISHER: Edward Artinian
DESIGNER: Quentin Fiore
COMPOSITION: Chatham Composer
PRINTING AND BINDING: Hamilton Printing Company

LIBRARY OF CONGRESS CATALOGING IN PUBLICATION DATA

Dragnich, Alex N.
    Politics and government.

    Bibliography: p.
    Includes index.
    1. Comparative government. I. Dorsey,
John T.   II. Tsurutani, Taketsugu.   III. Title.
JF51.D7   320.3   81-21726
ISBN 0-934540-13-6 (pbk.)   AACR2

Manufactured in the United States of America

10   9   8   7   6   5   4   3   2   1

Contents

Preface

This brief book is different, and we hope that it will open new vistas to students who are beginning to learn about government and politics in countries other than their own. Ultimately, they will be the ones to judge if we have succeeded. Before they begin the study of the various political systems, however, they should read the few introductory pages that follow, which are designed as a type of compass to point the way we propose to go, the objectives we hope to reach, and some of the problems or difficulties that may be encountered.

Professor Tsurutani wrote the chapter on Japan and Professor Dorsey wrote the one on Politics in the Third World. Professor Dragnich wrote the remaining chapters. All three of us collaborated on the introduction.

We wish to express appreciation to two of our colleages—Bernard E. Brown and Daniel R. Grant—for permission to borrow some phraseology from two chapters of an earlier collaborative effort. We are, of course, entirely responsible for what is in this book.

Introduction

The aim of this book is to provide useful and substantive knowledge about the political world to students who know very little about it or how to proceed learning about it. It is not a first course in professional training for prospective academic political scientists, but an "eye-opening" work for all students, whatever their disciplinary specialization or career plans. It is, in short, a book about government and politics in several selected countries having differing political systems, plus a final chapter that is largely concerned with problems of establishing viable political systems in the less well developed countries.

The number of political entities, variously called countries, nations, or states, existing today approximates 150. They vary considerably in geographic size, population, natural resources, and in technological and economic development. They are held together by a number of factors, among them being race, language, and attachment (a sense of belonging) to a particular piece of territory, and some common stock of shared beliefs (ideology)—all of which contribute to the people's rendering habitual obedience to a common political authority.

There are some exceptions to what has just been said, particularly in certain of the newer nations where significant segments of the population fail to render habitual obedience simply because they do not recognize a common authority. Such situations are not new; history abounds with examples. The best known to American students are the Revolution of 1776 and the American Civil War. Divisive situations exist to a degree in a number of well-established nations, for example Northern Ireland in Great Britain, Quebec in Canada, and the Flemish in Belgium. Consequently, some of our generalizations in the preceding paragraph are just that—generalizations—to which there are exceptions. And political scientists are far from agreement as to the mix of ingredients necessary for a binding political cement.

The modern nation-state, which really came into being only in the seventeenth century, is the political unit that commands the people's highest allegiance. In the era of the nation-state, people have been willing to fight and die for it; no city, province, or other geographic unit has commanded a comparable allegiance. This does not apply, of course, to those exceptions referred to above, where local or regional loyalties (for whatever reason) are in effect un-realized aspirations to nationhood.

Political scientists are interested in the form of government a given coun-try has. In the process, they ask at least three broad questions: (1) What are the purposes of government (ends of politics); (2) what do governments do (func-tions of politics); and (3) who exercises political power (processes of politics)? Each of the systems discussed in this book, by its very nature, tends to answer the first question. Generally speaking, democratic systems view the end of pol-itics to be the provision, protection, or preservation of an atmosphere or social climate in which individuals may freely seek to realize their personal or collec-tive aspirations. On the other hand, some dictatorships, notably the commu-nist ones, view the purposes of government to be the realization of certain goals that their ideology may envisage. Most of the discussion in the chapters that follow deals with the last two questions, particularly the final one. These questions are related and difficult to disentangle, but they do lead to the con-cept of political systems, the comparative analysis of which is the oldest and most honorable tradition of political science, going back to Aristotle over two thousand years ago.

Political systems have come into being and have evolved as a result of a complex combination of circumstances—basic beliefs and attitudes concern-ing human beings and their Creator, the influence of natural resources and other historical conditions or accidents, as well as the political ingenuity of those who rose to positions of leadership. While we cannot ignore the ques-tion of how political systems came to be what they are, the emphasis in this book is on seeking to understand how they function today.

Political systems are somewhat like living organisms in that they change over time. More accurately, political systems are what the political actors (government officials and those who choose to influence them) make them, but political actors cannot always do as they wish. In large measure they are constrained and conditioned by the acts of those who preceded them and the traditions and usages passed on by previous generations generally. Hence changes in political systems are, in large part at least, controlled and guided by forces beyond the sole powers of any set of generational political actors.

In a sense, it can be said that every political system changes or evolves (unless it is destroyed) according to shifting interactions between the forces of tradition and the imperatives of the changing environment, and between the creative-innovative impulse of political forces (leaders and parties) and cultur-al inertia (i.e., society's resistance to change).

One could argue that each political system is a creature of unpredictable combinations of circumstances, in some cases fortuitous and in others not or less so, such as the influence of tradition, the cultural predilection of the multitude, the perception of urgency and the capacity of the people to respond, the ideology and the skill of the political elite, as well as the material endowment and the technological development of the society. To a degree, it is the uniqueness of the combination in a crucial moment in the development of a given nation-state that renders its system distinct in the nature of political authority, in the quality of popular support, in the extent of its institutional integrity, in the manner of its functioning, and in the range and kinds of tangible and intangible benefits it confers upon the people.

One interesting consequence is that combinations of circumstances have produced some political systems that are similar to and some that are different from one another. At the same time, it is important to remember that in the case of most states political boundaries are rarely congruent with cultural, technological, or economic bases of cohesion. National boundaries have often resulted from military conquest, without much consideration for ethnic, economic, or similar factors. Moreover, structures of political authority are likely to be based on a combination of force and fear, habit and convention, identification and consent. Additionally, functional arrangements for securing governmental services vary among developed as well as between more and less modernized countries. Finally, differences between political systems are real, as one could observe if he or she were to live for a time in a religious theocracy and then move to a military oligarchy, or to live first in a constitutional republic and then move to a totalitarian dictatorship. At the same time, in a certain sense all political systems perform similar functions:*protection* from the forces of lawlessness; *economic services* such as a stable currency system, postal services, and sanitation disposal; and *institutions* for resolving disputes.

In the selection of political systems to write about we have been somewhat arbitrary, but our choices have not been random. In chapter 1 we treat Great Britain and the United States, which are said to have *homogeneous* political cultures (attitudes toward and values concerning politics, political leaders, and governmental processes) but somewhat differing systems of democratic government. In each there has been an acceptance of their respective political systems for a relatively long period of time. The one is described as cabinet government and the other as presidential government. The chapter also has a brief section on the government and politics of Canada, partly because of similarities (as well as differences) with Great Britain and the United States. In chapter 2 we take a comparative look at France and Germany, which are often referred to as having *fragmented* political cultures, and as examples of continental parliamentary democracies. In each, in contrast with Britain and the United States, there have been, for a relatively long time, sharp disagreements as to the acceptance of their respective political systems, contributing to a lack of stability. Only in recent decades have the systems in these two states gained fairly general acceptance.

In chapter 3 we deal with the best known of the communist systems, the Soviet Union, with some considerations of the Chinese and Yugoslavian variations. In chapter 4 we examine the political system of Japan, a non-Western developed nation embarked upon a new experiment in democracy. Economically powerful and culturally unique, Japan is the only advanced industrial democracy in a largely undemocratic non-Western world. In chapter 5 we consider, in broad outline, the political systems of the developing (or Third World) nations, a large number of whom gained independence only after the Second World War, although some are relatively old states. The large number of developing or modernizing societies, the similarity of their problems, and the probable impact of what happens in them on the more advanced societies — all are singular reasons for treating them in this book. By dealing with these societies, moreover, we are able to give to our introduction to politics and government a much broader perspective than would otherwise be the case.

We believe that our choice of political systems is at once fairly broad and representative. It constitutes a good beginning for anyone seeking a general introduction to comparative politics, as well as for anyone interested in an introductory approach to politics or the study of political science generally. Because several chapters each treat more than one political system, we believe that the result is a more genuinely comparative presentation.

In each of the chapters we discuss constitutions, their history and evolution, and the substance of their provisions, as well as present practice. Also, we examine the social forces that are contending for influence if not predominance. We identify major interest groups, their aims, their organizations, and how they seek to attain their goals. Next we consider political party systems, the nature and number of parties, how they are organized, how they seek support, and how they accept responsibility for governing. Finally, we deal with governmental institutions, their nature, powers or functions, and their relations to one another and to the public. In the end, we make some observations on the systems in action, their performance in the task of governing as well as their difficulties and failings, and their future promise.

Each chapter is followed by a list of selected works as suggestions for additional reading. We have attempted to choose substantive books, as well as seeking to pick those that concern themselves with various aspects of a political system. At the same time, we have endeavored to include some that are reasonably up to date and thus reflect contemporary developments.

1. Presidential and Parliamentary Systems: The United States, Great Britain, and Canada

The United States and Great Britain are both political democracies in the sense that decisions about public policies are made by popularly elected officials. Yet there are significant differences as to how these two systems are organized and the manner in which they function. The nature of these differences will become clear as we proceed in this chapter.

At the outset it may be useful to note that the United States is called a republic and Great Britain a monarchy. In the former case the head of state is popularly elected, whereas in the latter he or she comes to that position by heredity. In Britain, however, the head of state has no real political power; that power is exercised by the head of government (i.e., by the Prime Minister and colleagues). In the United States, the President is both head of state and head of government. The U.S. system is generally referred to as *presidential government,* suggesting that the President is the central or dominant figure in the American system, from whom leadership initiatives and management functions emanate. This was not always so. Good evidence of this is to be found in the title of Woodrow Wilson's doctoral dissertation, *Congressional Government* (1888), in which he pointed out that Congress was at the center of the American system. Be it noted that Wilson and other strong Presidents in this century played the major role in the change that has taken place.

The British system has also changed; today it is generally referred to as *cabinet government,* indicating that the Cabinet is the dominant institution in that system. Much earlier, Britain was an absolute monarchy. Subsequently, as Parliament gained supremacy, the British system was commonly designated as parliamentary government, a term that is still applicable in differentiating it from the U.S. system. The term is also still appropriate, as will be explained below, in that the Cabinet must have the confidence of Parliament (House of Commons) in order to stay in office. In recent years, because of increased powers of the Prime Minister, who has in any case normally been the dominant figure in the Cabinet, some British writers have described their system as "prime ministerial government."

The Constitutions

Modern democratic constitutions may be said to consist of the sum total of the basic rules, written and unwritten, that establish orderly political processes and provide for effective restraints on the exercise of political power. Constitutions allocate powers and in general define the spheres of governmental activity. They prescribe limitations on government, both in the form of certain prohibitions that safeguard basic freedoms from curtailment by government and in the form of procedural safeguards that force the government to exercise its powers in conformity with certain rules or principles that are considered just and fair. Viewed in this light, modern democratic constitutions serve to limit political power and to channel its exercise.

The constitutions of modern democratic states consist of several elements, the most obvious of which is a written document actually called the constitution. Of nearly equal importance—in some countries even more so—are certain basic statutes, binding judicial interpretations, and customs or precedents that have become an integral part of a nation's political practices.

The American and British constitutions are both democratic, yet are considerably different in the manner they were framed and in the ways their contents appear to us. In their substance—the popular choice of leaders, the guarantee of civil liberties, and the control of governmental processes—they are very much alike, in that they provide for a democratic form of government.

The British constitution is the result of centuries of slow growth. Its development began with the first successful efforts to limit the powers of the monarchy, proceeding to the point where Parliament (originally a judicial institution) was recognized as supreme in an actual or eventual confrontation. The monarch still appointed his ministers, through whom he governed, but increasingly found it difficult and ultimately impossible to do so unless the ministers commanded the confidence of Parliament. At that time Parliament was not a popularly chosen legislature, but in subsequent decades the lower house, the House of Commons, was democratized. Progressively its members were popularly elected, and in the process the House of Commons gained ascendancy over the upper house, the House of Lords.

The U.S. Constitution, on the other hand, was consciously framed at one time by a constitutional convention. The Constitution was based in part on the experience of self-government in the colonies and in part on the writings of English and French democratic thinkers. The framers were also considerably influenced by the weaknesses of the Articles of Confederation, the first constitution of the newly independent colonies. In short, they had to create a political system that would unify the colonies, providing for a national government that would not be weak and at the same time would be limited, while reserving maximum power for the states.

There was no real sense of unity among the American colonists until the years immediately preceding the Revolutionary War, when controversy with the mother country developed and the end of the French presence in Canada removed the most compelling need for British protection. Until then the colonists' loyalty had been to the British Crown and to their own colonies, but not to America. When the fighting began, however, the new "states" replaced their colonial charters with constitutions containing strong statements of popular sovereignty, bills of rights, and severe limitations on the power of government generally. This understandable but extreme reaction to their recent experience with strong government resulted in weak government bordering on anarchy, both within and among the new states.

The national government provided by the Articles of Confederation in 1781 was even weaker than the state governments. Though it rested on a written constitution and managed to preserve at least the idea of unity, it lacked such fundamental powers as the taxing power and the power to regulate interstate and foreign commerce. It could not require the states to honor either their own commitments or those made by Congress, and probably basic to all its other weaknesses, it could not pass laws applying directly to the individual citizen. Furthermore, the Articles provided no executive branch or national judiciary; required unanimity among the states for passage of amendments; and gave each state one vote in Congress, with members of Congress being appointed and recalled by their state governments.

Under such a regime, economic and political conditions within and between the states grew increasingly chaotic. Against this background of weak government and domestic difficulties, the radicals who had been so prominent in the Revolution began to lose power. The conservatives—property owners, creditors, shippers, and "solid citizens" generally—began to talk of ways of strengthening the Union, protecting property rights, and promoting business development. Eventually, representatives from five states, meeting in convention at Annapolis in 1786, petitioned Congress to call a convention of delegates from all the states to meet in Philadelphia in May 1787 "for the sole and express purpose of revising the Articles of Confederation."

Although the convention had been called only to "revise" the Articles, the 55 attending delegates (out of 74 appointed) soon concluded that a wholly new charter had to be drafted; that "a national government ought to be established consisting of a supreme legislative, executive, and judiciary." The days that followed were devoted in large measure in working out the three famous compromises. The first, the so-called Connecticut or Great Compromise, was a compromise between large and small states over representation in Congress. The Virginia Plan had favored the large states by basing a state's representation on population; the New Jersey Plan would have given each state equal representation in spite of population. The deadlock was broken with a proposal for a bicameral legislature with a lower house based on population and an upper house in which each state would have an equal vote. The large states considered this to be a serious setback, but finally accepted it as the small states' price for union.

The second or Three-Fifths Compromise ended a dispute between North and South over how to count slaves for purposes of representation in the lower house. To increase their quotas in Congress, the southern states wanted to count slaves; the northern states, having few slaves, did not. At the same time the question of counting slaves for purposes of apportioning direct taxes was involved, with southern states now opposing their inclusion. The resulting compromise made use of a practical, if less than humane, formula, previously used by Congress in requesting funds from the states: A slave was counted as three-fifths of a free person, for purposes of both representation and taxation.

The third compromise also grew out of North-South differences. Southerners feared the possibility that their predominantly agricultural interests might suffer at the hands of a northern majority in the passage of export duties, the negotiation of unfavorable treaties of trade and commerce, and even the abolition of the importation of slaves. The northern states, in turn, were keenly interested in having a government with full power to regulate trade and navigation, levy import and export duties, and ultimately to eliminate the infamous African slave trade. The outcome was a compromise that gave Congress broad powers to regulate interstate and foreign commerce and to levy duties on imports but not exports, and that forbade prohibition of the importation of slaves before 1808. In addition, the southern delegates secured as further protection the requirement of a two-thirds majority of the Senate for consent to the ratification of treaties.

But in understanding the politics of constitution making it is perhaps more important to examine the areas of *consensus* among the delegates than it is to look at the well-publicized conflicts and compromises. The general conservatism of the delegates was reflected in substantial agreement that the right to vote should not be extended to those who did not own property and the establishment of voting requirements should be left to the states. The concepts of a written constitution and of limited government were not subjects for debate, even by those few delegates who favored a monarch. Similarly, there was no real conflict on the basic principle of federalism. Finally, the framers were in strong agreement that provision for stability and balance in government was far more important than provision for change. This consensus is reflected in the various checks and balances built into the system to ensure that no single interest would prevail over others. The separation of the executive, legislative, and judicial powers and the provision of a difficult method of amending the Constitution were the product of a conscious effort to promote stability.

Even though the framers of the Constitution departed from the rule of unanimity prescribed by the Articles of Confederation for the passage of amendments and called for approval by only 9 of 13 states, ratification was by no means assured. The outcome in such important states as Virginia and New York was very doubtful, even after 9 other states had ratified. A close victory in Massachusetts was won only after the opposition of Samuel Adams and John Hancock had been cleverly appeased and the passage of a series of amendments to protect individual rights (the Bill of Rights) was promised. Virginia's ratification came after a debate between two groups of delegates that were almost as illustrious as those in the Constitutional Convention. New York became the eleventh state to ratify, but its two-vote margin came only after a masterful campaign by Alexander Hamilton, John Jay, and James Madison, who wrote a series of essays that have come to be known as *The Federalist*. The 85 essays, published in the leading New York newspapers, have since been hailed by historians as one of the most profound pieces on government ever written. North Carolina ratified in 1789, and Rhode Island made the Union complete in the spring of 1790.

The American Constitution is extremely brief, as written constitutions go, and comes closer to the idea of being concerned only with "fundamentals" than do most modern constitutions. There are, of course, unwritten provisions of the Constitution that have come to be accepted simply through habit, custom, and the mere passage of time. Political parties have become an indispensable part of the basic rules of the game, but they are nowhere mentioned in the Constitution. Although the framers of the Constitution considered the electoral college a brilliant invention, it has not functioned as they intended since as early as 1796. Other important institutions that are the product of custom are the President's cabinet, legislative committees, and the tradition that the members of the House of Representatives must be residents of the districts from which they are elected.

The basic characteristics of the American Constitution may be summarized as follows:

1. *Popular sovereignty.* Sovereignty — supreme power residing in the people — runs through the Constitution, although it is not always clear what powers are vested in the national government and what powers are reserved for the states. The controversy between national and state rights over nullification and secession is related to this question, and the nationalists won only after the bloodshed of the Civil War.

2. *Representative government.* The Constitution provides for a representative system, rather than pure or direct democracy. Although the initiative, referendum, and recall are used in varying degrees in state and local governments and although town meetings continue to be held in parts of New England, the pattern for the nation as a whole is one of government by elected representatives.

3. *A federal system.* This involves the distribution of powers between the national government, which was given delegated or enumerated powers, and the individual states. Technically speaking, "federal government" refers to the whole governmental system, including national and state governments, and it is incorrect to use the term "federal" to designate only the national level. In common American usage, however, in such terms as "federal courts," "federal administrators," and "federal Congress," "federal" refers to the central government.

4. *Separation of powers.* The separation of powers is a functional division among the executive, legislative, and judicial branches of the national government.

5. *Checks and balances.* Congress is checked by the existence of two houses, by presidential veto, and by judicial review. The President is checked by the rights of the Senate to approve treaties and certain appointments; and by judicial review. The judicial branch is checked by presidential appointment of judges and by the congressional power to impeach and to determine the size and appellate jurisdiction of the courts.

6. *Supremacy of the national government.* With the near anarchy of the Articles of Confederation fresh in their minds, the delegates to the Constitutional Convention placed the authority to settle jurisdictional conflicts between the national and state governments in the hands of the national government, specifying that the Constitution, acts of Congress, and treaties are the "supreme law of the land."

7. *Judicial review.* The right of the courts to declare acts of Congress unconstitutional has been exercised almost since the beginning of America's history as a nation — since 1803, in fact, when in the case of

Marbury v. *Madison* the Supreme Court first declared that an act of Congress violated the Constitution. The fact that the Constitution does not specifically grant the power of judicial review has made the practice the subject of considerable controversy through the years. But the power claimed for the judiciary in *Marbury* v. *Madison* has never been effectively challenged.

Great Britain is a constitutional monarchy in which the monarch exercises only such limited powers as the constitution prescribes. Formally speaking, all acts of government are performed in His (or Her) Majesty's name, but real political power is exercised by persons responsible to popularly elected representatives assembled in Parliament. Nor may the king or queen veto any act of Parliament.

This state of affairs is the end result of the transition from a more or less absolute monarchy to parliamentary democracy, a transition accomplished over a period of several centuries. Initially, Parliament was a gathering of non-elected feudal representatives who assembled to vote taxes required by the king. Its power evolved from successful efforts to present petitions to the king and to originate bills providing for expenditures and the raising of revenue. By the fifteenth century, Parliament had gained control over finance. But monarchs were slow in relinquishing power, with the result that there was a severe struggle over the relation of king to Parliament during most of the seventeenth century. In the course of this struggle the doctrine of the divine right of kings was proclaimed, the Stuarts were driven from the throne, civil war erupted, republicanism was tried, and monarchy restored. The whole process culminated in the so-called bloodless revolution of 1688, which brought to the throne William and Mary, who readily acknowledged the supremacy of Parliament. Since that time, the power and influence of the monarchy have steadily declined, and no monarch has challenged the supremacy of Parliament.

In practice, parliamentary supremacy has meant that the monarch appoints the heads of the important government departments (ministries) from among persons acceptable to Parliament. In other words, ministers must be selected from the political party or faction that can manage or has the confidence of Parliament, or more precisely of the House of Commons (i.e., the political party that commands a majority in the Commons). This body of the king's advisers (ministers), who came to be known collectively as the Cabinet, became in effect a committee of the majority party in Parliament.

A further development was the requirement that ministers resign whenever they met with an adverse vote, or a vote of no confidence, in the House of Commons. The phenomenon, known as *ministerial responsibility,* developed in the first part of the eighteenth century, although it was not until 1782 that responsibility became *collective,* in other words, that the defeat of one minister meant the defeat of the whole Cabinet. Subsequently the Cabinet acquired an alternative to resignation: the power to dissolve the House of Commons to ascertain, through new elections, whether or not the electorate's opinions were accurately represented by the House.

The source of political leadership in Britain, therefore, is the Cabinet. It is chosen from Parliament, or more precisely, from the political party having a majority in the House of Commons. The Cabinet is the real executive; it formulates policy and is collectively responsible for it and the way it is administered.

During the time that Parliament was gaining ascendency over the monarch, and subsequently when the principle of ministerial responsibility was being established, Parliament was anything but a democratic body. Even the members of the elected house, the Commons, were not democratically chosen. The democratization of Parliament, begun in 1832, culminated in the establishment of universal suffrage in 1928. The Reform Act of 1832 redistributed seats in the Commons to take into account the shift of population (occasioned by the Industrial Revolution) from the rural regions to the growing industrial towns. The act also extended the suffrage, nearly doubling the number of eligible voters. In 1867 a new Reform Act added nearly a million voters to the rolls and provided for a further redistribution of seats. In 1872 the secret ballot was introduced. In 1884 there was another redistribution of seats and a further extension of the suffrage, followed by an act designed to suppress corrupt practices. The process was continued with the extension of the franchise to all adult males in 1918 and to all adult women ten years later. Enfranchisement of large numbers of young people, through lowering the voting age to eighteen (in 1969), is the most recent step in this long process.

The broadening of the suffrage was perhaps the single most important constitutional development in nineteenth-century Britain. Its effect was to base political power on popular election, and thus to make political leadership accountable to a free electorate. Political power had passed from the monarch to Parliament and from Parliament to the party organizations that competed for a majority of seats in the House of Commons.

As parliament became more democratic, the power and influence of the Commons increased, while that of the upper chamber, the House of Lords, declined. After 1850 no Cabinet regarded an adverse vote in the upper house as requiring a confidence vote in the Commons. A test of power was precipitated, however, by the Lords' defeat of the budget in 1909. Following the election of 1910, in which the power of the Lords was the main issue, the struggle was resolved in favor of the Commons. The Parliament Act of 1911 stipulated that money bills must become law within thirty days whether the Lords act on them favorably or unfavorably or not at all; in the case of other bills, the Lords could delay action for as much as two years (reduced to one year by the Parliament Act of 1949). Although the House of Lords may still effect changes in legislation, it no longer is an equal partner with the Commons in the legislative process. In any test of wills, the Commons must prevail.

The British constitution is not written down in one document. Rather, the constitutional rules by which Great Britain is governed are found in a series of documents (great charters, statutes of a constitutional nature, judicial decisions) and unwritten political usages or conventions that have gained general acceptance. Usually, the elements of the British constitution are placed in two categories: the law of the constitution and the conventions of the constitution.

The *law of the constitution* is embodied in historic documents or charters, in statutes of a constitutional nature, and in the common law. The best known of the historic documents is Magna Carta (1215). Others are the Petition of Right (1628), the Bill of Rights (1689), and the Act of Settlement (1701). In one way or another these charters served to limit the authority of the monarch and provide for an orderly redress of grievances. Other historic documents, such as the Reform Act of 1832 and the Parliament Act of 1911, altered the basic political structure. Although they are less important than the great charters, parliamentary enactments dealing with the suffrage, election methods, and the powers and duties of public officials are nevertheless a part of the constitutional system. British political institutions have also been shaped by the common law, that body of judge-made legal rules that grew apart from any parliamentary action and in which are rooted most of the guarantees of civil rights. This body of rules, as well as the historic charters, has been altered by judicial decisions that from time to time have reinterpreted their meaning.

The *conventions of the constitution,* although less precisely formulated than the law of the constitution, are no less fundamental. Such important institutions as the Cabinet and the office of Prime Minister stem from custom and usage, not legislative enactment. Moreover, the basic attribute of the parliamentary system, the responsibility of the Cabinet to the House of Commons, has evolved through usage. The principle that the monarch cannot refuse to sign acts of Parliament and that the leader of the majority party in the Commons must be asked to be Prime Minister is likewise rooted in convention.

What basic characteristics of the British political system can be deduced from a study of the British constitution?

1. *Democracy.* Political decisions are made by popularly elected leaders. The monarch acts on the basis of their advice, being politically neutral.

2. *Supremacy of Parliament.* Legally, Parliament can do anything it wants. There is no provision that any court can declare an act of Parliament unconstitutional.

3. *Unitary government.* All power is vested in one central government; whatever powers are exercised by local units of government are granted by the central authorities and may be revoked by them.

4. *Fusion of legislative and executive powers.* The leaders of the majority party constitute the executive (the Cabinet) while retaining their seats in the legislature. There is no separation of executive and legislative powers in the American sense.

5. *Independence of the judiciary.* Although the political branches of government are fused, the judiciary is independent and free from political interference. Judges serve for life and have developed a tradition of impartiality in dispensing justice.

6. *Protection of civil rights.* Although the British have no neat enumeration of civil rights such as exists in the American Constitution, these rights are nevertheless protected.

Both the American and the British constitutions are amended in similar as well as in different ways. The American Constitution provides two methods of proposing formal amendments and two methods of ratification. Only one method of proposal has ever been successfully used—that of a two-thirds vote of both houses of Congress. Proposal by a convention called by Congress upon petition by legislatures in two-thirds of the states has been tried on numerous occasions unsuccessfully. Amendments may be ratified by legislatures in three-fourths of the states or by conventions in three-fourths of the states; except for the repeal of prohibition, all amendments have been ratified by legislative action. The American Constitution has been changed by judicial interpretation perhaps more than through formal amendment. The oft-quoted statement of former Chief Justice Hughes that "we are under the Constitution, but the Constitution is what the judges say it is" may be shocking to some, but it is basically true. Moreover, Congress has also shaped the development of the Constitution as it spins a legislative web in and around the general phrases found in the document. In addition, American Presidents have over the years construed the Constitution in particular ways, and often their interpretations have prevailed.

In Great Britain any act of Parliament that changes the processes, powers, or institutions of government is in effect an amendment to the constitution. On first glance this would seem to make the British constitution more flexible than the American. On further reflection, however, we realize that so much of the British constitution is based on custom and usage, and we know that custom changes exceedingly slowly.

Social Forces

American political behavior and institutions are in large measure a composite of such factors as the hopes, fears, customs, tensions, and drives of the American people. From an initial population of 4 million at the time the Constitution was written, the number of Americans has grown, through the effects of immigration and natural increase, to more than 225 million. Immigration from other nations has been the very lifeblood of the United States. The movement of 40 million Europeans to this country in a little more than a century is a development unparalleled in world history and has made America a fabled "melting pot." The early need for labor and the abundance of land supported a national policy of open doors to immigrants, but the disappearance of the land frontier in 1890, coupled with the growing power of organized labor and the recurrence of economic depressions, contributed to an eventual reversal of this policy.

With the possible exception of the American Indians, the American people today are all descendants of immigrants who brought with them and retained in varying degrees the political, economic, and social traditions of their respective mother countries. They are a complicated mixture of nationalities, races, and religions, whose outlooks have not all been reduced by the melting pot into one "American mind." Concentrations of peoples sharing the culture of a particular country—Irish, Italian, Spanish, or Polish settlements, for example—still constitute important political blocs in some parts of the United States.

American politics, especially that of the 1960s and '70s, cannot be understood when divorced from the statistics of race. Technically, this includes such minorities as American Indians and people of Chinese and Japanese origin, but in common parlance it almost always refers to Negroes, or blacks. The explosiveness of racial issues is rooted in revolutionary changes taking place—both qualitatively and quantitatively—in the black population in the United States. The number and location of American blacks in 1910, 9.8 million, with 91 percent living in the South, changed dramatically to 24.8 million by 1978, with only 53 percent residing in the South. Moreover, black population growth has become more rapid than that of whites, and is far more concentrated within the largest central cities, where the growing political significance of the black person in American politics is most apparent. "Black power," whether connoting growing voting strength, nonviolent demonstrations and confrontations for black causes, or violence and civil disorders, will undoubtedly write a major part of the history of central cities in years to come.

The U.S. population generally has shifted to urban areas. This change from 95 percent rural to approximately 80 percent urban helps explain much about modern American government that is often misunderstood: the expansion of governmental functions, taxes, and expenditures, for example, and the feeling that even local government has lost much of the "personal touch" it once had. It is the crowded, dependent, insecure urban wage earner who invites and even compels an ever-growing number of governmental activities to serve and regulate all phases of daily life. An added dimension to American urbanism has been the flight to suburbia of more than 50 million people, a flight vastly accelerated in recent years. Thus while centripetal forces have been luring millions from farms to cities, centrifugal forces have been scattering still more millions into sprawling suburbs. Indeed, the suburbs of the great metropolitan areas in the United States are fast overtaking the central cities in population.

The rise of suburbia and the decline and blight of the central city have had an important impact on local government, an impact that has required the coining of such new words as "metropolitanism" and "metropolitics." Metropolitics is concerned mainly with the struggle to secure area-wide decisions concerning governmental services and regulations in metropolitan areas fragmented into many (often hundreds of) autonomous decision-making governments. The stakes are high, involving such problems as mass transit, tax rates, crime control, local self-government, control of zoning, and metropolitan planning, with the proponents of metropolitan reform warning that the only alternative to more coordination among localities is state and federal intervention.

Even as the term "metropolitan area" becomes part of laymen's and journalists' language, some sociologists and political scientists have begun to talk about the developing "super-metropolitan area," or "megalopolis," formed when two or more metropolitan areas grow closer together. A 600-mile-long "linear city" on the eastern seaboard has been the most publicized; it would stretch from lower New Hampshire through Boston, New York, Philadelphia, Baltimore, Washington, D.C., and northern Virginia, reaching into ten states and containing 31.5 million people. A similar linear city is developing on the west coast from Los Angeles to San Diego.

A classic distinction between American and European society is supposedly the absence in America of a rigid class system. Certainly no class of landed gentry has flourished in the United States since the fall of the southern plantation system, nor can we point to closed aristocracies consisting of public servants, the clergy, or the military. Nevertheless, in some ways American society is stratified, and repeated studies of American communities have revealed a kind of class system based largely on wealth. People with comparable income, occupation, or social position tend to associate with one another and to vote alike. Although more than 80 percent of American people consider themselves members of the "middle class," studies of voting behavior reveal that a large number tend to fall into a "working class," consistently different from the middle and upper classes. Even more abhorrent to most Americans than the notion of classes in their society is the idea of a caste system—that is, a system of class based on birth and from which there is no escape. Yet the position of certain minority groups—blacks in particular—has undeniably had some of the characteristics of a caste system.

The religious traditions and affiliations of the American people contribute to the shape and direction of their political system, both in its historical origins and in the current issues of the day. Protestant Christianity is either the professed religious faith or the unprofessed tradition of the great majority of Americans, giving both religion and politics the individualistic and antiauthoritarian spirit of the Reformation. Nearly one out of every four persons is a Roman Catholic (based on an estimate of 45.5 million adherents), and an estimated 5.7 million are Jews. Political conflict over religious issues and religious differences is more intense in many nations than in the United States. And while interdenominational religious friction has affected the course of American politics from time to time, it has not threatened the very basis of community as such issues and frictions do in some other systems.

Political scientists and historians generally point to economic change as the most significant influence on the development of the American political system since the adoption of the Constitution. The growth of the large-scale industrial corporation, the continuing technological revolution with its accompanying specialization of labor and increased interdependence of persons, the divorcement of most of the people from the soil, and the growth of powerful labor unions—all have contributed to a governmental system that Thomas Jefferson would hardly recognize. American democracy has come to require its government to serve as the protector of the rights of weaker parties in economic struggles, particularly if the economically weak may be politically strong. This trend has been reflected in the development of the independent regulatory commissions; the guarantee of collective bargaining rights to organized labor; and more recently in the demands of women, blacks, the handicapped, the elderly, and any other group that considers itself disadvantaged.

The American economy is characterized by private enterprise, but it is hardly the pure capitalistic system implied by so many civic club speeches. Any realistic description of the close affinity of politics and economics in the United States must conclude that the system is a mixture of private, public, and hybrid enterprises. Although no "laissez-faire" separation of government from the economy has ever really existed in the United States, even in its early years, governmental regulation and intervention have steadily increased throughout the past century, tending to parallel the growth of big business and big labor.

Depression and inflation have come to be the twin devils of American politics. Both conservative and liberal economists now recognize the American government's responsibility to do whatever it can to prevent "boom and bust" cycles in the economy. Governmental provision of "built-in" stabilizing forces is increasingly accepted as a permanent fixture of the political economy. Of particular concern in recent years has been the high rates of inflation and unemployment ("stagflation") at the same time.

Also in recent years, economic concerns have been augmented to include questions of economic growth rate, pollution of the environment, and the early depletion of finite energy resources. For many decades American prosperity has been made possible by cheap energy (mainly oil) and an almost total disregard for the environment. With the sharp increase in the price of oil in the 1970s, dictated by the oil producing and exporting countries (as well as the higher costs imposed by measures to protect the environment), most of the industrialized countries (including the United States) have had to devote considerable energy to conservation and to finding alternate sources of energy.

Great Britain, unlike the United States, is geographically compact (about the area of Oregon), with a population of approximately 56 million, one-eighth of whom live in London, which is the political, cultural, and commercial center of the country. Great Britain is densely populated and highly urbanized, with problems not too different from those facing the American urban areas.

Although they are of mixed Celtic, Roman, Saxon, Norman, and Danish origins, the British have developed a strong sense of national identity. Except for the problem of Northern Ireland, there have been no boundary problems since the union with Scotland well over 350 years ago. During the past two decades, however, Scottish and Welsh nationalist movements have forced the national government to consider granting Wales and Scotland the right to have directly elected assemblies with powers to deal with local matters. More serious for Britain is the problem of the nonwhites who have emigrated from parts of the once large empire. These people now constitute over 3 percent of the population, and some racial disturbances have occurred in recent years, which have sorely tested traditional British tolerance.

All societies are beset with contending social forces, and change is the law of life. But the factors—historical, technological, political, economic, and the like—that contribute to change can be impeded or facilitated by the social and political organization of a particular society. Where change is impeded, violent revolution is the likely result. In Britain change has on the whole come about peacefully, although some of the transitions have not been without pain.

Great Britain, like other European countries, had its feudal period, with its manifold gradations of social rank. The descendants of the feudal lords, as the chief beneficiaries of the old system, wanted to preserve their vested interests. But by the late eighteenth and early nineteenth centuries, the Industrial Revolution could not be held back, and the struggle of those who stood to benefit from it was resolved in their favor. Subsequently, the growth of trade, a consequence of the Industrial Revolution, resulted in a contest between those who stood to gain from free-trade policies and those who would lose. This contest was won at first by the free-trade advocates, but in this century the protectionists had their day.

In addition to setting the stage for these conflicts, the Industrial Revolution also brought into being a new class—the industrial workers—and a whole host of new problems associated with urban civilization. In the eighteenth century, landed property owners had dominated politics; in the nineteenth, the interests of those involved in the development of large-scale industry and the growth of factory towns were gradually recognized in the system of parliamentary representation. By the beginning of the twentieth century, the industrial workers had their own political party, the Labour party, which by mid-century had not only reached the status of a major party but had also come to power and achieved some of its basic objectives.

The existence of a system of democratic representation had enabled labor to realize many of its goals more rapidly than did the bourgeoisie in the nineteenth century. Yet is it important to recognize that the Conservatives, the other major modern party, have accepted Labour's reforms. Just as a consensus had been reached between the landed and industrial classes in the previous century, a similar understanding was arrived at between Labourites and Conservatives in the twentieth, although certain disharmonies remain and the struggle to control public policy continues.

The political battle in Britain is waged according to certain agreed-upon rules. Those favored by the existing system are not inclined to give it up easily, but there is a tacit understanding among the British that their political system must take account of the forces, domestic and foreign, that make for change not only in the direction of British policy but also in the rules and personnel through which change is implemented. The significant thing to note is that the dominant social groups have repeatedly been able to devise political forms that eventually won their opponents' support. The social structure could change, and did. The new social forces generated by industrialization were able to play an increased role, while the influence of the farmers, the landed aristocracy, and the small shopkeepers waned. And the fact that the working classes were able to rise in influence may to a large degree explain the lack of communist success among British workers.

A final word should be said, however, about the persistence in Britain of classes in the social sense. Apart from differences resulting from occupation and income, British society has been stratified also by differences in appearance, accent, and manner. Before the last century, even a rudimentary primary education was unavailable to any substantial part of the population, a factor that contributed in no small measure to the perpetuation of social classes. The British social structure has been conducive to the creation of personal connections among those in established positions of power and prestige. Class consciousness is still prevalent in Britain, but the equalization of educational opportunities over the past two decades has gone a long way to open up the avenues to social as well as economic advancement for the children of most Britishers.

What accounts for the capacity of the British system to accommodate, without violence, profound social change? One factor may be a strong sense of national identity. Another element contributing to the British consensus grew out of the general British respect for the ideas of freedom, dissent, and toleration. The result has been moderation and a minimum of violence. A third component is the British moral sense. Politically civilized people are restrained people, but restraint must rest upon concepts of right and wrong. For the British, Christianity has been an important source of these concepts. To be sure, the British have had their differences over religion, but these very differences have contributed to political discussion and political debates and have given rise to tolerance for divergent views, although the troubles in Northern Ireland would seem to prove the contrary. In a more concrete way, the Anglican church and other Christian churches in Britain have contributed significantly to the abolition of the slave trade, to prison reform, to the elimination of child labor, and to factory reforms.

Education, too, has contributed to peaceful social transitions, although the British were slow to recognize a public responsibility to provide opportunities for the development of talent. Significant government financial support was not available for primary schools until after 1870 and not until 1900 for secondary schools, while the universities had to wait until after World War II. It is true that the government recognized the importance of education much earlier. It chose, however, to channel its support through grants to the church-supported schools. Since World War II the government has, in large measure, equalized educational opportunities, through specific legislation that provided for recognition of talent, financial aid, and the establishment of a number of new universities. While these measures have not reduced the demand for entrance into the independent schools, they have made it possible for children of all social classes to advance on the basis of ability and individual effort to a much greater degree than was heretofore the case.

Finally, peaceful social transitions have been aided to some extent by the enlightened self-interest of the propertied class. Class differences in Britain have been considerable, yet British capitalists have made important concessions to the workers, such as accepting their right to strike and acquiescing in considerable government regulation of business. The result has been a working class generally able to promote its interests politically through Parliament instead of feeling it necessary to resort to violence and revolution.

The ability of the major social classes to promote their interests politically has resulted in increased governmental activity in the social welfare field. This means, first, that the government assumes the responsibility of keeping the economy functioning at a high level and along certain lines and, second, that each member of society receives a certain minimum of the available goods and services. A high level of economic activity is achieved by public ownership of certain segments of the economy, by economic planning, and by government regulation. A minimum standard of welfare for the individual is achieved through such devices as minimum wages and the free provision of certain goods or services, such as medical care.

The British welfare state is often identified, erroneously in large part, with the postwar Labour government. Actually, a great deal of public economic control and considerable social security legislation existed long before Labour took over in 1945, much of it representing measures passed by Conservative governments. The first public health measures, for example, were enacted around the middle of the nineteenth century. Thus Labour, although desiring to go further and faster, was in fact building on past accomplishments.

In the postwar period, however, the choices open to either party were limited. Britain's international economic position was unstable; for the country to survive, it was imperative to expand the volume of exports. To do this, all sorts of controls were needed, particularly measures to curtail domestic consumption. In addition, Britain's economic plant needed rejuvenation. Its age created a domestic economic crisis that could only be met with a government-directed capital investment program. In short, had the Conservatives been victorious in 1945, they too would no doubt have been forced to engage in a great deal of economic planning and government enterprise.

The Labour program therefore had a broader popular consensus than is generally realized in the United States. This was made possible, in part, because the British have not been overly doctrinaire about free enterprise, but highly pragmatic and utilitarian in their approach. And the two major parties, although in apparent disagreement, seem constantly to be reaching new areas of agreement through a process of disagreeing.

That the Conservative and Labour parties have been drifting closer together may be explained in part by the fact that in recent public opinion polls fewer than half of those questioned declined to assign themselves to any class. Moreover, the proportion of middle-class support for Labour has grown, while worker support for the Conservatives increased markedly in the 1970s. Recent polls and the 1979 election have indicated that the positions taken by the Labour party leadership have not been those held by the vast majority of the people who normally vote for Labour candidates. For example, they preferred the Conservative positions on taxes, on regulating union activities, and on law and order. On the other hand, there is evidence of dissatisfaction with both major parties. In the 1974 and the 1979 elections, for example, the total vote for the two parties fell below 80 percent, down from an average of over 90 percent in the 1950s and '60s.

Nevertheless, the ability of the British political system to direct the forces of change along peaceful channels has resulted in the avoidance of severe stresses and strains, hence the absence of divisive ideological struggles. Differences have been discussed and resolved on the basis of alternative pragmatic solutions rather than in terms of doctrinaire ideological positions. In an age of ideological struggles, this relative insignificance of ideology is perhaps of major interest and significance.

In the late 1970s Britain, in common with most other industrialized nations, faced critical economic problems, brought on in large part by the steep increase in the cost of oil. While the discovery of oil in the North Sea has eased her difficulties considerably, other economic problems remain. Inflation has not been brought under control; unemployment remains high; and British exports have found Japanese, German, and other goods difficult to compete against. On the other hand, the people responded well to the government's policies of severe voluntary wage restraints and of deterring strikes. More-over, there has been a prodigious growth of fairly widespread prosperity. One British commentator found reason to hope that British political genius— "adaptability, pragmatism, and determination to avoid violent solutions" —will prevail. A former Cabinet minister, however, asserted that "political minorities in Britain are becoming more and more arrogant and contemptuous in their readiness to advocate and use violence against anyone who dissents from their views."[1] In the late 1970s a movement with an avowedly racist out-look, calling itself the National Front, appeared to be gaining ground in the decaying inner-city neighborhoods of Birmingham, Manchester, and London. In the 1979 elections, however, its candidates were able to win only 0.6 per-cent of the vote. One thing seems certain as of this writing: Britain's time of troubles is not over.

Interest Groups

In a free society, individuals combine to promote their aspirations; to this end, organizations arise in the political arena to advocate a variety of interests. This is natural because where there is power, pressure will be applied. Because of their activities, these organizations are often referred to as pressure groups, but since the word "pressure" may imply a value judgment, it is perhaps pref-erable to call them interest groups. We usually think first of economic inter-ests, notably "business interests," "labor interests," and "agricultural inter-ests"; but there are also "ethnic or minority interests," "urban interests," "religious interests," and a variety of professional interests (e.g., doctors, law-yers, teachers).

Among the interest groups in the United States that we hear most about are *labor* (American Federation of Labor–Congress of Industrial Organiza-tions, and several independent unions), *business* (Chamber of Commerce, Na-tional Association of Manufacturers, and a large number of trade associa-tions); *farm* (American Farm Bureau Federation, National Farmers Union, National Grange, and several commodity associations). The American Medi-cal Association, the National Education Association, the American Legion, the National Catholic Welfare Conference, the National Council of Churches, the National Association for the Advancement of Colored People—all have exerted political influence in a variety of contexts.

The above-mentioned communities of interest are less homogeneous than is commonly believed. For example, there was no single "farm interest" in the

1. Lord Chalfont, *New York Times*, 21 September 1977, p. 33.

long struggle to repeal a federal tax on colored oleomargarine, for the dairy farmers opposed any measure to help the sale of a "cheap imitation of butter," while the cotton farmers favored eliminating this "artificial restriction on the use of a cotton seed product." The clash of interests between different groups of farmers—wealthy ranchers and small renters, corporation farmers and single-family farmers, cotton farmers and hog farmers—makes it hazardous to speak with any certainty about the "agricultural interest." On the other hand, any congressman who seeks to promote the "consumer interest" by introducing a bill setting maximum prices for all agricultural products would doubtless find the diversified farm groups suddenly united in defense of the "agricultural interest."

Labor and business interests must be considered with similar caution. True, the common appeal of higher wages and a shorter workweek has traditionally united most industrial wage earners; but seeds of rivalry are found in the diverse interests of specialized labor groups—artisans and craftsmen versus large-scale industrial workers, New Englanders versus Southerners, coal miners in favor of the St. Lawrence Seaway versus longshoremen opposed to it, and on occasion, white laborers versus black laborers. Similarly, businessmen are generally united in the interests of lower taxes, curbs on "labor excesses," less government regulation, and less governmental centralization. But the "business interest," too, must be subdivided into such particular interests as those of union and nonunion companies, of importers and exporters, of big business and small business, and of groups of businesses competing with other groups in the same field of service or sales.

Because of the diversity of religious denominations in the United States, religious interests have from time to time become vocal. The two constitutional doctrines of separation of church and state and freedom of religious faith and practice have tended to keep the bulk of religious interests away from the floodlight of political struggles. In the 1980 U.S. elections, however, a group calling itself the Moral Majority asserted its determination to influence the outcome of political contests. Earlier, in two instances—1928 and 1960—the "Protestant interest" and the "Catholic interest" surfaced in political campaigns when Catholic presidential candidates Alfred E. Smith and John F. Kennedy encountered powerful religious opposition in strongly Protestant areas. It is particularly in state and local governments, however, that clergymen and lay denominational leaders frequently speak out for religious interests in legislative and administrative matters. In Britain, on the other hand, the Church of England is the state church and as such gets financial support from the state, while other religious denominations are merely tolerated.

Among the better-known British interest groups are the National Farmers Union, the Federation of British Industries, the National Federation of Property Owners, the National Union of Manufacturers, and the various trade unions. The pattern of interest-group activity in Britain, as in other nations, is diverse and complex, although the channels that British interests utilize are less conspicuous than those employed by their American counterparts. In the United States we are familiar with interest-group activity at the national as well as the state level. Lobbyists for special causes are freely at work, pleading their cases before legislative committees and individual legislators. The distribution of power in the American system practically forces interest groups to concentrate much of their activity on Congress and the state legislatures.

In Great Britain, on the other hand, such activity seems absent. This is understandable because British legislative committees are not powerful and cannot override the leaders of the government. The Cabinet's control over its majority is such that the votes of individual members cannot be changed by the actions of interest-group representatives. Consequently, lobbying of the type Americans are accustomed to is futile.

This does not mean that British interest groups are not effective but that they act in different ways. Because power in Britain is concentrated, they must focus their attention on those who make decisions: the Cabinet ministers and their advisers and associates. They must convince ministers that what they want is in the national interest, or at least that it can be so defended. Perhaps their most effective method is to work through the political parties — that is, by working for the nomination and election of candidates who will be sympathetic to their interests. In this way, interests come to be represented directly in Parliament. American interests also do some supporting of candidates, but mere election does not assure favorable action in Congress or elsewhere.

The British have not, generally speaking, been suspicious of the political activity of interest groups. In a sense, the Labour party is an association of pressure groups, and most business organizations are aligned with the Conservative party; contacts between lobbyists and decision makers have therefore not seemed out of order. As a matter of fact, interest groups are frequently consulted by the government. Consultative and advisory commissions, representing various interests, work closely with government committees and councils. Drafts of proposed laws are submitted to affected interests for their reaction, and whenever royal commissions are set up to study various problems, outside interests are liberally represented.

British interests also have an opportunity to state their views when new administrative regulations are being written. And they continually try to in-

fluence administrative agencies in an effort to gain the most favorable interpretation of laws and regulations that affect them. This form of activity has
been accelerated by the growth of welfare-state legislation, which has vested
an increasing amount of decision making in administrative agencies. It is here,
by and large, that decisions are made on what prices will be guaranteed to
farmers, what salaries are to be paid the doctors in the British Health Service,
and what licenses (import, building, and so on) are to be granted or denied.

The influence of interest groups depends on several factors: size, cohesion, status, leadership, organization, and program. While all of these may be
important in one or another context, prestige or status of a group in society
would appear to be especially important. Doctors, bankers, and lawyers, and
particularly the leaders of their professional associations, will usually enjoy
easier access to the decision-making circles of government than the representatives of lower-status groups. Similarly, the ideological content of the interest-
group's program has an important effect on its power position, with certain
programs doomed to hard sledding no matter how much professional public
relations assistance is employed. A clear-cut goal of "fair play," "correcting a
wrong," or "supporting the weak but worthy" will give a group a decided edge
over the group whose program has earned the brand of "obvious special privilege." In Britain the influence of an interest group often rests on the ability of
the group to supply the kind of expert knowledge ministers or administrators
require. One of the most effective groups in this respect is the medical profession, whose skill and expertise shape the policy of the British Health Service.

Political Parties

It would be difficult to visualize democratic government functioning without
parties, for it is through them that the popular will is ascertained and ultimately translated into action. Unlike interest groups, which seek the attainment of
limited goals by exerting direct or indirect pressure on government officials,
political parties attempt to attain a variety of goals by seeking public office for
their members and then assuming general responsibility for the conduct of
public affairs. Parties develop the programs and bring forth the leaders to
present to the electorate. Interest groups may seek control of certain governmental policies, they may even seek support from all parties, and they may
campaign to support certain candidates; but in general they do not seek to
nominate or elect candidates to office.

Political parties in the United States and Great Britain are of relatively recent origin. American political parties began very early despite the warning of
George Washington and others against the "baneful effect of the spirit of par-

ties." The fight for a strong constitution to replace the Articles of Confederation was accompanied by cleavage between the Federalists and the Antifederalists. The first real party lines began to develop toward the end of Washington's Presidency. Hamilton and Adams retained the Federalist's label for a new grouping of business, industrial, and financial interests in New England and the Middle Atlantic states; Jefferson and Madison organized the planters, small farmers, and artisans into a party that by 1816 had eliminated the Federalists. Known successively as Antifederalists, Jeffersonian Republicans, Democratic Republicans, and Democrats, this party is today one of the world's oldest.

Today's Republican party is the natural successor of two earlier parties — the Federalists of Hamilton and Adams and the anti-Jacksonian Whigs. The party of Lincoln succeeded in bringing together a coalition of northern industrial and financial groups and midwestern farmers and almost completely dominated national politics for the next half century, as the Democratic party found it difficult to throw off the image of rebellion. It was the economic distress of farmers and laborers in the 1920s and '30s that led more of these groups into the Democratic fold and provided the basis for the modern Democratic party. Each party has held the Presidency approximately 50 percent of the time during the past half century or so.

The two parties today stand close to the middle of the road ideologically. The demarcation line between the Republican and Democratic parties is badly blurred, and each party is divided into various wings, such as left and right, or northern and southern, with more unity often found across party lines in Congress than within each party. Party discipline in Congress is invariably strong in matters of personnel and organization, but often weak in matters of substantive policy. Furthermore, even though the major parties have clearly differed on particular issues at particular periods in history, these differences have changed through the years; and complete reversals have taken place, such as the Republican and Democratic "swap out" in the field of states' rights and national power. In spite of policy diversities within each party, however, it is usually safe to predict that in Congress a greater percentage of Republicans than Democrats will be found voting against proposals for government regulation of business, social legislation, and expenditures for international assistance.

British political parties can be traced back to about 1700 when two groups in Parliament began calling themselves Whigs and Tories. They, along with other factions and cliques, were loose groupings; they did not even call themselves political parties. There was no large-scale party organization outside Parliament, and in view of the fact that each member of the House of

Commons prior to the Reform Act of 1832 represented on the average 330 voters, there was little need for one. British parties in the modern sense date from early in the nineteenth century when the Tories began to be known as the Conservative party and the Whigs assumed the name Liberal. Although they received no formal recognition in British constitutional documents, these parties, as they evolved, have played an increasingly vital role in the political processes of the nation.

In Great Britain in the eighteenth century the Conservatives were dominated by landed interests. In the nineteenth century, especially after the Reform Acts of 1832 and 1867, merchants and manufacturers gained in political influence, and the importance of the landed interests declined. The Conservative party came to be identified with the new sources of wealth. In the process, however, particularly in their passage of the Reform Act of 1867, the Conservatives gained a sizable middle-class following as well as a good deal of working-class support, much of which they retain to this day.

The Labour party is relatively new. But it has grown rapidly, and forty years after its founding in 1905 it had a sizable majority in the House of Commons. The Liberal party, which attained considerable success in the nineteenth century and the early part of the twentieth century, began to decline after the formation of the Labour party. As it declined it was gradually replaced by the Labour party. The Labour party is basically a socialist party, although it has discarded many of the doctrinal precepts of traditional socialism. For example, it no longer espouses nationalization of land, and its advocacy of nationalization in the industrial sector of the economy has been tempered by a change in method; in more recent nationalizations, the government gained control of an industry by buying shares on the market. Labour's membership is based largely on trade unionism, although its appeal goes considerably beyond the trade unions.

One of the most striking characteristics of American and British political party systems is their two-party nature, in contrast with the multiparty systems of most European continental democracies. Various theories have been offered to explain the persistence of the two-party systems in the United States and Great Britain. In the case of the former, the nature of the electoral system seems most important. The single-member district plan for electing legislators tends to encourage coalitions of diverse groups within each district, as well as to overrepresent the majority and make it hard for a third party ever to gain a foothold. Similarly, the all-or-nothing basis of casting a state's electoral votes for President makes it easier for the two major parties to convince the voters that supporting a third party is "throwing your vote away." Although the Republican party is the only one to rise from third-party status to be one of the two major parties, it would be wrong to conclude that third parties are unimportant. Through the years they have played an important role as innovators of policy, with the major established parties taking over vote-getting planks of third-party platforms (such as those of the Populists, Greenbackers, Socialists, and Progressives) when it became apparent that the smaller parties were making serious inroads into major party strengths.

In Great Britain the electoral system is similar to that found in the United States in that the party getting the largest number of votes in a district wins that district's seat in the Commons. This has served to force the electorate to line up on one of two sides. Moreover, the tradition of strong government, in which the Cabinet is not buffeted about by an irresponsible legislature, has motivated voters to think in terms of getting a working majority in office. Whatever the reasons, the fact remains that British voters have preferred to vote for a party with a reasonable chance of forming a Cabinet, even though in the process they might elect a Parliament that was a less perfect reflection of popular views than a multiparty assembly can sometimes be.

American and British parties diverge sharply when it comes to organization. American parties are loosely organized, consisting mainly of a limited and often uncertain association of state parties, with national machinery being small and rarely capable of exercising any significant authority. A gulf frequently exists between national party headquarters and state and local party organizations. The relationship must be cooperative, with cooperation commonly at its highest during presidential campaigns and considerably lower at other times. The mere fact of fifty separate sets of state regulations for party machinery and elections places strong inhibitions on centralized party operations.

British parties, on the other hand, are highly organized and centrally directed by powerful national party machines. While the party organizations differ in some important respects for the two parties, they are similar in that they have three important components: the leader, the members of the party in Parliament, and the party in the country. Of the three, the leader is the most important in power and prestige, and is the actual or potential Prime Minister, and it is to him or her that party adherents look for day-to-day leadership.

The Conservative leader, both in the way he or she is selected and in the actual exercise of leadership, is more powerful than the Labour counterpart. Prior to 1965, the Conservatives staged no formal contests for the office. The leader emerged from a process of consultation involving important party stalwarts. Since 1965, the leader is elected by the Conservative members of the House of Commons. Once elected, the leader is seldom if ever challenged. He or she is free to select colleagues, and while advice may be sought, the responsibility for the formulation of policy is the leader's. Moreover, the leader has control, through appointments of key personnel, of the national party organization.

Organizationally, the Labour party, in and out of power, operates in fact if not in form much like the Conservative, although there are certain differences. In power and influence, the leader is all important and free to select his or her colleagues. Unlike the Conservative counterpart, the Labour leader does not formulate policy; he or she is in theory obligated to seek the implementation of a program determined by the party organization and the Labour members of Parliament. Nor does he or she exercise personal control over the party's head office. Furthermore, the Labour leader is elected annually so that the choice of a leader has proved more of a contest for the Labourites than for the Conservatives. Careful studies of British politics suggest, however, that even these differences are more apparent than real.

Next to the leader in importance is the party in Parliament, with the Conservative group popularly known as the "1922 Committee" because of its formation in that year, and more formally as the Conservative Members Committee. All Conservative members of the House of Commons who are not ministers are members, although ministers may appear before the committee. The Labour party organization in Parliament, known as the Parliamentary Labour Party (PLP), is similar to the Conservatives' 1922 Committee in that two-way communication between the leaders and their followers can take place in this manner. The PLP is more tightly organized, and the party leader and colleagues attend all meetings, because the PLP can make binding policy decisions. This function is not so important when the party is in power, for then the Cabinet is the real policy maker.

In the early years of the PLP's existence, Labour MPs were expected to take orders from the party's National Executive Committee (NEC), in accordance with party rules. This was abhorrent to a basic principle of British government — that members of Parliament do not take orders from an extraparliamentary body. With Labour in power after World War II, the Prime Minister and his colleagues were determined that they were the makers of policy, and in this they were successful until recent years. By 1979, however, the more radical elements gained control in the NEC, and at the Labour party conference succeeded, over the strenuous objections of the party leader, in passing a resolution that in the future the election manifesto (platform) should be drawn up by the NEC. At the 1980 conference left-wing elements in the party went further, stripping the PLP of its right to elect the party leader. In 1981 a formula was worked out whereby he would be chosen at the annual conference by a process in which the unions would have 40 percent of the vote and the PLP only 30 percent. The Labour party leadership has also been challenged in recent years on the question of nominations of candidates for the House of Commons. Earlier it had been customary to readopt (renominate) incumbent members for the next election. The more radical faction wants to eliminate this practice, as a way of more easily "dumping" MPs it does not like.

These developments caused a split in the Labour party, which in 1981 promised to produce the biggest political change in the British party structure since the emergence of the party as a major political force earlier in this century. In March 1981, twelve Labour members from the House of Commons, several of them former ministers, left the party in protest. They formed the Council for Social Democracy and soon thereafter a new political party, the Social Democratic party. Public opinion polls indicated that this was a popular development and by late 1981 the party had elected its first candidate to Commons.

Historically, there have been fewer internal tensions in the Conservative party, which has sometimes been described as a party of "tendencies," than in the Labour party, which has been referred to as a party of "factions."

Both party organizations outside Parliament are primarily electoral machines. They have annual conferences of delegates, who have little real influence on policy, although in theory the Labour conference is the ultimate authority of the party. In practice, the actions of the Labour conference have until recent years (as noted above) been largely advisory, much as are the actions of the Conservative conference.

Electoral procedures in the United States and Britain differ considerably. Nominations for most offices in the United States were initially performed by party caucuses or conventions. Increasingly, nominations came to be in the hands of the electorate through direct primaries. The President and Vice-President are nominated by party conventions, the vast majority of whose delegates, be it noted, are selected in accordance with presidential primaries.

There is no national elective office in Britain; the Prime Minister, as we have seen, is chosen from among the members of the House of Commons. Nominations for the Commons are party affairs. Candidates are selected by the respective party organizations at the constituency (district) level, in consultation with the national party office; they need not be residents of the constituency in which they run. There are no primaries or state or national conventions. Only those nominated by a party are entitled to use its label in running for office. Frivolous candidacies are effectively discouraged by the rule that each candidate must deposit the equivalent of several hundred dollars. The deposit is returned if the candidate polls at least one-eighth of the votes cast.

Minor party candidates often forfeit their deposits, and on rare occasions even a majority party candidate may have to do so.

Political campaigns, too, are different. American campaigns usually are underway even before the national conventions are held in midsummer and continue with accelerating vigor until the elections early in November. British election campaigns, on the other hand, are brief because the election takes place within a month of the announcement that Parliament is dissolved. British campaigns are more limited than American campaigns in other respects, particularly in the amount of money that is spent. It is illegal for anyone to spend money on behalf of a candidate unless authorized by the candidate or his election agent, and the total that can be spent by or on behalf of each candidate is severely limited. Television and radio time cannot be purchased, but each major party is provided an equal amount of free time, with minor parties getting less. Until recent campaigns, commentators did not discuss the campaigns or the candidates. Even newscasters stayed away from political news during the campaign, although the newspapers reported freely what the candidates said. With the advent of television, electoral campaign reporting in Britain has become fairly extensive.

The considerable discretion given to the broadcast media in the past decade on how to report campaigns has made for important changes in political campaigning. Now the parties' propaganda efforts are centralized, with more and more interest focused on the party leaders. In addition, there has been a decline in major speech-making tours by the leading politicians. There is no longer a confrontation on major issues, but on selective ones that are determined largely by the polls and the television broadcasters, which means that only a few of the issues cited in party manifestoes receive treatment.

In the United States the cost of campaigns has increased and indeed skyrocketed in recent decades. Beginning with the 1976 general elections, American laws provide that each of the two major parties may spend (on the presidential election) a certain sum ($29 million in 1980) appropriated by Congress. In addition each of the major parties is allowed to spend $3 or $4 million of party funds. Most estimates indicate that the total amount spent by the Republicans and the Democrats in the 1976 campaign did not exceed $30 million each. This is significant in that the Republicans alone spent perhaps twice that amount in the 1972 election. Proposals for government funding of elections for Congress have not been adopted as of this writing.

The date of American elections is generally set for the first Tuesday after the first Monday in November of any election year. In Britain, the law specifies that there must be an election at least every five years. In the case of an acute emergency, such as a war, an election may be postponed for a year at a time until the emergency comes to an end. The specific date of an election is determined by the party in power, or more particularly, by the Prime Minister, who presumably consults close Cabinet colleagues. Because it can choose the time for elections, the party in power has the advantage of selecting the time it thinks most propitious for victory, although its choice becomes increasingly limited as the end of the five-year period approaches.

Governmental Institutions: The United States

American political institutions at the national level include in the main the President, the Congress, and the judiciary. Because of the separation-of-powers scheme, they are independent of one another, and yet can be frustrated by each other. Because of the potential for deadlock in such a plan, especially between the President and the Congress, some observers have expressed wonderment that the system functions. Fortunately, political parties have helped bridge the gap between the President and the Congress (particularly when both are controlled by the same party), and in most critical situations common sense has prevailed, and even acceptance of unpopular results has been preferable to rejection of the system.

THE PRESIDENCY

The constitutional grant of powers to the President is made in general language without great detail. The "executive power" is vested in the President, who has power to appoint officials, subject to the advice and consent of the Senate (except where Congress waives the confirmation requirement), and to require opinions of such officials. The President is charged with seeing that the laws are faithfully executed and with keeping Congress informed of the state of the Union. The President can veto legislation, call Congress into special session, make treaties with the advice and consent of two-thirds of the Senate, is commander-in-chief of the armed services, and has the power of pardon in all federal cases except impeachment.

But the realities of presidential power are better seen in the history of what Presidents have actually done with these constitutional grants. George Washington established early precedents when he asserted presidential control of the cabinet, responsibility for suppressing domestic disorder (in the Whiskey Rebellion), and a monopoly on communication with foreign governments. Jefferson's initiative in the Louisiana Purchase without advance consent of Congress is well known. Jackson made his mark as a vigorous law enforcer, a vetoer of legislation on policy grounds (not merely on questions of constitutionality), and a strong leader of his party.

President Lincoln combined the roles of law enforcer and commander-in-chief in ways that greatly expanded presidential power. He blockaded ports, summoned state militias, and freed the slaves, all without congressional action. Presidents Theodore Roosevelt, Woodrow Wilson, and Franklin Roosevelt were influential in the growth of "administrative legislation" (rule making by administrators of federal agencies, having the force and effect of law) and "administative adjudication" (dispute settling by federal administrators, resembling judicial procedure). Much of it is performed by semiindependent agencies, such as tariff rate making or unfair trade practice determination, but subject to varying degrees of presidential influence. The depression of the 1930s, followed by World War II and the cold war, provided further impetus to the expansion of presidential power and a doctrine of "crisis leadership." President Truman, in recalling General MacArthur, dramatically reasserted presidential and civilian control of the military, but he exceeded the judicial limits of constitutionality when he seized the steel mills without congressional authorization.

Eisenhower's use of troops to enforce school integration in Little Rock left little doubt about the extent of presidential power in civil rights disturbances. Kennedy's dramatic rollback of Big Steel's price increases in 1962, and Johnson's less dramatic but equally decisive encounter with the aluminum and copper industries in 1965, demonstrate the withering impact of the formal and informal presidential power that can be mobilized in a contest with a segment of American industry. President Nixon's abuse of presidential power, however, led to his resignation.

The powers of the President have increased in response to such factors as war, depression, the failure of Congress to act in time of crisis, and popular demand for leadership, without regard to the party of the White House incumbent.

Although presidential power is obviously vast, recent studies of presidential decision making have described a growing tendency toward *institutionalization* of the Presidency, and some even suggest that the bulk of presidential decisions are actually made by the variety of staffs surrounding the President and even controlling him. He is surrounded not only by his immediate staff, or White House secretariat, but also by a complex of agencies whose heads report directly to him and which are grouped together in what is called the Executive Office of the President. These agencies include, among others, the White House Office, the Office of Management and the Budget (created in 1970, replacing the former Bureau of the Budget), the Council of Economic Advisers, the National Security Council, the National Aeronautics and Space Council, and the Office of Emergency Planning. Not all these executive agencies and assistants surrounding the President are of equal importance or influence. The Office of Management and the Budget ranks near the top in importance. It is not only the central control agency determining the financial needs of all government agencies but the President's policy clearinghouse for all proposals to Congress from the various administrative agencies. The Council of Economic Advisers is potentially as important as the Office of Management and the Budget because of its responsibility for advising the President on measures necessary to keep the nation's economy sound and growing, but its role in practice cannot compare with that of the Office of Management and the Budget.

The National Security Council was created in 1947 to help the President coordinate military and diplomatic policy with domestic resource mobilization capabilities and policies, and was given responsibility for direction of the Central Intelligence Agency. President Eisenhower made much use of the National Security Council, but its utility as a coordinating mechanism has been subjected to a considerable amount of criticism. Other agencies having close relationships with the President in his role as chief administrator are the Civil Service Commission and the General Services Administration (GSA), which is concerned with purchasing, construction, and other houskeeping activities in the government establishment.

Although members of the President's cabinet are obviously important officials, the cabinet in the collective sense has been vastly overrated as a political institution for advice, coordination, and decision making. Most studies conclude that cabinet members operate independently of any significant procedural or policy guidelines laid down by the cabinet as a whole and that the collective judgments required by the President have come to be institutionalized in the staff relationships referred to above.

CONGRESS

Although the paramount function of Congress is legislative, it has constituent powers relating to the proposal of constitutional amendments, electoral powers in certain presidential elections, impeachment powers, investigatory powers, the power to admit new states to the Union, and in the case of the Senate, certain administrative powers, such as the confirmation of executive appointments and the giving of advice on and consent to treaties. The powers of Congress through the years have increased in some respects, particularly as state powers have been eclipsed; but in other respects it has also lost out to the President, whose legislative leadership and quasi-legislative powers have taken away much of its policy-making initiative.

Bicameralism is an important factor in any comparison of Congress with legislative bodies in other countries. Congress shows no signs, for example, of following the British parliamentary pattern of steadily reducing the power and influence of one of the two houses. The 100-member Senate and 435-member House of Representatives remain virtually equal in legislative powers; such differences as exist between them stem more from their respective sizes and methods of electing members than from formal powers.

The role of House and Senate committees as "little legislatures" is also important to understand; the main work of legislative decision making is done in committees. Congressional committees generally have the power of life or death over bills. The House of Representatives is especially dependent on its standing committees, 20 in all, with an average membership of about 30; the Senate has 16 standing committees, varying in size from 7 to 27 members. Some committees are so large that they are divided into specialized subcommittees, some of which have come to have considerable power in themselves. Some 125 House subcommittees have been created.

One of the "sacred cows" of Congress in both House and Senate is the seniority rule governing the selection of committee chairmen. Thus the persons who fill these important positions are in effect locally chosen and locally responsible, because seniority depends upon the decision of voters within individual districts to send their legislators back to Congress time after time. The result has been a preponderance of southern chairmen when the Democrats are in the majority, and a preponderance of rural midwestern chairmen when the Republicans are in control. The party leaders in each house are not chosen on the basis of seniority; the Speaker of the House, for example, is elected every two years by a majority vote of the members of the majority party.

A "sacred cow" peculiar to the Senate is the strong tradition of virtually unlimited debate, with a resulting right of "filibuster" for minority groups determined to block a given piece of legislation. The larger size of the House has necessitated stricter rules limiting debate, but in the Senate cloture, or a vote to end debate so that the legislation before the Senate can be voted on, is a very rare event. As a result, either filibuster or the threat of filibuster by an organized Senate minority is sufficient to block the chances of certain kinds of legislation—particularly, until very recently, civil rights legislation. It should not be concluded, however, that only conservative southerners use the filibuster, for in recent years small groups of liberal senators have availed themselves of unlimited debating privileges.

Although the head of the executive branch, the President normally plays an important role in the work of Congress, both by virtue of constitutional provisions and by traditional extraconstitutional powers. The constitutional powers include the sending of messages to Congress, the proposing of legislation, the veto power, and the power to call special sessions. Extraconstitutional devices for influencing legislation include the threat of veto; discriminating use of the patronage power; personal persuasion through individual contacts with key congressmen; the use of the lobbying capabilities of administrative agencies; and direct appeals to the public through televised speeches, press conferences, and the like. While there are obvious limits to what a President can obtain from the Congress, skillful use of these legislative powers can often be decisive.

Throughout American history, Congress as an institution has been criticized more seriously than the Presidency, and for a greater variety of offenses. Overrepresentation of certain areas, groups, and interests, particularly rural areas and the party in power, has been a major offense. The device often used by state legislatures to accomplish this purpose is gerrymandering—the practice of drawing congressional district boundaries so as to augment the strength of one group at the expense of another. Even when compelled by the Supreme Court to apply the one-man-one-vote principle in determining the size of congressional districts, state legislatures may create a small number of congressional districts with an urban-rural population ratio of 10 to 1, for example, and a larger number of districts with a rural ratio of 3 to 2. But on the whole, because the number of congressmen allowed each state has been revised equitably by Congress after each decennial census, rural overrepresentation has been less of a problem in Congress than in the state legislatures.

The requirement of the consent of a two-thirds majority of the Senate for the ratification of treaties has received sharp criticism, particularly when a minority of the Senate was able to keep the United States out of the League of Nations after World War I. In more recent years, however, many important policies have been put into effect by executive agreements that do not require Senate consent, and by joint (simple majority) action by both houses. The European Recovery Program and the Point Four Program for aid to developing nations, for example, were both authorized by legislation rather than by formal treaty.

Congressional investigations have occasioned some of the severest criticisms that Congress has received. Few would deny that the investigatory function of Congress is an important and even indispensable corollary to lawmaking; many congressional investigations have brought to light important misconduct in and out of government. But in recent years several factors, not the least of which is television, have led to the use of investigations for the personal aggrandizement of certain committee members, or for campaign ammunition, or partisan malice. The Supreme Court has indicated that there are limits to the investigatory power and that it will not compel testimony if these bounds are overstepped.

One other frequent criticism of Congress is that too much of a congress-man's time is required to run errands for constituents. Congressmen have con-sistently refused to relieve themselves of this chore, for the fairly obvious rea-son that doing countless individual favors for constituents is one of the best ways to secure reelection. Although doing errands takes time away from law-making, there are some rather sophisticated arguments in support of congres-sional errand running. As big government gets bigger and seems more cold and impersonal to the citizen, the congressman can and does assume an inval-uable humanizing role as mediator between the bureaucracy and the citizen.

THE BUREAUCRACY

It is a common mistake to think of the mass of federal employees as part and parcel of the executive branch of government and directly subordinate to the President in a hierarchical structure. Actually, because of the complex combi-nation of the principle of separation of powers with the principle of checks and balances, the bureaucracy has an identity of its own and is characterized by dual and even triple responsibility—to the President and Congress as well as to the judiciary—under the law. This mixed pattern of bureaucratic respon-sibility is further complicated by such factors as responsibility to professional interest groups, political parties, and public opinion.

It is also common to think of those millions of bureaucrats "in Washing-ton," but the fact is that the great majority of them are not in Washington; they are scattered throughout regional, field, and local offices in every state. More than half of them—all civilians—work for the army, navy, air force, or other defense agencies, and only about 10 percent work for so-called welfare agencies; the welfare state is still relatively "small potatoes" in terms of the proportion of employees involved. An even smaller number work in agencies responsible for economic regulation.

The organization of the bureaucracy is rather heterogeneous, encompass-ing the "cabinet departments"; more than a score of government corporations, such as the Tennessee Valley Authority and the Federal Deposit Insurance Corporation; a group of independent regulatory commissions, such as the In-terstate Commerce Commission and the Federal Trade Commission; and close to forty other agencies of varying degrees of independence. The indepen-dent regulatory commissions are set apart primarily to keep them relatively free from presidential influence in their exercise of quasi-legislative and quasi-judicial powers.

THE JUDICIARY

Foreign students of the American governmental system, accustomed to courts performing narrowly defined legal functions with little publicity and scant public attention, never cease to marvel at the power and prestige of the American judiciary. There is probably no single reason for the great influence of American judges, though an important one is their possession of the power of judicial review. Judges have many more functions than reviewing the constitutionality of legislation, however, and probably spend only a very small part of their time in cases involving judicial review. Most of their activities center on the ordinary function of settling disputes on the basis of law and fact.

The founding fathers provided specifically for only one federal court, the Supreme Court, but authorized Congress to establish inferior federal courts and to determine their size, as well as the size of the Supreme Court. Congress ultimately set up a hierarchy of district courts, courts of appeal, and the Supreme Court. In spite of the principle of national supremacy as a general feature of American government, the relation of the federal court system to the fifty state court systems is not entirely a superior-subordinate relationship. Only state courts have jurisdiction over some kinds of cases; only federal courts have jurisdiction over certain others; and both court systems have jurisdiction over other kinds.

The Supreme Court was initially made a six-member body by Congress, but the number of justices has gradually been increased to the present total of nine, with one member serving as chief justice. All federal judges are appointed by the President with the advice and consent of the Senate for an indefinite term of "good behavior." Appointments have been made largely on political considerations from the beginning; even John Marshall's main qualifications consisted of his loyal and able service as a Federalist politician. Roger B. Taney had a more distinguished legal background than the inexperienced Marshall, but he too was appointed chief justice (by Jackson) because of his political services in the cabinet. President Grant made sure his prospective appointees were prepared to reverse a previous court decision declaring the Legal Tender Acts unconstitutional. Presidents in all periods of our history have paid attention not only to the party affiliation of prospective appointees but also to their political, social, and economic views.

We cannot escape the conclusion that judges are, in the true sense of the term, politicians. Their appointment with partisan and policy considerations in mind; their inescapable attachment to particular economic, social, political, and religious values; and their full knowledge of the important political implications of judicial decisions clearly make them actors in the American political process. Judicial eyebrows are still raised by such a statement, but it has become increasingly common to recognize that judges do often make the law, rather than simply discover it. There is a danger, to be sure, of overstating the case and concluding that judges are no different from other participants in the contest for the stakes of politics. Important differences do exist, for judges are considerably less accountable to elected legislatures and executives than other political actors; and the avenues of access to, and bargaining with, judges by various political groups are restricted by formal judicial procedures, the strong weight given to legal precedent, and the ethical norms of the profession. But on the whole it is more likely that the student of politics will fail to recognize judges as participants in the broad contest for the rewards of politics than that he will fail to recognize certain differences between judges and the various other participants in American politics.

AMERICAN FEDERALISM IN PRACTICE

The formal constitutional picture of national-state relations in the United States often leads the unsuspecting student of American government to adopt a rather rigid, "layer-cake" analogy of a careful parceling out of functions either to the states or to the national government, with the states in turn parceling out some of their functions to local government. Professor Morton Grodzins contended that a "rainbow" or "marble cake" analogy gives a far more accurate image of the federal system in practice, since it symbolizes better an inseparable mingling of functions at all levels, vertically, diagonally, and in whirls. Whether the layer-cake analogy was at one time true or not (Grodzins thought it never was), few would deny that federal-state-local relationships today are characterized far more by cooperation, coordination, and the sharing of power than by separation and competition. Issues of "states' rights" are seldom a concern when national, state, and local governments get together in joint action on a highway project, in fighting an epidemic, or in running down a "public enemy number one." The occasional controversy between a state and the national government over the administration of a "federal aid" program is an occurrence sufficiently rare to evoke newspaper coverage.

True, there continue to be occasional controversies, such as that between mayors and political leaders of some cities and the federal agencies that sought in Community Action Programs to organize and deal with local citizen groups directly, thus threatening the political base of local party and government officials, or between urban renewal and other federal officials and various state agencies and governors who feel threatened when federal programs establish direct relationships between metropolitan and federal agencies, bypassing the state level altogether. But the prevailing theme is not conflict over which government will monopolize what activity, nor loss of function by one level of government to another. It is expansion of function and increasing activity on the part of almost all agencies at all levels of government—federal, state, and local—as government has steadily accepted more and more responsibilities in "the welfare state."

The inevitable question in any discussion of this "cooperative federalism" is whether or not constitutional federalism in the United States as it once was known is now dead, or at least on its deathbed. It should be quite clear that in the formal constitutional sense, federalism has lost much of its vitality, not only because of the impact of grants-in-aid and other recent changes, but because of issues settled as early as the days of Jefferson and Lincoln. Nevertheless, in the political sense the states still play a prominent part in shaping the character of national party nominating conventions, determining the makeup of Congress, and influencing the selection of judges. Thus the political facts of American life are frequently "state" rather than "national" facts such as one might expect to find in England, France, and other nations not having a federal form of government. Although formal constitutional federalism seems to be withering considerably in the United States, political federalism remains vital principally because of the political vitality of the fifty states as states.

Governmental Institutions: Great Britain

The British have a way of preserving the form of their institutions long after their substance has been completely altered. This tendency is well illustrated by the position of the Crown. At one time, all power inhered in the person of the monarch. It was not conferred by Parliament or anyone else; and it was unlimited. Today the Crown retains full power to do anything and change anything—but only on the advice of ministers who possess the confidence of the House of Commons. Thus the powers of the Crown still exist nominally, and all political acts are done in the monarch's name; but these powers, as we have seen, are now in fact exercised by officials ultimately responsible to the people.

It is therefore necessary to bear in mind the distinction between the terms "queen" and "Crown," between the person of the monarch and the monarchy as an institution. The powers of the Crown have been transferred from the queen as a person to the Crown as an abstraction. Thus Queen Elizabeth's official acts are determined for her by her ministers. But the Crown is the agency through which these acts—the appointing of civil servants, the concluding of treaties, the calling and dissolving of Parliament—are given legal form.

British political institutions center on the Cabinet and Parliament. The former shapes policy and indeed governs the nation, but it must always have the confidence of the latter or it cannot stay in power. Parliament may pass or amend any law; there is no executive veto. And while there is an independent judiciary, there is no judicial review, that is, the courts cannot declare an act of Parliament invalid. When Cabinet and Parliament are in agreement, they are invincible—except that both must concern themselves with the winds of public opinion.

PRIME MINISTER AND CABINET

In the British system, as in other parliamentary systems, there is an essential fusion of legislative and executive powers. The Cabinet, consisting of about eighteen members, including the most important ministers, is the executive. Its members are chosen from Parliament, or more precisely, from members of the majority party in the House of Commons. Cabinet members retain their legislative seats while serving in the Cabinet. Most, certainly the most important ones, come from the House of Commons, although a few sit in the Lords. The leader of the majority party in the Commons is the leader of the Cabinet, the Prime Minister. When referring to the executive collectively, the British often use the term "the Government" in much the same way Americans employ the term "the administration."

The Prime Minister is more than a first among equals. Before becoming Prime Minister, he or she will have had some twenty years' experience in the Commons. This position is not achieved without having won the confidence and respect of party colleagues, upon whose support the Prime Minister must depend. As the queen's first minister, he or she appoints approximately one hundred high officials, including the ministers, the most important of whom will be Cabinet colleagues. The Prime Minister presides at meetings of the Cabinet and has the leading voice in the determination of policy. There may be times, however, when his or her views are at variance with the prevailing mood of the Cabinet, and he or she may not be able to prevail.

Collectively, the Cabinet governs. It is in charge of administration, but it also decides what legislation is needed. Its measures have priority over other business, and in recent years have taken up most of the time of Parliament. Broad policy decisions are hammered out in Cabinet meetings. Once a consensus has been reached, those who were in disagreement must be prepared to defend Cabinet policies in public or resign. The Cabinet is collectively responsible to the House of Commons for all its political and administrative acts. An attack upon one minister is an attack upon all of them; they must stand or fall together.

If the Cabinet meets defeat in the Commons, it must either resign or dissolve the House and set a date for new elections. The choice is determined by the Prime Minister after whatever consultation he or she chooses to make among colleagues. Since resignation would result in the leader of the opposing political party being made Prime Minister, invariably the decision is to hold new elections, giving the electorate an opportunity to pass on the issue or issues that precipitated the crisis. In view of the party solidarity that exists in

Britain, however, a Cabinet is not apt to meet defeat in the Commons so long as it has a majority there. Members of the Prime Minister's party know that a majority vote against the leadership is tantamount to a vote for new elections, in which the dissidents might conceivably lose their party's nomination. A vote against one's party leaders, therefore, is politically suicidal, and is likely to occur only in case of a most serious split in party ranks.

Under these circumstances, the Cabinet has the upper hand, a situation that has led some political leaders to assert that British government has deteriorated into "cabinet dictatorship." This charge would be difficult to substantiate because the Cabinet is continually in touch with its supporters in Parliament and is thus able to gauge what will or will not be acceptable to them. After all, the Cabinet's authority rests on its majority. It must always pay attention to what this majority thinks — for a new election is always in the offing. It must also pay attention to public opinion, for without popular support it cannot exist for long.

While the majority party names the Cabinet, the minority party has its "shadow cabinet," ready to assume the task of governing if political fortunes should provide the opportunity. The members of the shadow cabinet are the opposition-party members who, on the basis of experience and party standing, would assume ministerial posts if the Cabinet resigned or if a new election gave the party a majority in the Commons.

PARLIAMENT

Parliament is made up of two houses, the House of Commons and the House of Lords. The latter is largely a hereditary body, although in recent years it has included a small number of "life peers," men and women of distinction whose peerages exist in their lifetimes only and are not passed on to their heirs. Once superior to the Commons in political influence, the power of the Lords has diminished so that today they have power only to delay legislation — for one month in the case of finance bills and one year in other matters. Although the House of Lords still serves useful functions, such as providing more careful and deliberate consideration of bills by men of wide knowledge and great experience, its power has been so reduced that many observers speak of Parliament and the House of Commons as if the two were synonymous.

The House of Commons is made up of 630 popularly elected members. The chamber in which it meets is rectangular, with a wide aisle down the middle. The members of the two major political parties sit facing each other across the aisle on tiers of benches. At one end of the chamber is the Speaker's chair. On the benches to his right sit the members of the majority party and on those to his left the opposition. On the respective front benches sit the leaders of the two parties.

The presiding officer of the Commons, the Speaker, is elected from among its members but then withdraws from partisan politics and becomes completely impartial, unlike the Speaker of the U.S. House of Representatives, who is an intense partisan. There has been, moreover, an unwritten understanding (violated by Labour in some recent elections) that the Speaker will be automatically reelected to that post, and that in future bids for reelection to the Commons there will be no opposition.

All bills must be submitted to the House of Commons, although some may originate in the Lords. In the Commons they undergo consideration both by committee and by the whole House. The principal provisions of a bill are debated by the House before the bill is sent to committee; indeed, a bill is sent to committee only if the initial vote is favorable. Committees therefore know that every bill sent to them is assured of final passage, and must work to realize the aims and purposes of the bills under consideration. They cannot seek to change them radically. In the case of measures proposed by the Cabinet, the appropriate minister or his deputy is in the committee, helping to shape and guide the bill through. Bills introduced by ministers are known as government measures, while other bills concerning public policy are called private members' bills. Those of purely local concern, that is, with a local or personal application, are called private bills.

It is interesting to note that House of Commons committees are not specialized (for foreign affairs, agriculture, and so on), but are simply designated by letters (committees A, B, C, and so on). The Scottish and Welsh committees are exceptions. The membership of each committee changes to some extent with every new measure sent to it, so that a member of the Commons with special qualifications may be assigned to a particular committee that may be considering a measure in his area of competence. There is no seniority principle and no competition for committee membership. Committee chairmen, like the Speaker, are impartial. Bills do not carry the names of House of Commons members, nor are committees referred to by the chairmen's names.

As we have seen, Cabinet measures have priority in Parliament, assuring the government that its proposals will be acted upon. The Cabinet, moreover, has control of finance: It alone submits bills for the spending and raising of revenue. Standing orders—that is, the rules of the House—prohibit motions to increase expenditure, thus avoiding "pork-barrel" legislation. Motions to reduce expenditure are in order, but such motions would be regarded as expressing a want of confidence in the Cabinet, and treated as such. Finally, the government has no problem in bringing a measure to a vote. Debate can be cut off by an ordinary majority vote.

Since the Cabinet governs, the primary role of the House of Commons is criticism and control, a function the Commons exercises in several ways. Four times a week at the beginning of the day's session there is the Question Hour, a time when any member of the Commons may address questions to ministers about any matter within their province. Ministers generally reply fully and carefully, although on occasion (particularly when questions are in the realm of foreign affairs or defense) they may assert that it would not be in the national interest to answer. In addition to the Question Hour, there are debates on bills brought in by the Cabinet. And from time to time, motions of censure may be introduced, forcing the ministers to defend their actions and policies. Conversely, the Cabinet itself may propose a motion expressing confidence in the government, usually after criticism has been voiced by the opposition. By using these various means, the opposition can, on behalf of the public, extract information, ventilate its grievances, and voice its concerns about governmental measures and policies. The Cabinet, for its part, has the opportunity to explain and defend its acts.

It is significant that a considerable amount of parliamentary time is set aside for the use of the opposition. The Speech from the Throne, delivered by the queen at the opening of each session of Parliament but actually written for her by the Prime Minister and colleagues and presenting their program, is subject to considerable debate, following which a vote is taken on the Address, the House of Commons' general response to the Speech from the Throne. Moreover, the so-called Supply Days, consuming about a month's time, are for the exclusive use of the opposition, which determines what items in the Cabinet's budget are to be debated. Most of this debate concerns matters of policy rather than specific items in the appropriation bills. Finally, the opposition has little difficulty in getting two or three days set aside now and then to propose and debate a censure motion involving specific policies on such matters as foreign affairs, defense, or colonial policy. In brief, the opposition's rights in Parliament must not be underestimated.

THE BUREAUCRACY

In Great Britain most of the work of administration is carried out through some thirty ministries, each organized on a hierarchical basis. At the top of the hierarchy is the minister. Like the secretary who heads an American cabinet department, he or she is the political head of the ministry (department), shaping policy for it and presenting recommendations to the Cabinet. Unlike American cabinet officers, British ministers are also members of Parliament. At the same time, they are responsible for the daily administrative work of their departments. Assisting them are a handful of officials whom they appoint, principally their parliamentary secretaries, who belong to the same political party and are also MPs. If the minister sits in the Lords, the parliamentary secretary is always in the Commons, although the reverse is not necessarily true.

When political control of the House of Commons changes, therefore, only the minister and the few top aides change. For all practical purposes, each
ministry remains intact. Its work is supervised by a permanent secretary and a
number of assistant secretaries, all of whom are permanent civil servants.
They and those below them are recruited on the basis of ability, not political
preferment.

For a long time the recruitment and assignment of civil servants was under the Treasury, which in this respect exercised functions comparable to
those of the U.S. Civil Service Commission and the Office of Management and
the Budget. In 1968 this control was transferred to a new Civil Service Department under the Prime Minister. In contrast with the American practice, the
British practice is to recruit people for the civil service on the basis of their potential for growth rather than on the basis of training and preparation for a
specific job. This is especially true of recruitment for the administrative class,
the highest class in the civil service. The British attract the best university graduates, irrespective of their course of study, on the assumption that such people
can easily be trained for specific jobs and that they are the most promising candidates for really important positions in the future.

As we have seen, a minister is responsible to Parliament for the way his or
her department functions; permanent civil servants cannot be summoned by
the Commons or its committees to answer for their work. Consequently, civil
servants can serve their ministers to the best of their abilities without fear that
they may be called to account for advising courses of action that may be politically unpopular at the moment.

In recent years, the matter of responsibility has been complicated by at
least two developments. The first concerns the operation of nationalized industries. In some countries, responsibility of such enterprises is sought
through making them autonomous government corporations (much like the
American TVA); in others, through placing them directly under the control of
some established executive or administrative agency. Parliament decided to
put each such industry under the jurisdiction of a ministry, thus making the
minister responsible for it. At the same time, it wanted each nationalized industry to have some autonomy. The result was a compromise, with the minister being empowered to appoint the governing board of a nationalized industry and to pass on its basic decisions, for example, the borrowing of
money. In these matters the minister can be held to account, but not for those
over which he or she does not have control.

The second development is that of delegated legislation. With the increasing complexity of social legislation, Parliament found that it could foresee
fewer and fewer eventualities. Consequently, it began writing legislation in
broad outline form, empowering the agency charged with its administration

to draft such rules and regulations—called statutory instruments—as were necessary to give the legislation effect. These rules and regulations came to be known as delegated or subordinate legislation. Since ministers were overworked, civil servants far removed from Parliament were thus writing most of the subordinate legislation. To make ministers more truly responsible, Parliament requires such statutory instruments to be laid before it. Some require affirmative parliamentary action, but most go into effect if the House of Commons does not act adversely within forty days.

Some developments in the 1970s point to a politicization of the civil service. First, in 1974 the Prime Minister set up a special policy unit (six members) in his office, and subsequently authorized Cabinet ministers to appoint no more than two special advisers each. Their legal status was "temporary civil servants." When Margaret Thatcher became Prime Minister in 1979, all these positions were allowed to lapse.

Another seeming politicization of the civil service was the mushrooming of a large number of organizations, side by side with the regular civil service, known as *Quangos* (originally "quasi-nongovernmental organizations"). Appointments to these bodies (hospital boards, boards of prison visitors, etc.) are the personal gift of ministers. As of 1978 there were over 800 of these, with over 8,000 paid appointments and 25,000 unpaid ones. A large number of these are from civil servants currently in service. While there are few or no allegations that *Quangos* give "political direction to an important part of the public service," they do give party leaders "a new means to reward the party faithful" or provide a "fat retirement cushion" for those who have served the party well in the past.[2]

THE JUDICIARY

Great Britain is the mother of one of the world's principal legal systems, the common law, which the United States inherited. Common law is sometimes referred to as case law because it developed from the application by the king's judges of local custom to individual cases that came before them. After a time, these judges were applying similar legal rules throughout England, hence the term common law—law common to the whole realm. In some areas the common law has been augmented and in other ways superseded by legislative enactments. Moreover, both have been modified by court decisions. Here we are concerned less with the law itself than with the judicial system through which it is expressed and applied.

---

2. S. E. Finer, *The Changing British Party System, 1945-1979* (Washington, D.C.: American Enterprise Institute for Public Policy Research, 1980), p. 161.

The British judicial system is characterized by independence and the rule of law. British judges are appointed for life and serve during good behavior. Independence, however, does not mean judicial review, for as has been mentioned, no British court has the power to nullify an act of Parliament. The principle of the rule of law means that no one is above the law and that individuals can be punished only for those things that the law forbids. The end result of the application of these principles has been a high degree of impartial justice.

The English court system (Scotland has a separate judicial system) is organized into two hierarchies, one civil and the other criminal. Most appeals end with the Court of Appeal or the Court of Criminal Appeal. The final court of appeal for both civil and criminal cases is the House of Lords, or more precisely, those members of the House known as the law lords acting in the name of the whole House. These are not hereditary peers, but men with legal training who are appointed for life. In the main, the law lords hear appeals from civil cases involving particularly difficult points of law. It should be noted that appeals in Great Britain are much more difficult than in the United States. In virtually all instances, permission of the higher court is required, and appeals are normally restricted to cases in which the lower court's interpretation of the law has been challenged.

UNITARISM IN PRACTICE

Formally speaking, the British government is "unitary" rather than federal. All organs and actions of government below the national level are in principle legally the "creatures" of Parliament, which, in theory, may abolish or alter their structure and powers as it pleases. In fact, Great Britain has a long tradition of relatively autonomous government, that is, of local governments proceeding quite independently of direct national supervision or direction — perhaps because units of English local government were in existence long before there was a central government.

The areas of local discretion have increasingly narrowed, however. Although they are organizationally independent, local authorities have been more and more engaged in the local administration of national programs. Certain services once provided locally, such as public assistance, gas, electricity, and hospital management, are now a national responsibility. On the other hand, local authorities still exercise wide discretion over sanitation, street lighting, recreational and cultural facilities, and child welfare. In the field of education, national authority has also been on the increase, although actual administration (the hiring and firing of teachers, for example) is a local responsibility. This trend toward national responsibility has been facilitated by the circumstance that there is no constitutional division of authority between national and local authorities.

The central government exercises three forms of control over local authorities. The first is legal: Parliament can grant powers to local authorities and it can take them away. The second is financial: The national government provides over half the funds needed by local authorities and in large measure specifies the way they are to be spent. The third is supervisory: Various national ministries, through statutory instruments, memoranda, inspectors and district auditors, and also through their power to approve or disapprove local proposals in many areas of activity, influence and control the work of local government. The Home Secretary, for example, has significant supervisory powers over the police, and the Minister of Education over the schools.

Although units of local government have been in existence a long time, the machinery of local government was radically overhauled and modernized by several acts of Parliament during the nineteenth century. Today the principal institutions of local government are the elected councils in the cities and counties and the appointed full-time officials who perform the day-to-day tasks of local government. The councilors are the unpaid amateurs, though they are responsible for local policy and administration. Most of the actual work of the councils is performed by committees and subcommittees. Although some party politics enters local government, rigid partisan attitudes are rare. The full-time appointed officials are paid, and because salary and other benefits have improved in recent years, local administration is looked upon as a worthwhile career. Similarly, service on the local council is considered advantageous to those who aspire to a parliamentary career.

The British system of government is a good example of a democratic system that has been able to adjust peacefully and well to changing circumstances. It has long been of special interest to political scientists. Not only was it the first system to develop the forms of political organization that we now call the cabinet type of constitutional government; it has been very widely accepted as the classic model of this type. Many new nations all over the world have attempted to pattern their systems after the British. Understanding it and the ways in which it differs from other major systems is therefore of special importance when we try to compare political institutions and processes in different countries to arrive at a more general understanding of government.

Parliamentary Government in Canada

The British system has provided the model for the Canadian system of government. The North America Act of 1867 granted self-government to Canada, and after several imperial conferences early in this century, the right of self-government was recognized for a number of dominions by the Statute of Westminster of 1931. The act is quite precise in dealing with Dominion autonomy.

It asserts, first, that the formal executive, the Governor General, shall be appointed on the advice of the Dominion. Second, each Dominion is free to legislate concerning its own affairs. Third, judicial appeals from Dominion courts to the Judicial Committee of the Privy Council in London could be cut off should any Dominion wish to do so. Finally, each Dominion is sovereign in the realm of foreign affairs. Therefore, Canada (as well as the other dominions) is an independent self-governing nation, although maintaining a link to the mother country as a member of the Commonwealth (formerly the British Commonwealth).

Canada's political heritage, except for the French-Canadian population located mainly in Quebec, was British. With its extensive and sparsely populated territory, however, Canada found her political life influenced by the frontier spirit and became the home of immigrant pioneers to whom social class and other distinctions were not too important. This made for an environment favorable to the evolution of democratic ideas and institutions, of a tolerant pluralistic society based on liberal-democratic principles. Moreover, unlike the United States, Canada experienced no war of independence or civil war.

In the past decade, the problem of Quebec, with one-fourth of Canada's population (80 percent of which is French), has come to the fore. In the mid-1970s, the French nationalist party, Parti Quebecois, under the leadership of Rene Levesque, gained control of the provincial government. It immediately set about to make the province more French, among other things to insist that French be the dominant language, although English-speaking residents could still send their children to English schools. New arrivals in Quebec, whatever their linguistic or other backgrounds, would have to send their children to French schools. In addition, the Parti Quebecois promised to hold a referendum, which in effect would enable the residents of Quebec to vote for independence from Canada. In anticipation of this vote, many businesses (most of which were English-controlled) began to move out of Quebec, with no clearly predictable consequences.

After several postponements, the referendum was finally held on 20 May 1980. It was ingeniously phrased: not asking for a yes or no vote on independence, but asking citizens of Quebec to give the separatist government a mandate to negotiate for a sovereign Quebec that would still maintain an economic association (monetary union, free flow of people and capital, a free trade zone, and common tariff policies) with the rest of Canada. Long before the referendum was held, English-speaking Canada indicated that it had no interest in such an arrangement. The referendum went against Levesque by a wide margin (60 percent), indicating that many French Canadians had voted in the negative. Nevertheless, Levesque easily won the 1981 provincial elections.

Prime Minister Pierre Trudeau and the head of the Liberal party of Quebec, Claude Ryan, have supported a democratic bilingual Canada, wherein Quebec's grievances could be met in common cause. Be it noted that during Trudeau's several cabinets, much was done to remedy the economic injustices Quebec had suffered under the English-speaking elite that had in the past controlled most of the banks and other large enterprises.

Regional differences have become sharper in recent years in other ways. Natural resources, especially energy, are a source of discord. Ontario, for example, which has one-third of the country's population and one-half of its manufacturing capacity, has complained about the price of Alberta's oil, even though the oil has been selling considerably below the world market price. Quebec's determination to weaken the national government has struck a responsive chord elsewhere. The three western provinces, with a combined financial surplus that exceeds Canada's deficit of $13 billion, are not eager to share the wealth. And the impoverished province of Newfoundland was pleased to gain control over its offshore oil and mineral deposits, which are regarded as promising.

In any case, revision of Canada's constitution (the North America Act of 1867) is on the agenda. Given the somewhat diverse interests and demands of the various provinces, this could be a long and drawn-out affair. Prime Minister Pierre Trudeau in 1980 and 1981 acted to simplify the process by proposing that the British Parliament "patriate" the Canadian constitution, in effect making Canada the author of the North America Act, thereby giving Canada the power to amend it or to make a new constitution. Before doing so, however, he wanted the British Parliament to expand the constitution by including a bill of rights that, among other things, would limit the powers of the provinces. In this way, Canada's Parliament could adopt a constitution without asking the consent of the provinces. After several provinces went to Canadian courts in an effort to nullify Trudeau's plans with inconclusive results, Trudeau made considerable concessions and in late 1981 reached agreement on the principles of a new constitution with all the provinces except Quebec. The latter's Levesque, however, predicted "incalculable consequences."

Unlike Britain, Canada is a federal state, with ten provinces. The founders of the Canadian federation were determined to have a strong national government, and to that end stipulated that powers not granted to the provinces are reserved to the national government. Nevertheless, the provinces and their prime ministers have greater powers than do the states and their governors in the United States. For example, each province has sole responsibility for its educational system, and most Canadian workers bargain under provincial and not national legislation.

Canada has a parliamentary or cabinet system of government. There is no separation of powers in the American sense, and no judicial review. As in Britain, executive power is formally vested in the head of state, the Governor General, presumably representing the British monarch but actually the nominee of the Canadian government and now a Canadian. The powers of the Governor General are similar to those of the British monarch, with the major opportunity for discretionary political action occurring when no party has a majority in the legislature or when the incumbent Prime Minister dies or resigns.

Real executive power is exercised by the Cabinet, presided over by the Prime Minister, who is there by virtue of being the leader of the majority party in the House of Commons. While having the power to choose other members of the Cabinet, the Prime Minister must seek to include representatives from as many of the provinces as possible. As in Britain, the Cabinet is the real policy maker, and it is collectively responsible to the House of Commons.

In Canada's Parliament, the House of Commons is the dominant body. The upper house, the Senate, is similar to the House of Lords in London in that it may neither originate nor amend financial legislation and possesses powers of limited delay. The House of Commons is elected on the basis of a broad suffrage and single-member districts. While the more populous provinces have the bulk of the membership, each province is assured a minimum number of members irrespective of population. Members of the Senate are appointed by the Governor General on the advice of the Cabinet, and although all provinces are represented, the Senate is not viewed primarily as an aspect of Canadian federalism. Two provinces (Quebec and Ontario) have twenty-four members each, nearly one-half of the total Senate membership.

The internal organization of and procedure in the Canadian House of Commons is not too different from its counterpart in London. The Speaker is impartial in procedural rulings, but unlike the Speaker in Britain, the official serves only until another party gains control of the House. Moreover, at election time, the Speaker is actively opposed by a member (or members) of another political party. The procedure for the handling of bills and other matters is much like that in London.

For the most part, Canada has had a tradition of two political parties, based upon nationwide support and representing regional, economic, ethnic, and religious interests. They are the Liberal and Progressive-Conservative parties. Except for two brief interludes (1957-63 and 1979-80), the Liberal party has held sway over the national government since the 1930s. From time to time the Liberals have needed to form minority governments, that is, Cabinets made necessary by virtue of the fact that no party had a majority in the House of Commons. In such circumstances, a minority government can stay in power only if it can command some support from one or more minority parties, either in the form of actually voting with it or at least abstaining.

In 1968, the Liberals, under the leadership of French Canadian Pierre Elliott Trudeau, won a large majority. Subsequently, Liberal strength declined somewhat, with an actual loss in the May 1979 election, following which Trudeau announced that he was giving up the party leadership. With the fall of the Progressive-Conservative government after only nine months in office, Trudeau was persuaded to return, and in February 1980 the Liberals won a clear majority (146 seats). The Progressive-Conservatives won 103 seats, and the New Democratic party, formed in 1961 as a type of farm-labor-socialist party, succeeded in getting 32 seats (12 of them from British Columbia).

These results, as well as earlier ones, suggest a certain regional polarization in Canadian politics. In 1980, for example, of the 146 seats that the Liberals won, only 2 came from provinces west of Ontario; they won no seats in British Columbia, Alberta, or Saskatchewan. In Quebec, on the other hand, they won 73 seats, while the Progressive-Conservatives were winning only a single seat. Without the Quebec seats, the Liberals would be out of power and reduced to little more than a minority party. How the constitutional issue is resolved will have an impact not only on this regional polarization but also on the general future of the Canadian federation.

SUGGESTIONS FOR ADDITIONAL READING

ANDRAIN, CHARLES F. *Politics and Economic Policy in Western Democracies.* North Scituate, Mass.: Duxbury Press, 1980.

BRADSHAW, KENNETH, and PRING, DAVID. *Parliament and Congress.* London: Constable, 1972.

On Britain

BEER, SAMUEL H. *British Politics in the Collectivist Age.* New York: Knopf, 1965.

FINER, S. E. *The Changing British Party System, 1945-1979.* Washington, D.C.: American Enterprise Institute, 1980.

McKENZIE, R. T. *British Political Parties: The Distribution of Power Within the Conservative and Labour Parties.* 2nd ed. New York: Praeger, 1964.

MACKINTOSH, JOHN. *The British Cabinet.* 2nd ed. London: Stevens, 1968.

MORRISON, HERBERT. *Government and Parliament: A Survey from the Inside.* 3rd ed. London: Oxford University Press, 1964.

ROSE, RICHARD. *Do Parties Make a Difference?* Chatham, N.J.: Chatham House, 1980.

SMITH, GEOFFREY, and POLSBY, NELSON. *British Government and Its Discontents.* New York: Basic Books, 1981.

WILSON, HAROLD. *The Governance of Britain.* New York: Harper & Row, 1977.

On the United States

CAMPBELL, BRUCE A. *The American Electorate: Attitudes and Action.* New York: Holt, Rinehart and Winston, 1979.

COX, ARCHIBALD. *The Role of the Supreme Court in American Government.* New York: Oxford University Press, 1976.

KOENIG, LOUIS W. *The Chief Executive.* 3rd ed. New York: Harcourt Brace Jovanovich, 1975.

LADD, EVERETT C., and HADLEY, CHARLES D. *Transformations of the American Party System: Political Coalitions from the New Deal to the 1970s.* 2nd ed. New York: Norton, 1978.

MAYHEW, DAVID. *Congress: The Electoral Connection.* New Haven: Yale University Press, 1974.

OWEN, HENRY, and SCHULTZE, CHARLES L., eds. *Setting National Priorities: The Next Ten Years.* Washington, D.C.: Brookings, 1976.

PRITCHETT, C. HERMAN. *The American Constitution.* 3rd ed. New York: McGraw-Hill, 1976.

SANDOZ, ELLIS. *Conceived in Liberty: American Individual Rights Today.* North Scituate, Mass.: Duxbury Press, 1978.

On Canada

JACOBS, JANE. *The Question of Separatism: Quebec and the Struggle over Sovereignty.* New York: Random House, 1980.

MALLORY, J. R. *The Structure of Canadian Government.* Toronto: Macmillan, 1971.

MATHESON, W. A. *The Prime Minister and the Cabinet.* Toronto: Methuen, 1976.

VAN LOON, RICHARD, and WHITTINGTON, MICHAEL S. *The Canadian Political System.* 2nd ed. Toronto: McGraw-Hill Ryerson, 1976.

WHITE, W. L.; WAGENBERG, R. H.; and NELSON, R. C. *Introduction to Canadian Politics and Government.* 2nd ed. Toronto: Holt, Rinehart and Winston, 1977.

2. Continental European Parliamentarism: France and Germany

As we have seen in the previous chapter, there has been among the British and the Americans a basic acceptance of their respective political systems over a considerable period of time. A country having such a basic agreement (consensus) about its political system is said to possess a homogeneous political culture. Nations such as France and Germany, in which a similar consensus has been lacking, are said to have fragmented political cultures. Some observers assert that France and Germany are moving toward a homogeneous political culture, but only time will tell.

Both France and Germany have what might be called parliamentary regimes, but they differ from the classical British model and from each other. Following the French Revolution of 1789, France went through a century of turmoil, trying various political formations before the establishment of the Third Republic in 1875. Since that time she has remained a republic, even though consensus was often questioned and generally only skin deep. Defeat and occupation in the course of World War II led to the formation of the Fourth Republic, to be followed by the creation of the Fifth Republic in 1958, which is the present arrangement.

Unlike France, whose unity as a nation goes a long way back, Germany did not achieve unification until late in the nineteenth century, and then under the authoritarian dominance of one of the German states, Prussia. Similarly, Germany did not try democratic rule until the end of World War I when a parliamentary system was established, known as the Weimar Republic. This short-lived experiment came to an end with the creation of the Hitler dictatorship in 1933. After World War II, the Germans established a second republic in the Western occupation zones, known as the Bonn Republic, or formally, as the Federal Republic of Germany. Although different from Weimar in several respects, it is nevertheless similar in that it constitutes a parliamentary system.

The Constitutions

The most striking feature of French constitutional development has been the inability of the major social groups in the nation to agree on their fundamental political values and institutions. In all political systems a clash of interests takes place through channels provided by a constitution, but in France the constitutional arrangements themselves have been in dispute. This means an inability on the part of the principal social classes to "agree to disagree" within the framework of a common set of institutions. Some observers believe, however, that the Fifth Republic may be moving France in the direction of "legitimacy," that is, toward a general acceptance of the evolving political structure. Nevertheless, no one will deny that many uncertainties and challenges continue to exist.

There was in France a period of constitutional stability lasting over a thousand years under the old regime, overthrown in 1789. The Revolution was followed by a series of regimes, none of which was able to win lasting support from all the social forces within the nation. The partisans of monarchy, drawn mainly from the landed aristocracy, were pitted against the advocates of parliamentary republicanism, representing the commercial and industrial middle classes and later the workers. This conflict was in part resolved with the establishment of the Third Republic in 1875, which represented a compromise that was slowly winning the adherence of the people. Although the Third Republic weathered the First World War, it experienced crises in the 1930s and came to an end with World War II. The Fourth Republic, almost a copy of the Third, could not deal with the problems of the dissolving French empire, notably Algeria. In 1958 it came to an end, and the hero of Free France in World War II, General Charles de Gaulle, was given the mandate of drafting a new constitution, which gave birth to the Fifth Republic.

Since the Revolution of 1789, France has had nineteen constitutions, although this number is in dispute because some of them never came into force. The most lasting of these was the one that created the Third Republic in 1875. The assembly that produced it had a monarchist majority, but when after four years it could not agree on a pretender to the throne, it created a republic that most delegates did not believe would long survive. The constitution of the Third Republic consisted of three fragmentary "organic laws," which launched a parliamentary system that served France until the Second World War.

The basic structure of the Third Republic resembled that of a constitutional monarchy—with a President in the role of the constitutional monarch. Executive power was in the main exercised by the Council of Ministers (or Cabinet); legislative power was divided between a lower and an upper house (Chamber of Deputies and Senate). The Senate was indirectly elected, while the Chamber of Deputies was directly elected by universal suffrage and was considered to be the expression of popular sovereignty. The President of the

Republic was elected by a joint session of the two houses of parliament. He in turn designated a Prime Minister, who formed a Cabinet, subject to the approval of parliament. The relations between the Cabinet and parliament constituted the distinctive feature of French parliamentarism.

It was originally the hope of the monarchist majority in 1875 that the President of the Republic would become the dominant force within the system, thus facilitating the transition to a monarchy. The President, for example, was given the power to dissolve the Chamber of Deputies (with the consent of the Senate). The use of this power by President MacMahon in 1877 backfired when, in the election that followed, the republicans scored a decisive victory and virtually compelled MacMahon to resign. After that it became an article of republican faith to select a "weak" President, that is, one who confined his activities strictly to the performance of ceremonies and did not attempt to wield political power. The requirement that acts of the President be countersigned by a minister made it possible to enforce the custom.

Executive power then devolved upon the Prime Minister and the Cabinet. In order to prevent the utilization of the highly centralized administrative services for political purposes, parliament enforced continuing responsibility upon the political heads of the executive. Although it seemed that a rough balance had come into being between the executive, on the one side, and the national sovereignty (expressed through universal suffrage and parliament), on the other, parliament could overthrow the Cabinet with relative ease. Consequently, the French system came to be called "assembly government," because, unlike in Britain, it was the Chamber of Deputies that was dominant and not the Cabinet.

The Cabinet was weak not only because it could not dissolve the lower house and thus force new elections but also because every Cabinet was a coalition Cabinet, made up of representatives from several political parties. This was made necessary by virtue of the fact that no political party had a majority during the whole existence of the Third Republic. The Cabinet was also weakened because, again unlike in Britain, it did not have control of finance and its bills did not have priority in parliament.

The result in practice was Cabinet instability; the average life of a Cabinet was less than seven months. This fact is a bit deceptive in that each new Cabinet had many members from the outgoing one. But this game of political "musical chairs" was disruptive because most major problems had to be pushed aside. Coalition Cabinets could function only on the basis of agreement on the lowest common denominator.

Nevertheless, the French parliamentary system worked remarkably well until the end of World War I. Under its auspicies a succession of strong personalities was able to establish the Republic on firm foundations (against the attacks of monarchists and assorted rightists), reconstruct the shattered economy, pay off the reparations imposed in 1871 by the Germans, establish a farflung system of secular schools, build up the armed forces, create a diplomatic coalition that eventually brought about the isolation of Germany, and consolidate an empire in Africa and Asia. These achievements, crowned by victory over Germany in 1918, all redounded to the glory of the Republic.

What caused the failure of the Republic after the victory of 1918, in such sharp contrast to the success achieved after the defeat in 1871? In part it was the delicate balance between the executive and parliament, which was upset by the latter's withholding confidence in the Cabinet on the basis of partisan considerations that appeared unrelated to the serious task of constructing majorities. This happened at the very time when pressing needs of the economy and society required strengthening of the executive. Because of the executive-legislative deadlock, the practice developed of vesting the government with power to legislate by decree, even though this obviously violated the spirit if not the letter of the constitution. Yet there seemed to be no other alternative, since the legislature was unable to muster a durable majority.

The foregoing cannot be an adequate explanation, however. The French have demonstrated on numerous occasions their ability to combine universal suffrage, parliamentary control, and bureaucratic centralization in an effective manner. It seems that institutions began to function badly because the major social and political groups were unable to maintain sufficient unity to sustain effective government and were incapable of providing dynamic political leadership. Growing ineffectiveness of government and the rapid military collapse of 1940 were both reflections of a deep crisis within the French nation, although one must never forget that the latter resulted primarily from the superior armor of a determined foe.

The Fourth Republic did not differ too much from the Third, except that the powers of the upper house of parliament were significantly reduced and a not too successful effort was made to introduce the power of dissolution. In practice things proceeded much as before; "assembly government" continued. The lower house (called the National Assembly) continued to dominate, with all Cabinets being coalitions because no political party could gain a majority. Nevertheless, the Fourth Republic, much as its predecessor, gradually met a number of serious threats from extremists, consolidated popular support, and scored some respectable achievements through basic reforms that modified French economic, social, and colonial structures. It did not, however, bring about an equitable social division of the benefits derived from increased productivity.

Although the regime did not satisfy the communists, who were polling close to 25 percent at national elections, or the growing Gaullist movement, which was polling even more, it managed to reduce the strength of both in parliamentary seats so that government could continue. In short, the Fourth Republic functioned relatively well until it came up against the problem of Algeria. It managed to get out of Vietnam, but the inability of a series of Cabinets either to suppress the rebellion in Algeria or to negotiate a peace with the rebels that would guarantee the rights of the large French population (1.5 million) led to an explosion of nationalist sentiment and the overthrow of the Republic. When the leaders of the Cabinet realized that civil war could be avoided only by giving in to the demands of the nationalists that General de Gaulle be brought back, they gave in.

De Gaulle was made Prime Minister, and thereby the forms of republican legality were respected; but he accepted only when he was given power to govern and to revise the constitution. Within three months a new constitutional text was drawn up by his advisers, and in September 1958 it was approved in a popular referendum.

The constitution of the Fifth Republic contains the usual features of a democratic order. It retains the parliamentary system, although as we shall see, the way the office of President has evolved in practice leads some observers to conclude that France has moved to a form of presidential government. According to the constitution, the President is the head of state and the Prime Minister is the head of government. By comparison with the Third and Fourth republics, however, the powers of the President have been significantly increased, especially in times of emergency. The Cabinet continues to be responsible to the lower house, the National Assembly, but Cabinets are no longer as helpless as they were in the predecessor republics. Moveover, the powers of parliament are now enumerated, and thereby limited, since in the Third and Fourth republics the powers of parliament were considered unlimited.

Under the present constitution the position of the Cabinet in relation to parliament is made stronger. Cabinet measures now have priority, and the Cabinet has control over finance so that its budgets cannot be torn apart by an irresponsible assembly. The National Assembly may, in the final analysis, vote the Cabinet out of office. The Prime Minister is the key person in the Cabinet.

The judicial system remains as before, independent of political winds. The constitution does introduce limited judicial review before a separately constituted Constitutional Council.

As does Britain, France operates as a unitary system, although it is even more centralized than Britain. What is referred to in Britain as local government is generally viewed as administration in France.

The French constitution may be amended by a majority vote in each of
✳ the houses of parliament (National Assembly and Senate), subject to ratification either by a three-fifths majority vote in a specially called joint meeting of
the two houses or by popular referendum at the discretion of the President of
the Republic. If the proposed amendments are initiated by members of parliament, ratification must be by referendum. De Gaulle was able to circumvent
the amendment process in 1962 by submitting his proposal for the popular
election of the President to a popular referendum without action by the houses
of parliament. His second attempt to utilize this unconstitutional process in
1969 resulted in the defeat of the proposed amendment and in his resignation
as President.

Constitutional instability and a lack of consensus in Germany stemmed
from late unification and a lack of experience with democracy. The Congress
of Vienna, which met in 1815 to make the peace treaties after Napoleon's defeat, reduced the total number of independent states in Central Europe to thirty-nine, which joined together in the German Confederation. This feeble organization (existing from 1815 to 1866) was unable to function effectively. The
wave of national and liberal revolutions in 1848, which spread through most
of Europe, failed to produce a meaningful unification of Germany. Unification was finally achieved or, more appropriately, imposed from above by the
strongest of the German states, Prussia, and her Iron Chancellor, Otto von
Bismarck, who through a series of military and other actions succeeded in creating the German Empire in 1871.

The empire had a central government of limited powers, a federation in
which the member states retained most of their powers except over foreign affairs. Moreover, the empire was dominated by the strongest of the states,
Prussia, whose king was also emperor of Germany. The Chancellor, who was
the first minister both in the empire and in Prussia, was appointed by the emperor and responsible to him and not to the legislature. There were some trap-
pings of democracy, such as a popularly elected lower house of parliament,
but they did not seriously limit the exercise of executive power. The lower
house (Reichstag) did have power to vote the budget and loans, but this power
was restricted by the exclusion of the most important expenditure, the military budget, which grew at a staggering rate up to World War I. Not only was
parliamentary authority limited but certain extraparliamentary forces (the army, landed aristocracy, and the bureaucracy) exercised considerable real
power. Under the bellicose leadership of Emperor William II, Germany embarked on an aggressive campaign to build up her military establishment, a
process that led to World War I and the end of the German Empire.

Following the surrender of the nation and the flight of the emperor, a republic was rather hastily proclaimed, and in 1919 a constitution was drafted in the quiet little town of Weimar. The government established by this constitution preserved some forms of federalism, but essentially it created a centralized system. Moreover, the constitution provided for a parliamentary system, although it delegated significant power to a democratically elected President. The latter appointed a Chancellor and a Cabinet that were responsible to the Reichstag, the lower house of parliament.

The Reichstag was elected on a nationwide system of proportional representation (i.e., each political party getting seats in proportion to the vote it received), a system that encouraged many parties. The result was something like that in France; no party ever had a majority in the Reichstag, and all Cabinets were coalitions representing several parties. The result was Cabinet instability and frequent elections. These factors, combined with the critical problems (loss of territory, reparation payments, inflation) that the nation faced in the 1920s, capped by the worldwide depression of 1929, were more than the system could endure. These circumstances might well have brought about the collapse of more effective governments; they were just too much for the first feeble German attempts at democracy.

As conditions in Germany became worse, the strength of the radical parties increased. More and more people began turning to Adolf Hitler and his National Socialist German Workers (Nazi) party. At the same time, communist strength was increasing. Together, the Nazis and communists polled half of the vote in the 1932 elections, enough to bring government to a standstill; but of course they could not collaborate to govern the nation. In January 1933, President von Hindenburg called Adolf Hitler to serve as Chancellor, which, despite the retention of certain forms, spelled the end of the Weimar Republic.

Upon assuming the chancellorship, Hitler began to establish a one-party state under his dictatorship. After the arrest of the communist members of the Reichstag, the Nazis and the Nationalists commanded sufficient votes to bring an end to German democracy "legally." Civil rights were terminated on the pretext of protecting the people and the state. Powers to legislate, to determine the budget, and to amend the constitution were transferred from the parliament to Hitler and his Cabinet. In accordance with the delegation of power embodied in these acts, Hitler's government decreed in July 1933 that the Nazi party was the only legal party in Germany. Upon the death of von Hindenburg in the following year, Hitler consolidated his power by combining the office of Chancellor with the office of President. After considerable success in his economic recovery programs and large-scale remilitarization, he led Germany to war, with disastrous consequences for Germany and many other countries.

After twelve years, Hitler's "Thousand Year Empire" came to an end. The main allied powers (United States, Soviet Union, Great Britain, France), by prior agreement, divided Germany into zones of occupation, an arrangement designed to be temporary until a new German government could be organized and peace negotiated with it. When it soon became evident that the Soviet Union was embarked on policies to make communist satellites of her zone of occupation (East Germany) and the other countries of Eastern Europe, the Western powers ceased their policies of treating Germans in their zones as conquered foes. Instead, they first established economic cooperation among the three zones and then set about helping the Germans to establish their own political institutions. In 1949 the German Federal Republic was established in what had been the Western zones. The Soviet Union countered by forming the German Democratic Republic, a communist state, in East Germany.

The constitution promulgated in West Germany in 1949 was drafted in Bonn, now the temporary capital, by German representatives of the states and was subject to the approval of the occupation authorities. It is called the Basic Law rather than the constitution in order to emphasize its temporary nature, because the drafters assumed that a genuine constitution could be drawn up only after Germany was reunited and all Germans were given an opportunity to be consulted on their form of government. This terminological distinction does not conceal the fact that, for all practical purposes, the Bonn Basic Law is the constitution of the Federal Republic.

Some of the basic characteristics of the Bonn constitution are suggested by the country's name, German Federal Republic. It provides for a republic by establishing a President, elected by a special electoral college, as chief of state, and for a federal system rather than a unitary one by specifically reserving certain powers to the states. One of the conditions specified by the Western powers was that the states must be kept strong. Although the powers of the national government have grown in the intervening years, the essential features of federalism remain. In addition, by guaranteeing an elected parliament to which the head of government, the Chancellor, is responsible, and by prohibiting antidemocratic activity, the constitution provides for responsible democratic government.

The constitution also contains a bill of rights with such traditional features as a guarantee of freedom of speech, press, and assembly, as well as certain novel provisions, such as those guaranteeing economic freedom, however that may be interpreted. Various guarantees of the rule of law are also included, and for the first time in German history, a constitutional court with powers of judicial review is able to ensure the rule of law against encroachments by organs of government. Finally, there are provisions designed to prevent the abuse of executive decree powers such as occurred in the last days of the Weimar Republic.

The constitution may be amended by a two-thirds vote of the members of each house of parliament (Bundestag and Bundesrat). Some provisions are said to be unamendable. These include the federal system, the sections that provide for the basic form of democratic organization, and the sections that protect fundamental civil rights.

Social Forces

In Britain the gradual evolution of the political system as a constitutional monarchy was accepted by all parties. But in France the landed aristocracy remained devoted to the principle of hereditary monarchy, while the new middle class and the workers tended to be republican. As we have seen, the Third Republic represented a compromise between monarchists and republicans that gradually stabilized itself and won widespread acceptance. Yet the old social and ideological divisions continued to bring into question the forms of the state. The social groups that previously had supported the monarchy or Bonapartism—notably the aristocracy, clergy, army officers, elements of the peasantry, and part of the middle class—clamored for a stronger executive. On the other hand, the workers and the more recently prosperous elements of the middle class tended to identify the Republic with the dominance of universal suffrage, as expressed through parliament.

The social structure of France has changed less than that of any other major Western nation in the past two centuries. Since 1789 the population of the United States has increased fifty times, from 4 million to over 200 million, and that of Great Britain has tripled; but France's population has grown only about 50 percent. Furthermore, the Industrial Revolution had less of an impact in France than elsewhere in northern Europe. Thus the agricultural sector has been more important in France than in Britain or Germany, and the industrial sector proportionally less important. In political terms, this has meant that the new social forces generated by advanced industrialization (a managerial class, skilled workers, technicians, engineers, and the like) until recently played a relatively limited role in France; whereas the traditional social formations (the peasants, small shopkeepers, landed aristocracy, family business groups, and unskilled workers) continued to retain much of their old political power. It also means that classic ideological controversies (involving, for example, the form and activities of the state and the position of the church) have had a longer life in France than in other advanced nations.

While the number of people engaged in agriculture has declined in this century by over 50 percent, they nonetheless represent one-fifth of the working population. The increase in the number of people engaged in manufacturing and services corresponds with the trend in other advanced nations, but has not been as marked. Also, the family shop or enterprise remains an important form of economic organization. Again, the political implications are obvious: In France the working class and managerial groups are less important, and the peasantry more important, as voting blocs and political forces than in most other Western democracies.

Stability of the social structure is also reflected by figures on the distribution of the population between rural and urban areas. Only about one-fourth of the population live in cities with more than 50,000 inhabitants, while nearly one-third live in communes with less than 2,000 inhabitants. Paris is the only city with a population of over 1 million, with 3 million people within the city limits and 7 million in its metropolitan area. Rural areas in France are more populous, and hence more powerful politically, than in the other advanced democracies.

Governments and even constitutions come and go in France, but the principal social groups remain and manifest their political views with remarkable fidelity, if not monotony. Under the Fifth Republic, as under the Fourth and the Third and indeed in every election held since the Revolution of 1789, certain communes and even *départements* (basic administrative units roughly comparable in size to large American counties) have voted to the Left, others to the Right. For example, the peasants of the east (along the German border) and the northwest (Normandy and Brittany) tend to be conservative, if not reactionary; the peasants of the south and the center tend to be radical. In many areas of central and southern France, the peasantry has always voted for the party on the extreme Left — Radical Socialist in the late nineteenth century, Socialist until 1939, and Communist thereafter.

The working class, like almost every large professional, social, or economic group in France, is split along ideological or party lines. A majority of the industrial workers have been voting Communist since World War II, though there is significant working-class support for the Socialist party, the Christian Democrats, and even the Gaullists. It is impossible to identify the other social groups with any one party or political orientation. In a country with so many parties and ideological divisions, there are partisan and ideological organizations among all classes and groups. Thus there are Socialist teachers, shopkeepers, workers, civil servants, and veterans at the same time that there are Communist, Christian Democratic, and other organizations among the same groups. Nonetheless, certain social groups tend to vote or support certain parties more than others. Teachers and civil servants tend to be on the Left, although the higher civil service is generally on the Right. Workers are on the Left, but they frequently respond to nationalistic appeals, as is evidenced by General de Gaulle's success among them. The peasants are on the Left or the Right according to region and income; the landed aristocracy and capitalists on the Right; businessmen sometimes in the Center, but more often on the Right. The clergy and the religious faithful were historically on the Right, but since World War II a segment of the Catholic community has supported the Christian Democratic party.

Despite this long history of stability in social structure and political alignments, sweeping changes have been taking place in the French economy and society in the past fifteen years. It is likely that the historic orientations of both geographic regions and social groups will be utterly transformed as a result. Since 1949 France has been experiencing a remarkable economic expansion. In certain key sectors of the economy—railroads, aviation, electricity, chemicals, and automobiles—technological progress has approximated or surpassed that of Western Germany and the United States.

The widespread use of modern household devices and ownership of private automobiles are changing shopping and living habits. Many uneconomic family enterprises are disappearing. The rapidity with which the "quick lunch" and "self-service" have caught on in France attests to a major revolution. The tempo of life is shifting from a traditional to a modern pace. Work incentives and leisure-time aspirations are increasingly similar to those of the more advanced industrial states. France as a result is losing some of her "Old World charm"—which is regretted by the foreign tourists, but not by the French. Despite losses during World War II and in both the Indochina and Algerian wars, France's population is growing rapidly and undergoing a structural change as well; today France has one of the youngest populations of any country in Western Europe.

Many observers of the French political scene have hailed these social and economic developments as presaging an inevitable transformation of French political life as well. They reason that the newly created or expanded social categories—technicians, managers, economists, scientists, engineers, rural elites using modern techniques, white-collar workers—are no longer interested in the old, sterile ideological quarrels. The hope has been expressed that the political parties will respond by becoming more pragmatic, that is, by proposing practical solutions to pressing problems without regard to old ideological issues.

Paradoxically, the center of political gravity in the Fifth Republic (which is above all an attempt to create dynamic government) originally was to be found among the inhabitants of the small communes of France. These people continue to be preoccupied with agriculture and wine cultivation; their major concern is still the protection of the small artisan and the family farm or business; their political experience has been gained mainly by extracting favors or concessions from the state while taking care to shift the tax burden onto other. These are the social elements least affected by the Industrial Revolution — the most likely, indeed, to resort to violent protest against programs of modernization. There is some evidence, however, that the center of political gravity is shifting away from these groups.

In the long run, modernization of the French economy is bound to bring with it changes in political parties and opinions, but evidence of such changes is not yet abundant. The traditional political parties have not freed themselves of concern with doctrinal and ideological disputes, nor have they been successful in recruiting the elite of the new social groups. President de Gaulle's total domination of policy making after 1958 undercut or partially paralyzed the parties. It is still unclear how the process of modernization will affect parties and public opinion in the near or more distant future, although some decline in the importance of ideology in the political process would seem to be evident.

West Germany has many natural advantages for industry, which give it a more favorable situation than Britain or France — although, aside from coal, it does not have the mineral resources for all its industrial requirements. It is a highly urbanized society; it no longer has the benefit of what were significantly agricultural areas, which are now in East Germany. Moreover, the agricultural regions it possesses are characterized by small peasant holdings that are worked by the peasants and their families, where it is difficult to increase production. This combination of circumstances has resulted in Germany's importing nearly a third of its food supply.

Because of the country's geographic diversity, the German people have tended to maintain strong attachments to their native regions. This is one reason for the late unification of the country. The extent of regional identification is perhaps best indicated by the fact that although there is only one written language, known as High German, dialects of this language spoken in one section of the country are not understood by people in another. Some of the boundaries dividing the ten states were drawn rather arbitrarily at the end of World War II, and thus many of them no longer coincide with the historic regional boundaries. To some extent, this has diminished some aspects of regional identification.

Closely related to regionalism is the more divisive issue of religious differences, an issue that has resulted in many conflicts—from the Thirty Years' War to current conflicts over religious education. Before partition, Germany was two-thirds Protestant and one-third Catholic; in West Germany today the two groups are almost equal in number. Religious cleavage has generally reinforced regional particularism. The formula of the Peace of Augsburg (1555), which imposed the religion of each German prince on his subjects, provided a geographic basis for religious affiliation that has continued down to the twentieth century. Political parties are thus compelled to use involved systems of ticket balancing so that both Catholics and Protestants are represented. The critical political conflicts based on religion center on state support of religious education and religious institutions.

Potentially more explosive than religion were the problems that derived from partition and the influx of refugees from the east. In 1961 it was estimated that 13 million people, almost 25 percent of the population of the Federal Republic, were exiles and refugees. For a country that had just been devastated by war, the problems created by millions of people pouring in with only the clothes on their backs would have seemed insoluble. Simply housing these refugees in an area in which 22 percent of the housing units had been destroyed might have seemed impossible. Moreover, the differences in economic status between those who had been completely dispossessed and those who still had some property could have added to the social tension.

Yet West Germany rose to the challenge and has been largely successful in absorbing these refugees. The most important single step was the Equalization of Burdens Law, which provided that those who still held property in 1948 would be required to pay one-half its value in installments over a twenty-year period in order to compensate for those who had nothing. This equalization fund has been used to provide housing, welfare assistance, and compensation for lost household goods.

Nobody could have predicted the success the Germans have had in rebuilding their economy since World War II. At the end of the war Germany lay prostrate, with its factories and its transportation and communication systems destroyed. Organized social life had come to an end, and the Allies had to provide aid simply to keep the population alive. The first few years after the war were very difficult, but beginning with the currency reform of 1948, rapid progress was made in rebuilding the economy through a combination of government action and free enterprise known as the "social market economy." West Germany not only absorbed the refugees but so successfully achieved full employment that it was able to provide jobs for many workers from other countries. These opportunities have diminished and German unemployment has risen, however, although not as much as in some other Western nations.

The economic miracle, the most tangible element in German cohesion, has tended to make regional, religious, and other differences less explosive. With more new cars, TV sets, and houses, and with one of the most comprehensive social insurance systems in the world, the Germans have been less inclined to social conflict than they were earlier, although the rising unemployment may change this. Less tangible but perhaps equally important as the economic welfare are a strong national patriotism and a necessity for maintaining a united front in a country on the frontier of the worldwide East-West conflict.

The German cohesion has been marred by the actions of terrorist gangs in the 1970s, which have evoked demands for action along with the sprouting of right-wing extremist organizations. German authorities seem baffled as to how to respond. The terrorists are not separatists, like those in Northern Ireland, nor are they nationalists like the Palestine Liberation Organization. They seem to be bent on destroying the system. If they can provoke the state into more repression they will have achieved one of their goals—to expose what they allege is a "fascist face beneath the democratic mask."

The government has responded with laws that liberal democrats assert go too far in limiting traditional liberties, and that others regard as inadequate and wretched. Among other things, these laws outlaw the formation of terrorist associations, permit surveillance of correspondence between defense counsel and the accused, allow judges to exclude defense lawyers from trials under certain circumstances, and empower the search of whole buildings and not just specific apartments in the hunt for terrorists. These enactments are hemmed in with certain limitations, which do not satisfy those who see in the laws an erosion of democracy, nor those who are convinced it will take much more than these laws to put an end to terrorism.

Interest Groups

Social interest groups put forward their demands through a complex network of organizations as well as through the political parties. Under the Fourth Republic, interest groups were very much in evidence. Each major lobby could count on a core of solid support in the National Assembly and on established contacts with the appropriate administrative agencies. Some groups (especially labor unions, business interests, and religious organizations) were loosely affiliated with political parties. Cabinet instability frequently made it difficult for governments to resist the demands of interest groups, since the small margin of a government's parliamentary support might be destroyed if even a few of its supporters deserted it in response to a group's demands. Perhaps the most notorious example of pressure politics under the Fourth Republic was the success achieved by the alcohol lobbies, made up of beet growers, wine cultivators, and distillers, in maintaining state purchase of alcohol at premium prices. It has been estimated that 4 million people in France derive profit in some way from the manufacture, sale, or transport of alcohol.

The chief organized groups in France include those speaking for broad socioeconomic interests: business interests such as the National Council of French Business and the Union for the Defense of Artisans and Shopkeepers; trade unions such as the General Confederation of Labor (pro-Communist), the Democratic Federation of Labor (pro-Christian Democrat), and the pro-Socialist Force Ouvrière (Workers Strength); and agricultural groups such as the National Federation of Farmers Unions. Each of these can draw support from a significant portion of the population—6 to 8 million workers, 8 million farmers, and several million people engaged in commerce and business. In addition, there are a host of more specialized groups: veterans, religious faithful seeking subsidies for schools, secular champions of the public schools, students, and so on.

These groups utilize techniques we are familiar with in the United States: mobilization of public opinion, provision of information to administrators, and especially application of pressure to parliamentarians and ministers. Recourse to drastic measures (refusal to pay taxes, blockade of roads by the peasants, strikes, seizure of public buildings, and sabotage) has not been infrequent since World War II. The army's intervention in politics as an aftermath of the uprising of May 1958, the resort to terror by conspiratorial associations in both Algeria and France since then, and the student revolt of May 1968 may be considered spectacular examples of the recourse to violent methods by pressure groups.

The framers of the Fifth Republic anticipated that the power of lobbies would be reduced under the new constitution, and to a certain extent their claims have been borne out. Since the government rests essentially upon a solid bloc of deputies, it need not court the support of small coteries defending particular interests. But the great interests, and many smaller interests as well, are largely represented within the Gaullist and Independent parties and their allies. Thus the alcohol-producing groups, the associations in favor of religious schools, the business groups in general, and the peasants have many defenders in the Assembly and within the Cabinet. The most important interest groups whose political power initially declined under the Fifth Republic are the labor unions, since the parties with which they are affiliated, particularly

the Communists and Socialists, had their parliamentary representation sub-
stantially reduced. In the 1981 elections the Communists reached a post-World
War II low, while the Socialists won a majority in the Assembly.

Although Germany also has the kind of voluntary associations that characterize other democratic societies, an outstanding feature of its interest
groups is that some of them are established by public law and membership in
them is obligatory. These include business, farmers', and workers' organizations. For example, a handicraft worker must join a handicraft council, a
manufacturing business an industrial council, and in some states all farmers
are required to belong to the state agricultural council. These organizations
act not only as pressure groups in promoting the interests of their members but
also perform such regulatory functions as setting standards, licensing, and
educating apprentices. They are organized in a hierarchy on local, state, and
national levels.

In addition to the public law bodies in which membership is compulsory,
there are many other interest groups. Almost every German business concern
is associated with one or more business organizations. One national group of
business organizations, the Federation of German Employers Association, has
a membership in its local branches that takes in 80 percent of private enterprise. Another, the Federation of German Industry, represents 90,000 employers. These two organizations in turn support another one, the German Industry Institute, which is the propaganda organization for business interests.
Businessmen also support the civic and sponsors associations, which are the
overtly political agencies of business. Among their political goals, business
groups naturally favor lower taxes, but their position on government regulation is ambivalent in that they seek more restrictions (on competition, imports, new products) favorable to their interests as well as fewer restrictions
unfavorable to their interests.

The German Farmers Union favors higher subsidies and high tariffs for
agricultural products, and thus has hampered German steps toward a common agriculture policy in the Common Market. Although, unlike the state
agricultural groups, membership is not compulsory, almost all farmers belong
to it.

There are several labor organizations, but the largest is the German Trade
Union Federation, with 6 million members in 16 industrial unions. This federation has adopted an official party neutrality difficult to maintain at times,
since most of its active leaders are Social Democrats. In addition to such traditional goals as seeking higher wages and better protection for workers, it has
sought to increase the power of organized labor. It has been particularly active
in promoting "co-determination," the German term for workers' participation

in the management of industry. Under the laws of the Bonn Republic, labor names half the members of the boards of iron, coal, and steel concerns and one-third of the members of the workers' councils in private plants outside these basic industries.

Because the heritage (or origins) of the German Trade Union Federation has long been associated with Marxism, some Catholics have organized the Christian Trade Union, which now has almost 2 million members. In addition, the Salaried Workers Union and the German Civil Servants Union each have almost a half million members.

More clearly than in America, the German churches and their auxiliary organizations are political interest groups. The intimate relations between the churches and the government require that religious groups concern themselves with politics. For instance, the states collect church dues with regular taxes and provide religious instruction in public schools and state aid for parochial schools.

The Roman Catholic church, whose membership is 45 percent of the population, has long been involved in German politics. Although bishops and priests have been somewhat restrained in overt support for Catholic candidates in the Bonn Republic, Catholic auxiliary organizations such as the Christian Trade Union movement have been quite active.

Although 51 percent of the population is Protestant, German Protestant traditions in politics have been quite different from those of the Catholics, in the sense that Luther's stress on salvation by faith alone has led many of his followers to be less concerned about the social order. However, Hitler's persecution of Protestants and the catastrophe he brought to the country have convinced many of them that their Christian duty does require a greater concern about the social order. Therefore in 1948 they organized the Evangelical Church in Germany. This organization of twenty-seven state churches divided along geographical and denominational lines has no clear-cut political position other than a defense of Christianity and a particularly great concern about reunification, which would bring back their Protestant coreligionists in East Germany. As far as voting habits go, Protestants are distributed among all the German political parties.

By offering financial support and campaign assistance to the parties at elections, interest groups seek to influence the electoral outcome. In the early years of the Bonn Republic business groups formed associations to provide contributions to the non-Socialist parties, but this was ruled illegal by the Constitutional Court. Farm groups have been equally active in supporting right-wing parties and in placing their officials in legislative bodies and on the agricultural committees. The Trade Union Federation has been more circumspect in its relations with the Social Democratic party, but its officials have been elected to offices and its functionaries have "unofficially" campaigned for Socialist candidates at elections.

Besides taking an active interest in parties and elections, the interest groups maintain close relationships with officials in the executive branch of the state and national government. In some cases, these relationships are formalized by allowing the organized groups to name members of advisory bodies attached to executive departments. In other cases, the relationships involve informal but regular consultations with the officials. But however it is done, it is customary for executive officials to consult the organizations that might be affected before issuing administrative orders or proposing legislation. Because executive action is so important in Germany, lobbying in executive agencies is more extensive than in legislative halls.

Political Parties

Political parties, as we suggested in the previous chapter, are the bone and sinew of democratic politics. It is through them that the popular will is ascertained and ultimately translated into action. Major parties in two-party systems such as those in Britain and the United States are invariably coalitions of groups, interests, and forces that in France would be separate political parties. In the former countries, collaboration among interests takes place *within* the major parties; in France, the process of compromise takes place among independent parties. In brief, France has a multiparty system, with nearly a dozen parties presenting candidates in the 1981 elections. Germany, too, during the Weimar Republic had a multiparty system, but during the Bonn Republic it has moved steadily toward a two-party alignment, with a third party often providing the critical balance.

IN FRANCE

French parties traditionally enter into alliances for electoral purposes, much as various factions making up an American party will unite temporarily every four years in order to nominate a candidate for the Presidency. Collaboration by the parties is continued in Cabinet coalitions, although not always on the same basis as the electoral alliances. In this search for mutually profitable arrangements, the classic distinction between the Right and Left has been of overriding importance, although the issues have changed. As we have seen above, the original issue between Right and Left involved a choice between hereditary monarchy and republicanism. In the twentieth century the main constitutional issue has been the relative power to be accorded to parliament and to the executive.

Among the other issues dividing the Right and Left are state aid to religious schools, with the Right for and the Left opposed; state interference in the economy, with the Right opposed and the Left in favor; colonial policy, with the Left for decolonization and the Right generally nationalistic. Sometimes these two broad political orientations tend to shift. For example, middle-class radicals have been on the Left with respect to the republic and the status of church schools but on the Right in matters of social and economic policy. On the other hand, Christian Democrats have been on the Right in the issue of church schools but on the Left when it came to republicanism and economic policy.

Nevertheless, since World War II there have been three fairly stable currents of party opinion in France: the Communists and Socialists on the Left; a combination of small parties making up a Center; and the Gaullists and Independents on the Right. In the mid-1970s, there appeared a trend toward a bipolar situation. A tenuous alliance between the Communists and the Socialists, who traditionally have been critical of each other, represented a strong bloc. Counterpoised against this combination were the Gaullists and the Independents and some centrist allies. Even though sharp divisions existed between the leaders of the Gaullists and Independents, this combination managed to gain majorities in the National Assembly in the elections of 1973 and 1978, but lost in 1981.

French Communist Party (PCF). The party was founded in 1920 when the Socialist party split over the question of adhering to the international association of Communist parties (Comintern) organized by the Soviet Communist party leadership. By and large, the militants organized the party along Soviet lines, that is, as a party that would be admirably suited for carrying out the orders of the leadership without much risk of dissension. It did not do well initially, but increased its electoral support greatly in the mid-1930s. After some falling off before World War II, it managed to get about 25 percent of the vote in several postwar elections, dropping to around 15 percent in recent electoral contests.

The PCF espouses the classic Left position on the nature of the regime, the status of the church, and the role of the state in public control of the economy. Because of its allegiance to Moscow and its support for the Soviet Union, other parties have distrusted the PCF, convinced that if victorious it would establish a one-party dictatorship in France, which would be incompatible with the democratic ideal not only of the moderate and conservative parties but of the Socialists as well.

The Communists made an effort, after Stalin's death, to break out of political quarantine by offering cooperation to other parties on the Left, but the gap was too great to be bridged easily. Some electoral agreements were made in the 1960s, but these did not seem to accomplish much. In the 1970s, however, cooperation between the Communists and Socialists became more meaningful. In 1972 a common program of action was signed, and the Communists became more and more critical of the Soviet Communist model and declared themselves loyal to traditional French political and cultural values. In 1977, in anticipation of 1978 national elections, the Socialists and Communists met to update their common program, but they could not reach agreement on such important subjects as nuclear defense or the extent of nationalizations. Public opinion polls nevertheless indicated that the Communist-Socialist alliance (which also included the small Leftist Radical Movement) would capture a majority of the seats in the National Assembly. As election day approached (March 1978), this prediction seemed less certain, and indeed did not materialize. In 1981 there was no common program, but the Socialists won a majority and thereupon gave the Communists four Cabinet seats.

The Socialist Party (PS). The party was formed in 1905 by a fusion of revolutionary and moderate Socialist factions, then called the French Section of the Second International (SFIO). For thirty years it remained in opposition (except during World War I) to the "bourgeois" regime. For a brief period in the late 1930s it accepted the responsibility of governing, but its more meaningful participation came after World War II, when it polled around 15 percent of the popular vote. With the coming of the Fifth Republic in 1958, it again went into opposition. Even before then, it had seemingly reached a point of stagnation, which continued.

In the 1960s it worked toward combining with other small parties of similar views, and in 1969 and 1971 succeeded in scrapping its old structure and under new leadership broadened its appeal. It adopted the simplified name Socialist party. In the 1973 national elections it polled nearly 20 percent of the vote and doubled its representation in the National Assembly. Results in subsequent local elections led it to aspire to 30 percent of the vote in 1978. In fact, it was disappointed in receiving less than 23 percent on the first ballot in March 1978, and it did not increase its strength in parliament. In 1981, however, it scored a resounding victory, with a majority in the National Assembly.

While the Socialists have employed revolutionary jargon, they have long been committed to change by peaceful democratic means. Perhaps their agreement with the Communists on a common program, mentioned above, frightened some voters, especially when public opinion polls in 1978 indicated that the combination might win a majority in the National Assembly. The Socialist party convention in 1974 pushed the party farther to the Left in that it called for more nationalizations, although far fewer than the Communists wanted.

In addition, Socialist wavering on nuclear armament was also the source of doubt among some voters. But in 1981 the electorate produced a Socialist tide, perhaps preferring an outright Socialist victory to an outcome in which they would have to share power with the Communists. The Socialists nevertheless gave the latter four Cabinet seats, but the Communists had to pay a price. They were forced to sign what most observers regarded as a "surrender document," wherein they pledged in writing full support and cooperation on the major principles of the Socialists' domestic and foreign policy programs. At its inception in mid-1981, no one could predict the outcome of this token sharing of power.

Other Leftist Parties. Note should also be made of two small parties on the Left, the Leftist Radical Movement (MRG) and the Unified Socialist Party (PSU). The former is a splinter group of the centrist Radical party, and it advocates a "moderate path of socialism." The PSU is made up largely of people who became disillusioned with or were expelled from the Communist, Socialist, and Radical parties. Originally the PSU aimed to unite the Left by making the Socialist party more radical and the Communist party more democracy-oriented, but its impact has been minimal.

Rally for the Republic (RPR). Formed in 1947 by General de Gaulle as the Rally of the French people, this party changed its name several times but always made clear its support for the institutions of the Fifth Republic. It scored its greatest successes during de Gaulle's presidency in the 1960s, at one point winning a majority of the seats in the National Assembly. It was the largest party there (154 seats) until the 1981 elections when it became a poor second. It is generally a right-of-center party, and some would say that it constitutes the Right. For most of its existence its positions have been the positions of its leaders. Its most recent leader, Jacques Chirac, was Prime Minister for a while in the mid-1970s, but resigned after disagreements with then President Valery Giscard d'Estaing. In 1977 Chirac was elected mayor of Paris, which constitutes the base of his political operations.

Union for French Democracy (UDF). An electoral combination of centrist parties, it has the third largest number of deputies in the National Assembly. The largest and most important of these parties is the Republican party (PR). Its members were once known as Independents, and later as Independent Republicans. In 1977 the party changed its name simply to Republican. It is the party of former President d'Estaing and prides itself in being a modestly reformist party somewhat left of center. The second largest party in this combination is the Center of Social Democrats (CDS), a merger in 1976 of two centrist parties, the Democratic Center (CD) and the Center for Democracy and Progress (CDP). The Democratic Center evolved from the Popular Republican Movement (MRP), which was a Christian democratic party and for a time the largest one in the Fourth Republic, but fell apart with the coming of the Fifth Republic in 1958. During the presidency of d'Estaing it considered itself the "left wing of the majority." The CDP is made up of former supporters of the opposition center, and its leanings are the same as the CD; together the CD and CDP now make up the new CDS and were participants in the earlier governing coalition.

French parties vary a great deal in their organizational structures and their leadership systems. The most highly organized and disciplined are the Communists, with a hierarchical organization and a card-carrying membership that unquestioningly obeys the top leaders. Of the non-Left parties, the RPR has the most intricate organization with several governing bodies at the national level, as well as district and regional organizations. All the parties have conventions or congresses that meet annually or every few years. In between congresses, party affairs are handled by steering committees or political bureaus, usually a two-tiered arrangement, with one a larger representative body and the other a smaller and more compact leadership group.

In Germany

Germany, as indicated earlier, also had a tradition of multiple political parties, with no party having a majority in parliament. This tradition appeared to continue after the establishment of the Bonn Republic in 1949 when a number of parties put forth candidates. After a few elections, however, only three parties were able to elect deputies to parliament, with the two largest parties getting nearly 90 percent of the popular vote and thereby coming close to developing a two-party system. Because of the nearly equal vote received by the two parties, the third party has played a key role, first joining in a coalition with one of them and, after subsequent elections, forming a coalition with the other. The one exception was the period of the so-called Grand Coalition (1966-69) when the two major parties made up the governing combination.

Christian Democratic Union (CDU). In all national elections but one (1972) from 1949 to 1980, the CDU, along with its Bavarian wing, the Christian Social Union (CSU) has been the strongest political party in the Bonn Republic. In 1953 and 1957, it won majorities in the Bundestag (lower house of parliament), the only times that a German party achieved this goal. Since 1969, it has been out of power, a fact that has contributed to strained relations between the CDU and the CSU. The latter in late 1976 decided to end its long alliance with the CDU, suggesting that it would become a separate political party, a suggestion that did not come to pass. Instead, its controversial leader, Franz Josef Strauss, became in 1980 the CDU/CSU candidate for Chancellor, but after the party's defeat, the search for a new leader began.

The origins of the CDU extend back to the Catholic Center party of the Bismarck era, but the bringing in of a large number of Protestants after World War II resulted in a broadly based party. In addition to bridging religious differences, the party also had some success in bridging class divisions by enlisting the support of a fair number of workers for a party closely associated with business and farm interests. This diversity, however, has contributed to the party's weakness as well as to its strength. When selecting candidates, for example, the ticket must be balanced so that various groups are represented, and yet this does not ensure cohesion after the election. Moreover, as a broad collection of diverse elements, the CDU has tended to stress general principles and promote popular candidates, rather than to spell out issues in detail. Perhaps the only exceptions are the party's strong pro-West stance and its suspicion of the Soviet Union and Communists generally.

Geographically, the CDU/CSU has been strongest in Catholic Bavaria and the Saar and weakest in Protestant North Germany. Economically, the CDU has commanded more support from business interests and from farmers than from workers. It has also drawn more support from women than from men, and from older people than from the younger ones. Moreover, it seems to excite more people in national elections than it does in local ones.

Social Democratic Party of Germany (SPD). The oldest party and the one with the largest membership, the SPD had difficulty in winning the people's trust, mainly because of its Marxist heritage. Founded in 1875, it has changed over the years, most notably in 1959 when it formally turned from Marxism. In doing so, it rejected Marxist views toward national defense and the church. Moreover, it even endorsed some free enterprise in the economy. The party adopted the slogan "As much competition as possible—as much planning as necessary." In addition, instead of nationalizing industries, the party proposed "people's shares," a plan such as that used for Volkswagen ownership, in which preferential prices for lower-income groups would make corporate shares available to the masses. While endorsing a pro-Western foreign and defense policy, the party also is in favor of improvements in pensions, health insurance, family allowances, and public housing. This was perhaps less socialism than the majority of the party members wanted, but the retreat was necessary to appeal to voters who were not the party's regular supporters.

The SPD's electoral strength grew in successive elections, forcing the CDU to accept a coalition of the two parties after the elections of 1965. In new elections in 1969, the SPD continued to gain and became the major partner (with the Free Democrats) in a governing coalition. In the 1972 elections, the SPD for the first time elected more deputies to parliament than did the CDU. In 1976, the SPD suffered a setback while the CDU gained, and the SPD was able to continue its coalition with the Free Democrats by the narrowest of margins. In 1980 the SPD gained slightly (4 seats), while the Free Democrats gained 14 seats, giving the coalition increased strength. The SPD's most colorful leader was Willy Brandt, the popular young mayor of West Berlin. Because of a spy scandal in his office, Brandt was forced to resign as head of the government in 1974, although he has managed to remain the leader of his party. He was succeeded as Chancellor (prime minister) by Helmut Schmidt, whose stature has grown, despite intraparty bickering and unresolved German domestic problems.

Free Democratic Party (FDP). The only one of the minor parties that has been able to elect deputies to parliament since 1961, the FDP is difficult to characterize. Initially it was compounded of nationalism, nineteenth-century liberalism, sheer opportunism, individualism, and anticlericalism, with the actual combination of these elements varying from state to state. It supported big business and lower taxation, which meant that its appeal was greatest among upper-income groups, and hence a natural to join in coalition with the Christian Democrats. By the mid-1960s, however, its leaders began to present the FDP as liberal and reform-minded, making it more attractive to liberals, intellectuals, and students. The result, in part at least, was that the party ceased its coalition with the CDU in 1966, and following the elections of 1969 it joined the Social Democrats to form a coalition Cabinet, a combination that as of this writing continues to rule Germany.

The electoral fortunes of the FDP suggest that it could never become a major party. In 1957 it elected 41 deputies, increasing to 66 in 1961, but dropping to 30 in 1969. In 1972 it elected 42 deputies; in 1976 it was 39 and in 1980, 53. Its share of the popular vote in 1969 was 5.8 percent (increased to 7.9 in 1976 and 10.6 in 1980). In 1969 it came perilously close to losing all representation in parliament because the electoral law requires at least 5 percent for a party to be entitled to seats in the legislature (see discussion of electoral procedures below).

Other Parties. Two extremist parties, the neo-Nazi Socialist Reich party and the Communist party, were outlawed by the Federal Constitutional Court as unconstitutional organizations seeking to overthrow the government. This was in accordance with the constitutional provision that parties could be formed only if they supported the democratic system established by the constitution. The Communists had polled 6 percent of the vote and elected 15 deputies in 1949, but their vote declined to almost 2 percent in 1953, and they elected no deputies. The Socialist Reich party never came close to electing any deputies.

In the main, German political parties are highly organized and centrally directed, although each has its own problems. The Social Democrats have their factions and the Christian Democrats their Bavarian partners. All parties have periodic conventions where some of their internal differences are aired.

ELECTORAL PROCEDURES

French and German electoral procedures are somewhat different. Both have experimented with proportional representation, the French during the Fourth Republic, as well as earlier, and the Germans under the Weimar Republic. Under this system, seats in a legislative body are divided among political parties according to the percentage of votes they have received. When many parties offer candidates, the result under this sytem will be that rarely if ever will one party have a majority in parliament. This was certainly true of France and Germany.

With the establishment of the Fifth Republic, the French reverted to the system used during most of the existence of the Third Republic. Under this arrangement, the nation is divided into single-member districts. If no candidate receives a majority of the valid votes cast, there is a runoff election (*ballottage*) two weeks later, at which time only a plurality is required for election. Candidates who receive less than 12.5 percent of the votes of the registered electorate on the first round cannot be on the ballot for the runoff election. The exception is in the event of only one candidate receiving the required 12.5 percent. Should that occur, the candidate with the next highest number of votes is permitted to run on the second ballot. Moreover, no new candidates may appear on the second ballot. All candidates are required to make a deposit the equivalent of $250, which is refunded if the candidate obtains at least 5 percent of the votes cast.

Since the vast majority of the deputies are elected in the runoff election, the various parties usually engage in some electoral agreements between the two elections (and some even much earlier) as to who is going to support whom under certain given circumstances. The Communists and the Socialists have in recent elections agreed to support each other's candidates in the runoff (i.e., to support the one who did the best in the first round). Other parties have had similar arrangements. The supporters of the various parties have not, however, always acted upon the advice of party leaders. Many Communist voters, for example, have found it difficult to vote for a Socialist on the second ballot, and vice versa.

There is no limitation on campaign expenditures. Television seems to be of limited importance. Parties that contest at least 75 seats do get a limited amount of free TV time.

The French electoral law also provides that each candidate must have an alternate who would step into the position in case of death or acceptance of a position regarded as incompatible with the position of parliamentary deputy. This proviso stems from the fact that under both the Third and Fourth republics some ministers in coalition Cabinets, who were also members of parliament, often voted against the Cabinet in the hope that they or their party would do better in a succeeding Cabinet. In the expectation of remedying this cause of frequent Cabinet resignations, the framers of the present constitution provided that if a member of parliament is made a minister, he or she must give up the parliamentary seat, which is then taken by the alternate.

The Germans, too, failed to give any political party a majority during the Weimar Republic, and thereby experienced considerable Cabinet instability. In the hope of improving the situation after World War II, the Allied occupation powers urged the Germans to give up the system of proportional representation, which they believed was responsible for so many parties and the consequent Cabinet instability. The Germans went half way. They adopted a system that provides for both single-member districts and for proportional representation, with approximately one-half of the members of parliament being elected under each system. Each German voter has two votes: one for a member from his district and one for a party list in his state. There are 248 single-member districts, and voters elect one person from these districts by plurality, just as elections are conducted for the U.S. House of Representatives and the British House of Commons. In addition, another 248 deputies are elected on the basis of proportional representation.

Each state party organization submits a list of proportional representation candidates for its statewide slate and ranks them from first place down for the total number of seats on its list. Position on the lists is of great importance because those on the bottom of the list are not likely to be elected. The rank on the lists is also important, for if a member dies or resigns during the legislative term, the next person on the list just below the last member elected becomes a member of the lower house of parliament.

The number of seats won by a party in single-member districts is subtracted from the total to which the party may be entitled under proportional representation before additional seats are assigned to it under the latter system. Because of the way in which the single-member districts are drawn, this does not mean that each state will elect an equal number of deputies by each of the two methods. North Rhine-Westphalia, for example, elects 155 deputies, but only 66 of them by direct vote, because it has only that many electoral districts. In a number of other states the reverse is true. Under the present system it is possible for a party to win more seats in some states via the single-member district method than it would be entitled to under both methods. In such an eventuality, which is rare, the party would keep the extra seats won, thereby enlarging the size of the lower house by a few seats.

To discourage small parties from getting seats, the electoral law provides that to qualify for any seats under the proportional representation scheme, a party must win 5 percent of the total national vote on the state party lists or win seats from three single-member districts. This provision has been the primary reason why the number of parties electing deputies was reduced from ten in 1949 to three in 1965 and in all subsequent elections.

As in France, there is no limit on campaign spending, but the three main parties have reached an agreement on several aspects of campaigns (money, posters, newspaper ads, leaflets, skywriting). A sizable portion of the money comes from the government treasury. About two hours of television and radio time are available to the major parties; smaller parties get less.

As in Great Britain, there are no primary elections in France and Germany. Nomination of candidates is in the hands of party organizations. Hence, if a person wishes to influence the choice of a nominee, it is necessary to be active in party affairs.

In France deputies must be at least twenty-three years of age; twenty-five in Germany. In the former they are elected to five-year terms; four-year terms in the latter. In France the voting age has been lowered to eighteen; in Germany it remains twenty-one. Electoral lists are kept up to date, ensuring the maximum number of eligible voters. Elections in both countries are held on Sundays, and turnout has been about 85 percent in recent elections.

Governmental Institutions: France

The political institutions of the Fifth Republic were in the main inspired by Charles de Gaulle and Michel Debre. The latter was chairman of the study group that drew up the first draft of the constitution and then became the first Prime Minister when the constitution was ratified. Their main aim was to strengthen the executive (the President and the Cabinet) and to weaken the parliament. De Gaulle had outlined his ideas much earlier (at the time of the debate over the constitution of the Fourth Republic), insisting that in France the political parties were too divided to provide effective and dynamic leadership for the nation. By conferring significant powers on the President, the Fifth Republic departs from the classic French model; instead of "assembly government," typical of the Third and Fourth, the Fifth comes close to creating a presidential government or at best a greatly modified parliamentary system.

THE PRESIDENCY

The President is told that he "shall see that the constitution is respected. He shall ensure, by his arbitration, the regular functioning of the governmental authorities, as well as the continuance of the State. He shall be the guarantor of national independence, of the integrity of the territory. . . ." This sweeping grant of powers by Article 5 of the constitution implies a virtual presidential veto over all policy making. The President may refuse to sign a decree or make a nomination; he may send personal messages to parliament that do not require ministerial approval or countersignature.

As "national arbiter," he may dissolve parliament at any time and for any reason (but not twice within the same year), subject only to "consultation" with the Prime Minister. President de Gaulle used the threat of dissolution on several occasions in order to strengthen the position of the Prime Minister. And twice he actually dissolved the National Assembly (1962 and 1968), and he was supported in the elections that followed.

The President also retains the traditional powers of the office: the right to designate a Prime Minister; the appointing power, legally defined in a more sweeping fashion than before; and the power to request the parliament to consider a bill. In a concession made to the classic parliamentary system, the constitution does *not* give the President power to dismiss a Cabinet, which remains solely responsible to parliament. By exercising his power of "mediation," the President could no doubt make it difficult for a Cabinet to stay in office. Since the founding of the Fifth Republic in 1958, several prime ministers have resigned at the simple request of the President.

In accordance with General de Gaulle's concern that the chief of state have legal power to act on behalf of the nation in circumstances similar to the surrender in 1940, the constitution gives the President broad emergency powers. He can take "whatever measures are necessitated by the circumstances" in the event that the nation is threatened or the function of its institutions interrupted. He is required only to "consult" the Constitutional Council and inform the nation by message, but he may not dissolve the National Assembly during this period. This power was invoked by General de Gaulle in 1961 when four retired generals attempted to seize power in Algeria with the aid of a few military units.

The President can also bring certain issues before the people by way of referendum. He *may* submit to the people any bill dealing with the organization of the public powers, on the proposal of the government or on joint resolution of parliament. But he is not compelled to call the referendum; hence this too remains a personal power. President de Gaulle used the referendum extensively as a means of establishing a direct relationship with the French people, without the intermediary of parliament, and stated that the referendum had become a part of the political *mores* of the people.

The use of the referendum led to President de Gaulle's downfall in 1969. In 1962 he created a political crisis because he sought (successfully) to amend the constitution via referendum to provide for the popular election of the President rather than by an electoral college. This action ignored the amendment procedures specified by the constitution, and provoked the National Assembly to vote to censure the Cabinet for its part in the affair. In 1969 de Gaulle submitted a proposal to the people that would have merged the upper house (Senate) and the Economic and Social Council and would have created a new structure of local government. When the people voted in the negative, de Gaulle resigned as President, even though the Gaullists had an overwhelming majority in the National Assembly, elected less than one year before.

Under the change made in 1962, the President is elected by popular vote, with provision for a runoff if no candidate receives a majority on the first ballot. In all elections since this system was inaugurated, it has always been necessary to have a runoff election.

Presidential candidates must deposit the equivalent of $2,000. This is refunded, along with a grant of about $20,000 for campaign expenses, provided the candidate polls at least 5 percent of the vote. Each candidate gets two hours of free TV and radio time. This is cheap broadcast time for anyone who wishes to spout his or her views, and there have been several proposals to increase the deposit required to a much higher figure.

THE PRIME MINISTER AND THE CABINET

During the Third and Fourth republics, real executive power was vested in the Prime Minister and his Cabinet colleagues, but as we noted earlier, they were subject to the whims of the legislature. Under the Fifth Republic, as noted above, they have lost significant power to the President, who is no longer a figurehead. At the same time, they have gained power in relation to parliament.

The constitution says that the Prime Minister and the Cabinet have power to "determine and conduct the policy of the nation." It further declares that the "Prime Minister directs the action of the Government," is responsible for national defense, assures the execution of the laws, and exercises extensive decree powers. The traditional character of the parliamentary system is preserved in that the Prime Minister submits a declaration of his program to the National Assembly, and is invested only after his program has been approved. Theoretically, the Prime Minister and the Cabinet dispose of important powers, presumably more important than those of the President. In practice, especially in the de Gaulle years, the Cabinet was overshadowed by the President.

This was made especially easy because the President and the majority of the National Assembly were of the same political persuasion. Should this change, and someday it must, France could experience an interesting confrontation.

The Cabinet has gained power in that the legislature has been made weaker. No longer can parliament ignore Cabinet measures, and no longer can it act irresponsibly in the area of finance. Cabinet bills have priority, and the Cabinet has control over revenue and appropriations, two areas where the British Cabinet, as we have seen, is strong. There are complicated constitutional provisions that make it possible for the Cabinet to adopt the budget by simple decree if the National Assembly and the Senate have not given their approval within seventy days after its presentation.

THE LEGISLATURE

The parliament of the Fifth Republic, like those of the Third and Fourth, is bicameral. The lower house, the National Assembly, consists of some 490 deputies who are elected by universal suffrage. Teachers account for the largest percentage of deputies, followed by civil servants, doctors, and lawyers. Although legislative power is shared with the Senate, the latter is not too powerful. Senate members are elected mainly by councilors from the municipalities and the geographic regions (departments), and serve for nine years (one-third renewed every three years). The Senate may not introduce motions of censure; the Cabinet is responsible only to the National Assembly. In case of disagreement between the two chambers with respect to a bill, the Prime Minister may convene a joint conference committee to work out a compromise text. If the discord between the chambers continues, the Prime Minister may ask the National Assembly to "rule definitively"; thus, in effect the Cabinet and Prime Minister can decide whether or not the Senate is able to exercise a veto. And the Senate can serve as a check on the National Assembly only if the Cabinet agrees.

In order to strengthen the Cabinet's hand in dealing with the National Assembly, the new constitution limits the parliament to two sessions per year— two and one-half months beginning in early October and three months beginning in late April. Thus the parliament can sit for a maximum of less than a half a year, whereas earlier it generally sat most of the year. A special session can be convened at the request of the Prime Minister or of a majority of the Assembly. President de Gaulle refused to convoke an extraordinary session in March 1960, however, even though requested to do so by the requisite majority of the Assembly.

The lawmaking power of parliament is now restricted to matters specifically listed in the constitution. On all other subjects, the government may legislate by decree. The Cabinet also draws up the agenda of the National Assembly, thus determining the order of business. In order to further strengthen the executive power, the constitution allows for the creation of only six committees. To be represented on a committee a parliamentary group must have at least thirty members. Instead of being created for the purpose of considering specific bills, as in the past, the committees are standing, specialized bodies. Above all, debate in the Assembly must take place on the Cabinet's text of the bill and not, again as in the past, on the committee's counterproposal.

In spite of these significant limitations upon the powers of parliament, it must be stressed that the Cabinet remains responsible to the National Assembly. If it loses the Assembly's confidence, it must, as in the past, resign. After being nominated by the President, as noted above, the Prime Minister presents his program to the Assembly, which must approve it by a simple majority before the Cabinet can be invested. Once invested, however, every effort is made to ensure Cabinet stability. A motion of censure, for example, may not be debated or acted upon unless signed by 10 percent of the members of the Assembly. Moreover, the motion carries only if an absolute majority votes for it, which means that abstentions help the Cabinet. In addition, if the Cabinet makes its bill a matter of confidence, that bill becomes law unless a censure motion is introduced within 24 hours and is subsequently passed by an absolute majority. Thus a law may be enacted without a vote on it, simply because the opposition may not be able to muster an absolute majority. Censure motions have been ineffective in controlling the Cabinet. This is not surprising in view of the pro-government majorities. One innovation of the Fifth Republic constitution that enhances the role of the National Assembly is the setting aside of one session each week for questions by members of the Assembly and answers by Cabinet members.

THE JUDICIAL SYSTEM

The distinctive features of French judicial organization remain unchanged under the Fifth Republic. The legal system is very different from its Anglo-American counterpart, although some of the differences appear to be lessening as the systems seem to borrow practices from each other. French law is based on the Napoleonic Code, which in turn was influenced by Roman law; that is, the principles that govern large areas of human activity are codified and then applied in specific cases by trained judges. Juries are used only in serious criminal trials, such as homicide.

One major reason for the use of codes in France was the conservative orientation of judges and lawyers throughout the medieval and revolutionary periods. Unlike the situation in England, where judges adopted the law of custom to the needs of a changing society, the courts in France were a stronghold of feudal privilege. Napoleon carried forward the revolutionary urge to refashion the entire legal system. Under his direction a legal code was drawn up based on abstract principles of justice rather than local custom. In France judges are recruited not from the ranks of the legal profession but from law graduates of the universities. Those who pass special qualifying examinations enter the Ministry of Justice and subsequently study at the National Center for Judicial Studies. After appointment and service in judicial posts, promotions come in due course.

There are two distinct court systems: a hierarchy of regular courts, which deal with the usual civil and criminal matters; and a system of administrative courts, headed by the Council of State, which handles disputes involving the state and the individual. The Council of State also gives the government technical advice on the drafting of bills and decrees. It is relatively easy, and inexpensive, for the individual to sue the state in the event of abuse of power by servants of the state. The French system of codes, specially trained judges, and administrative law was widely copied in continental Europe in the nineteenth century.

French courts, like those in Britain, traditionally have not had the power to declare acts of parliament unconstitutional. An innovation of the Fifth Republic is the Constitutional Council. Its main function is to decide whether bills are compatible with constitutional provisions relating to the organization of the public powers. In 1974, however, the constitution was amended to permit judicial review of laws that may infringe on individual liberties. Originally, the only persons who could bring a matter to the Constitutional Council were the President, the Prime Minister, and the presiding officers of the two houses of parliament. The 1974 amendment permits any group of deputies (60 from either the Assembly or the Senate) to approach the Constitutional Council if they believe that a new law violates civil liberties. But private individuals cannot bring a case.

The French Political System in Perspective

The most persistent feature of French political life has been the intensity of political debate, which involves not simply alternative policies but even the nature of institutions. In the century following the Revolution of 1789, rivalry between republicans and their enemies produced a series of regimes none of which won the support of all major social groups. Toward the latter part of the nineteenth century, the republicans seemed to win out, but agreement failed to emerge on the exact balance between the executive and the legislature. Strong parties have always existed on both the revolutionary Left and the nationalistic Right, repudiating the principles of moderate republicanism.

Yet in spite of the fragility of the consensus on which the political system rested, techniques were developed by parties of the political Center, enabling them to formulate policies and govern the country with reasonable effectiveness. A centralized bureaucracy, the main structure of which goes back to the old regime and to Napoleon, furnished an essential element of continuity and expertise. While no one party enjoyed a stable majority in parliament or in the country, coalitions were formed that provided majorities on important issues as they arose. Once a decision was made on these and a new issue demanded attention, the old coalition broke up and was replaced by another. Hence, through the institutionalized "cabinet crisis," the party system was able to produce policy even though no one group or party constituted a majority. Above all, the democratic system was preserved and the extremes prevented from coming to power. But the constant shuffling of Cabinet posts and party coalitions frequently left the public bewildered and confused. Some of the real achievements of the Third and Fourth republics were therefore obscured or even negated in the confusion generated by the system.

The Fifth Republic is an attempt to create effective and dynamic government in a country that lacks a stable party majority. Essentially, the solution is to buttress the Cabinet's authority with respect to parliament by constitutional guarantees and then to create a chief of state vested with sufficient power and prestige to protect the Cabinet in case of difficulties. The personal powers granted to the President do not concern the daily business of government, which remains the province of the Cabinet. His powers rather permit him to occupy a position above the rancor of party politics, from which lofty place he may descend from time to time in order to separate the combatants and remind them of their duty to the nation.

Political responsibility in a democratic system cannot, however, easily be evaded. Where basic political decisions are referred to the people in elections, it is exceedingly difficult to preserve a sphere of political irresponsibility. Assume, for example, that the President of France exercises his power to dissolve the National Assembly or calls for a referendum to strengthen the Cabinet's hand. If the latter's policy is approved by election or referendum, then the Cabinet's dependence on the President is accentuated—that is, the regime becomes increasingly presidential. This indeed was a noticeable consequence of the three referendums in 1961 and 1962. President de Gaulle's policies were vindicated. In 1969, however, the referendum on the reform of the Senate and of local government was defeated, which resulted in de Gaulle's resignation. What if a Cabinet named by the present or future President is repudiated in a future legislative election? Then the triumphant opposition might associate the President with the defeated Cabinet and compel him either to "give in or get out." The likelihood of such a confrontation at some time in the future cannot be excluded. Some observers were afraid that it might happen in 1981, but presidential and parliamentary elections in that year gave the Socialists a victory in both.

In practice, the trend has been toward concentration of power in the hands of the President. Even though de Gaulle's successors have not possessed his prestige, the office of the presidency seems to have become the driving force of the French political process. It remains to be seen, as French society moves into the mainstream of twentieth-century technological civilization, whether the problem of integrating various elements of that society into the social and political system will prove to be manageable. Perhaps the most important challenge confronting French Presidents and Cabinets, as well as the political parties, is to adapt the nation's political institutions through which the insistent problems of a rapidly changing society may be resolved.

At the beginning of the 1980s, it appeared that the system fashioned by de Gaulle and his successors had progressively gained the acceptance of the vast majority of the French people. A real dialogue between the "government" and the "opposition" seemed to be in the making. President Giscard d'Estaing found it desirable and necessary to consult with the "opposition" leaders on important national issues. And the National Assembly permitted both the "government" and the "opposition" to raise questions once a week on matters they regarded as important or urgent.

Moreover, socioeconomic changes (modernization, profit sharing, nationalization of certain key industries, greater opportunities for upward social mobility, etc.) have contributed to some breakdown of class antagonisms and of regional differences. Ideological fragmentation is on the decrease. New social legislation dealing with health, unemployment, and old age has reduced feelings of insecurity. Activities of voluntary and professional organizations have increased, and electoral campaigns have taken on an aura of more meaningful participation.

Socialist party victories in 1981, however, raised anew questions about the direction of French politics. The election of François Mitterrand as President and the subsequent election of a Socialist majority in the National Assembly, with promises of nationalization of additional sectors of the economy, seemed to represent a significant change of the political course.

A far-reaching reform of France's administrative structure was launched by Mitterrand and his Socialists in July 1981. Its aim is to reduce severely the administrative authority of the ministers in Paris and to confer on regional and local councils a substance of real power. Under the old system, devised by Napoleon, ministers acting through the head (*prefect*) in each of the country's 95 departments had unlimited control in implementing legislative and administrative decisions made in Paris. A change in name, as well, has been made; the prefect has been replaced by a "Commissioner of the Republic." For the first time in some 175 years, therefore, the French may be getting significant power for their institutions of local government.

France's intellectual mood, historically characterized by procommunist sympathies, changed as she entered the 1980s. This change was shaped by several major international and domestic events of the late 1970s. The first was the publication in 1975 of Solzhenitsyn's *Gulag Archipelago*, which detailed the oppressive nature of the communist regime in the Soviet Union. The second was the Cambodian tragedy, the beginning of which was evident as early as 1976 among French intellectuals, most of whom had been critical of American actions in Vietnam. Third was the death of Mao Zedong and the subsequent criticism of his Cultural Revolution. Maoist sympathies had been strong in France. Fourth was the disenchantment with Eurocommunism and the failure of the Communist-Socialist common program. Capping off these events was the Soviet invasion of Afghanistan in 1979-80 and the 1980 exodus of people from Cuba. Taken together, they had a profound impact on French intellectuals, as well as the public, which began a marked increase in the purchase of anticommunist publications.

Governmental Institutions: Germany

Unlike France, Germany is a federal state composed of ten states, known as *Länder*. The pattern of German federalism is exceedingly complex, although it has much in common with what has been called "cooperative federalism" in the United States. The German national government enacts general legislation, provides funds, and sets standards; the states, on the other hand, enact more specific implementing legislation and administer programs. In the main, Germany exhibits more national legislative authority than the United States, but the German states have more administrative authority.

The Bonn Basic Law spells out specific areas in which the national government has legislative powers. These areas can be classified into three general categories: (1) those in which the national government alone has power to legislate, such as foreign affairs, defense, communication, and public transportation; (2) certain areas in which both the national government and the states can legislate, among them legal, economic, and fiscal matters, but the national government has exclusive authority if it chooses to act; (3) areas in which the national government can pass skeletal laws establishing standards, but the states may then pass laws to carry them out (e.g., civil service, the press, and motion pictures).

Those legislative powers not granted to the national government are reserved to the states. Included among them are local government; police protection; cultural affairs; and, most important, education. In 1969 the constitution was amended so as to give the national government increased powers in the areas of taxation and education. In the case of the latter, the aim was to bring about greater uniformity in the educational requirements of the states.

THE EXECUTIVE: PRESIDENT AND CHANCELLOR

Germany has a parliamentary system of government. It has a President who is chief of state, largely a ceremonial role. Real executive power is exercised by the chief of government, the Chancellor, a position similar to that of a prime minister. The President is elected by an electoral college composed of the members of the lower house (Bundestag) of the legislature and an equal number of electors designated by the legislatures of the states. Aside from his ceremonial functions, the President has the important task of selecting the Chancellor, wherein he would have discretion only in the event that no candidate has an obvious majority in the Bundestag. Closely related to this is his power to dissolve the Bundestag if it rejects his choice of Chancellor and fails to elect another candidate by a majority of the members. In that event, the President may either accept the candidate who has won the largest number of Bundestag votes on the third ballot or dissolve the Bundestag and require new general elections. Thus far it has not been necessary to use these alternative provisions because the Bundestag has had no difficulty in choosing a Chancellor. All other presidential acts must be countersigned by an appropriate Cabinet minister.

The Chancellor as the chief of government is the commanding personality in the entire system. His authority stems both from the Basic Law and from the personality of the first Chancellor, Konrad Adenauer, who held the office for the first fourteen years of the Bonn Republic. The constitution intentionally established a strong Chancellor, partly in reaction to the weak ones who were unable to maintain stability during the Weimar Republic. One means to this end was to weaken the President by providing for his election by an electoral college rather than by popular vote so that he does not compete with the Chancellor for popular support. Similarly, the Chancellor has been given the emergency decree powers of the Weimar President, but with some careful safeguards, discussed below.

More important in the long run may be the unique tenure provided for the Chancellor. After the Bundestag has elected him, he can be removed only if that body elects a successor by majority vote. This "constructive vote of no confidence," as it is called, is intended to prevent a repeat of the Weimar experience, in which parties of the extreme Left and extreme Right joined in overthrowing Cabinets even though they obviously could not agree on who should succeed, thus sometimes leaving the nation for weeks without a head of government.

The Chancellor and the Cabinet constitute what is officially designated as the government (in American terms, the administration). The government's powers are extensive. It executes laws but it is also a lawmaking body (similar to the British Cabinet) in that it initiates most bills passed by parliament. It determines the budget, which is subject to Bundestag approval, but the latter cannot increase expenditures or revenues beyond what the government proposes. Furthermore, many laws passed by parliament simply establish general lines of policy, with the Chancellor and his colleagues implementing these policies by filling in the details with decrees, which do not need legislative approval unless they affect the states (in which case the approval of the upper house— the Bundesrat—is needed).

Extensive as these powers are, they are not shared jointly by the Chancellor and the Cabinet. It is the Chancellor who determines the general lines of policy, and he alone is responsible to the Bundestag. Since the Cabinet is not collectively responsible (as in Britain), the stature of the German Chancellor far exceeds the position of the British Prime Minister. Cabinet ministers are therefore in a subordinate role. They serve at the pleasure of the Chancellor. They need not be members of the Bundestag, but in fact most Cabinet appointments have been made from that body. Most of them head executive departments.

National ministries in the German administrative system are skeletal affairs. Traditionally, they do not have field offices throughout the country to administer programs; this is done by state and local administrators. National ministries are concerned with planning, setting standards, and supervising administration. The minister is usually the only political appointee in his department. The other top officials are drawn from the top level of the civil service.

Although government by bureaucratic experts raises serious questions of democratic responsibility, few persons question the competence of the civil service. Germany in the nineteenth century was the first nation to establish a professional bureaucracy, and it early developed a tradition of honesty and efficiency. The civil service, both at the national and state levels, is regulated by national law. Since legal education is the prevailing preparation for the higher civil service, German bureaucrats generally have an almost exclusively legalistic approach to administrative problems.

The Bonn Republic has departed from past practice by permitting civil servants to participate in partisan politics. If they do, they go on leave but retain their civil service seniority and pension rights. Similarly, a civil servant may preserve his rights while accepting employment from an interest group, usually one whose activities he may have been regulating in his capacity as a government official.

THE LEGISLATURE: BUNDESTAG AND BUNDESRAT

The two houses of the German parliament do not have equal powers. In fact, authorities differ on whether the parliament should be called bicameral or unicameral. Most of the powers are held by the popularly elected Bundestag. Although the Bundesrat (upper house) has some legislative authority, it functions as an agent of the states. Bundesrat deputies are chosen by the cabinets of the individual states, paid by them, and may be recalled by them. Voting in the Bundesrat is by state delegations acting under instructions from their governments rather than on an individual basis.

In its capacity as defender of states' rights, the Bundesrat exercises concurrent legislative authority with the Bundestag over categories of legislation that affect federal interests. Examples would include territorial changes and the establishment of new federal agencies. Such legislation cannot become law without the consent of the Bundesrat, and its broad interpretation of what constitutes legislation affecting the states has made this power important. In other legislative matters, the Bundesrat exercises only a suspensive veto, which can be overridden by the Bundestag by a vote proportional to the vote against the measure in the upper house. For example, if two-thirds of the Bundesrat vetoed a measure, a two-thirds vote would be needed in the Bundestag to override the veto.

In addition to its legislative functions, the Bundesrat performs others, such as voting on amendments to the Basic Law, which require the consent of two-thirds of its membership as well as two-thirds of the Bundestag members. In addition, it has the power to appoint half the members of the Constitutional Court and to approve ordinary decrees affecting the states, as well as decrees based on the emergency powers.

The Bundestag has certain powers of election and appointment: It participates in the election of the President; it appoints federal judges; and, as noted earlier, it has the important task of electing the Chancellor. Its primary functions are legislative, however. Most of the bills it considers are introduced by the Cabinet, although a few are initiated in the Bundesrat. But the Bundestag also may introduce bills. In addition, it has the authority to question the

Chancellor and Cabinet members, and it may conduct investigations. To date, the latter powers have not been much used.

Government bills are sent first to the Bundesrat and then submitted through the Cabinet to the Bundestag. Bundesrat proposals are also submitted to the Bundestag through the Cabinet. Proposals originating in the Bundestag can by introduced only by a *Fraction,* which, under the rules, is a group of at least fifteen members. Each of the three parties now represented in the Bundestag constitutes a *Fraction,* but any fifteen members could, if they agreed, make up such a group. Individual members do not have the right to introduce bills. This rule was designed to prevent a few extremist individuals, should they get elected, from taking up valuable Bundestag time with measures whose aim would be mainly obstructionist.

Consideration of bills is similar to the process in the British House of Commons. First the basic principles are discussed and voted upon. If the vote is favorable the bill is sent to committee, where the specifics are discussed in greater detail. Membership on committees is roughly proportional to the strength of the parties in the Bundestag. There are no hearings on bills, but the committees may call expert witnesses, ministers, and civil servants to testify. The committees do much to work out compromises among the parties as well as among the groups affected by the legislation. Indeed the latter are often represented directly on the committees by interest-group functionaries who have been elected to the Bundestag. When the bill is returned to the Bundestag, the general practice has been that members vote in accordance with their party's position, but there has been some deviation in this respect, especially among CDU and FDP deputies.

Bills passed by the Bundestag are sent to the Bundesrat, whose consent is required if they affect the states. Other bills, as indicated above, may be passed by the Bundestag alone, provided they receive a favorable vote comparable to the negative vote in the upper house. Constitutional amendments, however, require the approval of a two-thirds majority in each chamber. Disagreements between the two bodies are worked out by the mediation committee, a joint standing committee composed of members of each house. Compromises through the mediation committee are necessary for legislation affecting the states, and in the case of ordinary legislation they obviate the necessity of overriding vetoes. The mediation committee has become especially important because the Bundesrat has insisted that proposals affecting the states be interpreted rather broadly. Bundesrat members of the committee are not bound by instructions from their state governments. The committee has considered most of the bills in dispute and has worked out compromises for nearly all.

In the main, the Bundestag is not a strong legislative body. It can be considered as a decision-legitimizing institution rather than a decision-making one. To a considerable degree the prestige of the Bundestag was diminished by the way the first Chancellor (Adenauer) treated it. For example, he often refused to explain his policies to the body to which he was formally responsible, and he at times ordered ministers to refuse to appear before the Bundestag or its committees. This policy of the first Chancellor is principally responsible for the relative unimportance, until recently, of parliamentary investigations and the posing of questions, devices that in Britain provide members of the House of Commons important opportunities to influence government policy. More recent chancellors have had a far more respectful attitude toward Bundestag members. The concept of question time has indeed been expanded, and parliamentary undersecretaries have been created, whose major responsibilities are to stand in for ministers at question time.

From the beginning of Germany's new experiment with democracy, there was a general feeling that the government needed additional special powers that would enable it to deal with an emergency stemming from internal or external circumstances. Yet in view of the fact that the emergency powers of the Weimar constitution had been used to bypass parliament and indeed to destroy democracy, the Germans were understandably wary of providing for them. After ten years of debate and discussion, however, the Basic Law was amended to provide for emergency powers, but the amendments were so drafted as to assure the protection and survival of the democratic order in times of crisis. These amendments, often referred to as the "emergency constitution," specify in considerable detail many procedural and substantive safeguards. Among other things, the dissolution of the Bundestag during the period of the emergency is forbidden. Moreover, the Constitutional Court cannot be tampered with. Finally, the Bundestag, with the approval of the Bundesrat, can at any time repeal emergency decrees, and can declare the emergency itself at an end.

THE JUDICIAL SYSTEM

The German judicial system is similar to the French in that both are based on code law, sometimes referred to as Roman law. The legal codes are enacted by the national government so as to ensure uniformity throughout the states. Most of the courts, however, are operated by the states. They are staffed much the same as the civil service: Law graduates enter a hierarchy at a bottom level and are promoted up through the ranks in accordance with their professional qualifications. The national and state ministries of justice administer the judicial system and determine its personnel policies.

The state court systems include local, state, and supreme courts, the latter having mainly appellate jurisdiction. Juries are not used but, as in France, there are two lay assessors who have a vote along with the judge. In serious criminal cases such as murder, six lay assessors are used. At the appellate level, several judges make up the tribunal that hears the case.

There is a Supreme Federal Court, which is primarily an appellate court, although one section does have original jurisdiction over a few categories of offenses that are national crimes. Judges of this court are appointed by the minister of justice. He is assisted in his selections by a committee representing the Bundestag and the state ministers of justice.

A new feature of German government is the Federal Constitutional Court, which has been given explicit powers of judicial review—powers that did not exist before the Bonn Republic. Its jurisdiction extends to conflicts between the national government and the states, conflicts between the states, interpretations of the respective rights of the national government and the state governments, interpretations of the rights of national government organs (President, Chancellor, Bundesrat, Bundestag, etc.), and interpretations of the constitutionality of national and state laws. Unlike in France, individuals may bring cases to the Constitutional Court. Some cases may reach it on request of lower courts. Questions may also be brought by request of the national or state cabinets or by one-third of the members of the Bundestag. Thus, unlike American practice, the court can render opinions without waiting for litigants in specific lawsuits to raise constitutional questions. Because it would be impossible to hear all cases, a screening committee determines the cases that actually reach the Court.

The Bundestag and the Bundesrat each elect one-half of the judges of the Constitutional Court. The Ministry of Justice maintains a list from which most new judges are chosen. Some members must be chosen from among federal judges, and prior to 1971 they served for life; other members served for eight years and were eligible for reelection. Since 1971, however, all judges are chosen for twelve-year nonrenewable terms.

This constitutional tribunal has played a significant role in the Bonn Republic. Its jurisdiction clearly authorizes it to decide questions that in most instances American courts would avoid as "political" and therefore not subject to judicial determination. Accordingly, the Court has ruled on some of the most controversial political issues, such as the status of civil servants, remilitarization, and the outlawing of extremist political parties. The practice of judicial review has proved so popular in Germany that the individual states have created state constitutional courts.

In addition to the regular courts, there are various special ones. The most important of these are the administrative tribunals, which, as in France, hear claims based on alleged wrongful acts of government officials. There are local, state, and national administrative courts; the latter are primarily charged with maintaining uniformity throughout the country as they hear appeals. Other special tribunals include labor, social, and fiscal courts.

THE GERMAN SYSTEM IN ACTION

Germany began her second experiment in democracy with many observers doubting her ability to make a go of it. Thirty years later, there is a good deal of admiration, some of it grudging, for the way the Germans have managed their system of self-government. Problems there are. The German economy, which was once described as a miracle, has had its problems, although they are less serious than in some of the other democracies, including the United States. The fabric of the social consensus that the Germans appeared to be shaping has been torn to a degree, and yet the government has met the terrorist threat without sacrificing the principles of tolerance that are necessary if political differences are to exist.

Throughout its first fourteen years the Bonn Republic was dominated by the first Chancellor, Konrad Adenauer, who was chosen for that position in 1949, 1953, 1957, and 1961. Some features of Germany's political system derive exclusively from this strong-willed and skillful politician. He weakened other institutions by concentrating power in his own hands. His motives were to overcome the evils of the Nazi heritage and establish strong ties with the West, but his methods were often criticized as autocratic. Yet his regime brought prosperity and stability, and thus contributed to democracy by providing the conditions under which a democratic government could exist.

Under Konrad Adenauer's successors (Erhard, 1963-66; Kiesinger, 1966-69; Brandt, 1969-74; Schmidt, 1974—), Germany has given the appearance of a well-ordered democracy. The post-Adenauer Chancellors have demonstrated more respect for parliament than was true under Adenauer, and have been much more inclined to share power with their Cabinet colleagues. Moreover, the shift of power in 1969 from the Christian Democrats to the Social Democrats signified an orderly transfer of power from one major party to another. All these were positive signs of a functioning democracy.

Although the orderly transfer of power to new Chancellors has been successful, some observers question whether the social basis for democracy exists in the German system. Admittedly, extremist parties have had little success in the Bonn Republic, and the Nazis have been discredited by the catastrophe they brought to the country. Yet many observers are still taking a wait-and-see attitude. Some doubts linger because of aspirations and attitudes with respect to reunification of East and West Germany. These are far from clear. For a time it was thought that the German people were reconciled to the notion of permanent division into two nations, but there have been more recent signs that a strong sentiment for national unification is a latent and potentially powerful force in German politics. As the history of Bismarck's and Hitler's Germany both demonstrate, tides of national fervor can dominate and transform the political and governmental system of a country, given a chance.

The prestige of the Presidency was well established by President Heuss (1949-59). He and his successors have by and large performed their duties with dignity and impartiality. Some Presidents, however, failed to sign certain laws that they thought unconstitutional, and were upheld by the Constitutional Court. President Walter Scheel even challenged the authority of some Cabinet ministers to dismiss top ministerial aides, but was firmly blocked by the Chancellor and parliament. In the main, Presidents have left politics to the party leaders in the Bundestag, and the latter have acquitted themselves in a manner becoming seasoned democrats.

SUGGESTIONS FOR ADDITIONAL READING

REVEL, JEAN-FRANCOIS. *The Totalitarian Temptation.* New York: Doubleday, 1977.

On France

ANDERSON, MALCOLM. *Government in France: An Introduction to the Executive Power.* Oxford: Pergamon Press, 1970.

ARDAGH, JOHN. *The New French Revolution.* New York: Harper & Row, 1969.

CHARLOT, JEAN. *The Gaullist Phenomenon.* London: Allen & Unwin, 1971.

MACRAE, DUNCAN, JR. *Parliament, Parties, and Society in France, 1946-58.* New York: St. Martin's Press, 1967.

MACRIDIS, ROY C. *French Politics in Transition: The Years After De Gaulle.* Cambridge, Mass.: Winthrop, 1975.

THOMSON, DAVID. *Democracy in France since 1870.* 5th ed. London: Oxford University Press, 1969.

On Germany

CONRADT, DAVID P. *The German Polity.* 2nd ed. New York: Longman, 1982.

DAHRENDORF, RALF. *Society and Democracy in Germany.* Garden City, N.Y.:
    Doubleday, 1967.
GROSSER, ALFRED. *Germany in Our Time: A Political History of the Postwar
    Years.* New York: Praeger, 1971.
HEIDENHEIMER, ARNOLD J., and KOMMERS, DONALD P. *The Governments of
    Germany.* 4th ed. New York: Crowell, 1975.
KOMMERS, DONALD P. *Judicial Politics in West Germany: A Study of the Fed-
    eral Constitutional Court.* Beverly Hills, Calif.: Sage, 1976.
LOEWENBERG, GERHARD. *Parliament in the German Political System.* Ithaca,
    N.Y.: Cornell University Press, 1966.
SCHELLENGER, HAROLD K. *The SPD in the Bonn Republic: A Socialist Party
    Modernizes.* The Hague: Martin Nijhoff, 1968.
SMITH, GORDON. *Democracy in Western Germany: Parties and Politics in the
    Federal Republic.* New York: Holmes and Meier, 1980.

3. Communist Political Systems: The Soviet Union, Yugoslavia, and China

Unlike the political systems studied in the preceding chapters, communist-controlled governments are dictatorships. Although there are many dictatorships in the world, the communist variety represents dictatorial rule that is in some ways an innovation of the twentieth century, often referred to as totalitarian. There has been some disagreement in recent years among political scientists as to the utility of that term, but it does have some value in that it depicts systems that strive for a complete or total remaking of society, leaving nothing to chance. The present chapter deals with the political system of the Soviet Union (formally Union of Soviet Socialist Republics, or USSR), with brief observations in the concluding sections on the Chinese and Yugoslav variations.

Any student of the Soviet Union must first recognize that the pre-Soviet government of Russia was in almost all respects unlike its Western contemporaries. One of the constant enigmas of the present-day Soviet system is the extent to which some particularly distinctive, interesting, or important feature is a characteristic of twentieth-century Soviet government or an outgrowth of the tsarist system that preceded it. There is considerable disagreement on this point among scholars, but all of them seem to agree that the Soviet system represents a pattern that is quite foreign to the experience of most Westerners.

One obvious reason for studying the Soviet Union is its status as one of the world's two superpowers. Whatever the Soviet government does necessarily has enormous effects on the political events and lives of people almost everywhere else in the world. Equally important is the fact that the Soviet system of government is one of three or four systems consciously used as models by nations around the world. The communist-ruled nations of Eastern Europe—Bulgaria, Czechoslovakia, Hungary, Poland, Rumania, Yugoslavia—have been patterned in greater or lesser degree on the government of the Soviet Union. The same is true of the Chinese People's Republic (Communist China).

99

Moreover, many political leaders of developing nations in Asia and Africa have consciously compared Soviet, British or French, and American institutions and practices as they have sought to build modern governments in formerly colonial areas.

At the same time, there are now (and have been) authoritarian dictatorships that explicitly deny kinship with the Soviet form of government, and in many cases, set themselves up as bitter antagonists of the Soviet Union—for example, Nazi Germany, Japan before World War II, Salazar Portugal, and Franco Spain, to name the most familiar. In examining the development and workings of government in the Soviet Union, therefore, we shall be laying the groundwork to do more than just have some descriptive familiarity with that particular system.

Constitutional Development

Russia has a long history that can be divided into more or less distinct epochs, set off by crises or decisive turning points. But two chief themes persist: the expansion of Russia into a large empire and the retention of autocratic political systems. Not until this century did democratic constitutionalism make a brief and uncertain breakthrough, only to be eclipsed by the Soviet dictatorship in 1917.

The history of the Russian state goes back to the period when the chief city of Russia was Kiev, an era that lasted from about the ninth century to 1240. The conquest of Russia in that year by Mongol hordes ushered in a period of Tartar rule that continued for some 250 years. The reestablishment of Russian rule in the sixteenth century under the leadership of the princes of Moscow was accompanied by autocratic rule and internal troubles. Ivan IV (the Terrible or Dreaded), who ruled from 1547 to 1584 and was known for his ruthlessness, was the real unifier of Russia in the post-Mongol period. After his death, the country entered a period of strife—the "Time of Troubles"—when civil war and palace intrigue threatened to undo Ivan's work. But the election of the first Romanov as tsar in 1613 ended this epoch. The rule of the Romanovs, which came to an end in 1917, saw Russia expand into a great empire and rise to a position of power among the nations.

Most of Russia's achievements in the Romanov period are associated with a few of her great rulers, particularly Peter I (the Great), who ruled between 1682 and 1721, and whose overriding aim was to Europeanize Russia in one lifetime. But these rulers did not tolerate, much less promote, democracy. Some were less ruthless than others, but all ruled by autocratic methods, and even the weaker ones did not readily accept limitations on their power. The most "liberal" of them, Alexander II, who ruled between 1855 and 1881 and who is known for his liberation of the serfs, would accept no restrictions on his absolute power.

The most vocal defender of tsarist absolutism was the Russian Orthodox church, whose leaders viewed Western influence as inimical to Russian interests. Nurtured in the Christianity of Byzantium, Russian church leaders saw the West as hostile to "holy Russia," the true interpreter and defender of Christianity. Thus the church early became an ally of Russian nationalism, although a fullblown Russian version of the divine right of kings theory was not developed until late in the nineteenth century.

Another source of support for tsarist absolutism was the landowning, serf-holding aristocracy. Although it was initially illegal to sell serfs apart from the land, the practice had become so common by 1675 that it received legal sanction. More and more voices came to be raised against serfdom, however, and it became the most persistent issue during the long history of Russian autocracy. The reforms of Alexander II (1861) offered some promise of resolution, but many things were left undone, and no final and acceptable solution to the most acute problem of Russian society was ever found under the tsarist regime, although promising steps were taken in the decade before the First World War.

Protests against serfdom and Russian autocracy took several forms. In the seventeenth and eighteenth centuries they consisted mainly of intermittent and small-scale peasant revolts, although two revolts of major proportions were led by nonpeasants (Stenka Razin, 1667-71; Emilian Pugachev, 1773-74) and were brutally put down. In the nineteenth century, protests were mainly literary and political. The first major political protest, known as the Decembrist Revolt, occurred in December 1825 and was led by nonpeasants, chiefly nobles and army officers who had fought against Napoleon. It, too, was quickly and ruthlessly suppressed. The intellectual atmosphere that had made the uprising possible, however, also gave rise to a literary protest against the evils of tsarist autocracy. This literary upsurge produced Russia's greatest writers, among them Pushkin, Gogol, Lermontov, Herzen, Chekhov, Turgenev, Dostoevsky, and Tolstoy. The intellectual protest against serfdom and tsarist autocracy was also the forerunner of late-nineteenth-century political revolutionary movements, among them the Russian version of Marxism.

Although reforms were slow in coming to Russia, those inaugurated by Alexander II gave considerable promise at the time they were promulgated. The emancipation of the serfs in 1861 was hailed as a great act and earned for Alexander the title Tsar-Liberator. In actuality, the serfs were only partially emancipated. The government bought one-half of the land owned by landlords, but the peasants who received this land had to pay for it over a period of forty-nine years, an obligation that was to prove increasingly burdensome. As time went by, moreover, it became evident that more and more land would have to be bought from the landlords if peasant needs were to be satisfied, but this the government failed to do.

Another great reform of Alexander II was his partial democratization of the institution of local government (the Zemstvo) in 1864. This reform was in large part the consequence of the emancipation of the serfs, who were no longer content to see the landlords govern the local communities. The reform of the judiciary in the same year fell in somewhat the same category: It was intended to give the free peasants a share in the dispensing of justice. Among other things, juries and lawyers were introduced for the first time.

Other notable reforms made the budget public (1862), introduced self-government in the universities (1863), reorganized municipal government (1870), and placed military conscription on a nonclass basis (1874). Additional reforms were under consideration when Alexander was assassinated in 1881.

Unfortunately, the assassination of the Tsar-Liberator doomed prospects for further reform and ushered in a period of reaction, during which some of the reforms were reversed or diluted. Alexander III and his antireform advisers hit hard on all fronts, but especially at education and the press. The political police (Okhrana) were given far-reaching authority. And the procurator-general of the Holy Synod of the Church developed a Russian version of the doctrine of the divine right of kings.

THE BEGINNINGS OF CONSTITUTIONALISM

Although for the most part it could not be manifested publicly, there was a good deal of political ferment in Russia in the last decades of the nineteenth century. Few political movements could function openly, and those that could were not productive of change. More and more energetic people were therefore driven to work in underground organizations, some dedicated to democracy and others to direct action and violence. Among the former were the Social Revolutionaries and the Constitutional Democrats. Among the latter were the Russian Marxists, officially called the Russian Social Democratic Workers' party, who found new ammunition in the evils resulting from the industrialization that had recently burst upon Russia.

But political ferment in itself would not have produced the Revolution of 1905. This was triggered by the disastrous consequences of the Russo-Japanese War (1904-5). The revolution was brought about by the Zemstvos, the local assemblies whose work had in the past been impeded by the government. The first All-Russian Congress of Zemstvos met in the capital in November 1904. It demanded the creation of a representative assembly with real legislative powers, the elimination of class and racial discrimination, and the protection of civil liberties. As things were going from bad to worse, both at home and on the war front, the tsar in June 1905 promised a joint deputation from the Zemstvos and municipal councils that he would convoke a national assembly "as soon as possible." But when it was announced in August that the Duma (legislature) would have only consultative powers and that it would be chosen on the basis of a narrow franchise, the unrest grew, culminating in a general strike in October.

Although his initial answer to the revolution was the imposition of martial law, the tsar at the same time proclaimed a moderate constitution. Russia, in theory at least, became a constitutional monarchy. The Duma was to have legislative powers and would be elected on the basis of universal manhood suffrage. Moreover, a cabinet of ministers was made responsible to it; and guarantees of free speech, press, assembly, and conscience were promulgated.

Because of these newfound freedoms, the underground political groups came out into the open. All of them promoted active discussion of contemporary political, economic, and social problems. Through meetings, newspapers, and political tracts, they attempted to propagate their views and their programs for reform.

But the promise of this seemingly auspicious beginning for representative government was not to be fulfilled. The tsar refused to play the role of a constitutional monarch. From the outset he committed unconstitutional acts, among other things dissolving the first Duma within three months of its convening, although it had been elected for a term of five years. A second Duma, newly elected, was convened in March 1907, but met a similar fate four months later. The electoral law was then changed, without consulting the Duma, to do away with universal manhood suffrage. By thus manipulating the electoral regulations, the government was able to facilitate the election of two conservative Dumas, both of which served their full terms. But the Duma did not become a true parliamentary body. It never was able to call the ministers to account, nor did it gain control over finance. Moreover, administrative officials continued to ignore it and to make use of emergency powers that were still on the statute books.

THE COLLAPSE OF THE OLD ORDER AND THE BOLSHEVIK SEIZURE OF POWER

In spite of these halting steps toward a constitutional regime, Russia by 1914 was making progress in the economic, social, and political realms. To be sure, there were some discouraging situations, but on the whole the signs were favorable. Had it not been for World War I, the revolutions of 1917 might never have occurred. But war did come, and with it the whole tsarist structure was swept aside.

Initially, the war against Germany was not unpopular. The spirit of resistance was strong, and in spite of heavy losses the Russian army fought well. As the war progressed, however, and particularly as evidence of general inefficiency on the home front piled up, dissatisfaction spread. As the situation deteriorated at the front and seeming helplessness prevailed at home, leaders of the Duma and the Zemstvos demanded the appointment of a responsible cabinet, but their call went unheeded.

The beginning of the collapse came with food riots in the capital in March 1917. When the troops refused to fire on the rioters, tsarist authority was at an end. The Duma thereupon asked for and got Tsar Nicholas' abdication. Tsarism was overthrown with very little bloodshed. The Duma leaders quickly formed the Provisional Government, which was to exercise a tenuous authority until its overthrow by the Bolsheviks in November 1917.

The overthrow of tsarism engendered a struggle for power between two competing forces, the Provisional Government and the Soviet (Council) of Workers' and Soldiers' Deputies.[1] The latter organization had come into existence with the collapse of the old order, and from the beginning sought to share in running the country. Its famous Order Number One, for example, asked military units to obey the Provisional Government only to the extent that its orders did not conflict with those of the Soviet. Although the Soviet allegedly sought to help the Provisional Government, the latter found itself increasingly harassed by the former.

In its struggle with the Soviet, the Provisional Government was handicapped by two crucial decisions it had made when it first came to power: to continue the war against Germany and Austria-Hungary, and to postpone domestic reforms until after the end of hostilities. With no decisive victories at the front, the government was more and more challenged by those who wanted to get out of the war and get on with needed reforms at home. These forces gathered momentum in the newly formed soviets in various cities throughout Russia, particularly in Moscow and Petrograd.

In the early months of the struggle between the two authorities, the Bolsheviks, the Lenin-led maximalist wing of the Marxist Russian Social Democratic Workers' party, were skeptical about working in the Soviet, which they

---

1. The first soviets, or councils, grew out of the strikes in the spring and summer of 1905, as bodies to represent the workers in a number of cities throughout Russia. They were not associated with any political party.

believed to be too close to the Provisional Government. But as the Soviet began taking an increasingly independent stand, the Bolsheviks started to work among the various local soviets, seeking to take them over; by September 1917 they had succeeded in gaining majorities in the soviets of Petrograd and Moscow. Thereupon they determined that the soviets should have military revolutionary committees. Although the Bolshevik leaders had serious doubts about their prospects of success if they sought to seize power, one of them, Vladimir Lenin, insisted that they must do so. On the eve of the Second Congress of Soviets in Petrograd, the Bolsheviks struck, seizing the government buildings, the railway station, and the telephone and telegraph networks, and arresting the members of the Provisional Government. The next day (8 November 1917), they asked the Congress of Soviets to install them as the new government of Russia, which was done.

Once in power, the Bolsheviks proceeded to consolidate their gains, a process that required several years. The Provisional Government had promised the election of a Constituent Assembly to determine the future form of government in Russia. The Bolsheviks permitted this election to take place, even allowing the Constituent Assembly to convene in January 1918. But since they could not control it (they had about 25 percent of the seats), they disbanded it by force. Moreover, they concluded a separate peace with Germany (the Treaty of Brest-Litovsk), which many Russians regarded as treason to their allies. Many of the military commanders actually sought to rally their forces against the Bolsheviks. The result was several years of civil war, which the Bolsheviks finally won.

The young Bolshevik regime was led by Lenin until his death in 1924. Thereupon a struggle for power ensued among several leading communists, principally Leon Trotsky and Joseph Stalin. By 1928 Stalin was firmly in the saddle, but several more years elapsed before he liquidated his main enemies (real and imagined) and established a personal dictatorship that lasted until his death in 1953.

SOVIET CONSTITUTIONALISM

Soviet ideas of constitutionalism have been consistently different from those found elsewhere. In the West, for example, constitutions historically have come to be looked upon as instruments by which government is restrained and the rights of citizens are protected. In addition, Western constitutions have provided for procedural safeguards to prevent abuses in the exercise of the powers granted to governments. The Soviet concept of constitutionalism contains none of these ideas. The Soviet constitution provides neither limitations on the powers of government nor any meaningful procedural safeguards. In the Soviet view, the constitution is an instrument for defining government goals and establishing political and administrative institutions to carry them out.

When the Bolsheviks came to power, they did not have a blueprint of the kind of government they wanted. Lenin and other Marxists had insisted that it must be a dictatorship of the proletariat, but even this was not precisely defined. According to Marxist theory, the dictatorship of the proletariat was to be temporary—the transition stage between capitalism and communism. Once private property—the basis of all class struggles—was abolished, classes would cease to exist. The state, the instrument of the dominant class in any epoch, would no longer be needed and would wither away. The dictatorship of the proletariat would thus pave the way for a classless, stateless society, which, according to Marxist doctrine, is the ultimate in social development.

In the early months of their rule, the Bolsheviks operated their "dictatorship of the proletariat" without a constitution. After they disbanded the Constituent Assembly by force in January 1918, they went about drafting a constitution, which came into force in July 1918.

This first Soviet constitution in effect ratified the evolving governmental structure based on the soviets. It proclaimed the revolutionary nature of the regime, declaring power to rest in a dictatorship of the urban and rural proletariat. Moreover, it announced the inauguration of socialism and the suppression of the bourgeoisie. Political power was to be exercised through a hierarchical organization of executive committees of the soviets, culminating in a Council of People's Commissars at the top.

The first constitution was for Russia proper, or the Russian Soviet Federated Socialist Republic, as it was then officially called. After the end of the civil war, parts of the old Russian empire were forcibly brought back under Moscow's domination, and a Union of Soviet Socialist Republics was created in 1922. A new constitution, not too different from that of 1918, was ratified by the Congress of Soviets in January 1924. Although technically a federation, the USSR was a highly centralized state, all powers of significance being vested in one central government.

In 1936 a completely new and much-heralded constitution was adopted. The building of the new society had presumably proceeded to such a point that a new constitution was needed to reflect the changed state of affairs. A drastic economic and social transformation had in fact taken place. But the drawing up of the new constitution seems actually to have been motivated more by external factors, particularly the rise of Hitler in Germany. To counter the Nazi-Fascist threat, the Soviet Union needed allies in the West. By providing proof of an allegedly evolving democratic system in the Soviet Union, the Moscow leaders hoped to convince the Western democracies that they had something in common with the new Soviet regime, and that therefore they should cooperate in meeting the Nazi-Fascist challenge. Moreover, the Soviet leaders hoped to gain a propaganda victory abroad with a constitution that contained declarations of universal suffrage and workers' rights and that provided for secret elections.

In 1977 a new constitution—for the most part a recasting of the 1936 constitution—was promulgated. Under it the regime remains a dictatorship, although now referred to as the "state of all the people" instead of as the dictatorship of the proletariat. All legislative power continues allegedly to reside in the soviet structure (that is, the series of local, regional, and national assemblies). At the national level is the Supreme Soviet, made up of two houses, the Council of Union and the Council of Nationalities. Both are popularly elected, the former based on population, the latter designed to represent national units (the republics and other subordinate units). Each republic, as well as each local unit of government, city and rural, has a unicameral soviet, also popularly elected.

Executive power is divided. The formal executive functions are vested in a presidium of thirty-nine members, elected by the Supreme Soviet and exercising the latter's powers when it is not in session. Powers of government are allegedly vested in the council of ministers, elected by and responsible to the Supreme Soviet. As we shall see, all these governmental institutions are but instruments of the party dictatorship.

Social Forces

The various social forces that normally exist in every society do not have free play in a dictatorship. Some may be repressed and others favored, but a facade of unanimity is usually erected. In a communist dictatorship, the aim is allegedly a classless society: hence the elimination of competing social forces.

The ideological foundations of the Soviet system are to be found in the doctrine formulated by Karl Marx (*Communist Manifesto* and other writings) as interpreted by Vladimir Lenin, founder of the Soviet state. This doctrine—in the Soviet Union referred to as Marxism-Leninism—holds that all political institutions and all political systems can be traced to man's struggle to satisfy his material needs (food, shelter, etc.). The instruments or means (forces of production) used to satisfy these needs (e.g., a horse) are valuable, and those who control them will see to it that laws (and whole political systems) are created to protect them, especially from those who do not have them. This situation results in class struggles. Hence the Marxist notion that the state (political system) in any epoch is the instrument of the dominant class. All other institutions (social, religious, etc.) will be shaped by this fact.

Instruments of production change as a result of inventions and consequent alterations in the economic organization of society, which leads to a new dominant class. This new class will not be bound by old political forms that shackle it. Hence it will revolt and create a new political system to safeguard its position and privileges. In this scheme of things Marx believed that he had discovered the law of social development.

The modern epoch, in Marx's view, represents the culmination of the process of social development. First, because the class struggle has been simplified—the bourgeoisie or capitalist class versus the propertyless wage earners or the proletariat. Second, because when the proletariat revolts it will create a system that will do away with private property, the basis of all classes and class struggles, along with the property-owning bourgeois class. The absence of classes, therefore, would mean that there would no longer be a need for the state because, according to Marxist theory, the state comes into existence as the instrument of the dominant class.

To bring the classless, stateless society into being, according to this theory, will require a transition period, a dictatorship of the proletariat. The driving force in this dictatorship, acting for the proletariat, is a communist party. As the instrument of the proletariat, the dictatorship is charged with establishing the new society, after which the state is to wither away.

It was to be expected, therefore, that in the initial years of the new regime the Soviet leaders would move against the surviving capitalists. As a matter of fact, the so-called remnants of capitalism became the scapegoats for nearly every failure of the new regime. The alleged discovery of innumerable "wreckers," "spies," "diversionists," and other malefactors produced countless trials, executions, and imprisonments. But although the Soviet regime is in its seventh decade, there is still no sign of the abolition of classes and the consequent withering away of the state. Wide social and economic differences persist in the Soviet Union. There are great disparities in earning power, perhaps greater than those found in most capitalist states, with consequent disparities in standards of living. The few privileged—members of the Communist party, the higher bureaucracy, university professors, military officers, top writers and artists, and the technical-administrative intelligentsia—live relatively well. The bulk of the people are on one common level, with a standard of living considerably below that of some Eastern European and all Western European countries.

Thus, while most private property is abolished, privileges continue. This is made possible because the "new class" (the communist ruling group) can manipulate property even if it does not "own" it. The justification is that this is a temporary situation and that the leaders need better living conditions if they are to contribute to the maximum of their abilities. At some future date, presumably, there will be plenty for all; in the meantime, the top leaders decide who "needs" to share the available privileges with them—that is, who is most needed in the pursuit of the aims of the regime.

In other words, although the actual structure of Soviet society may have altered in the years since the Revolution, social classes continue to exist. It is only natural, after all, that those who share the available material privileges should develop a feeling of oneness—a class consciousness—and should be loath to give up their privileges. They know, however, that they owe them to the high party leaders, and are consequently careful not to offend the party.

Their less fortunate fellow citizens constitute groups that in Western democracies would organize for political action to promote their interests, but in the Soviet Union are immobilized. They are given "crumbs" and are constantly told that their day will come. But as the day recedes more and more into the future, awareness of class differences becomes stronger, and the regime's promises develop a hollow ring.

Without admitting it openly, the Soviet leaders have learned that basic social conflicts cannot be assumed away. They therefore seek to keep them in check by a rigid organization of society in which nothing is left to chance. All organizational life is controlled and directed by the party. There can be no autonomous groups or organizations, only those the party sanctions. The party, because it seeks a total transformation of society along definite lines, gives direction to all group activity and attempts to prevent any it considers inimical to its aims.

Political Groups: The Communist Party

In every society there is competition for the things that society has to offer. In democratic societies people are relatively free to compete individually and in groups, although the government acts as a kind of umpire, enforcing the rules under which competition takes place. There is also competition to see who will do the umpiring, as exemplified by the struggle for power among political parties. But many rules and norms of conduct are not government-imposed or government-enforced. In short, a number of forces are at work, a situation that has led some to describe modern democracies as "pluralistic societies."

Pluralism also exists in totalitarian dictatorships, but it is of a different order. Although there is still a struggle for goods and services, the limits of this struggle are carefully defined and rigidly controlled. In the Soviet Union the controller is the Communist party. It is the self-appointed rule maker and umpire, and no one can challenge its decisions. Consequently, in the Soviet Union what is generally described as politics takes place primarily within the Communist party. Furthermore, Soviet citizens have neither the legal right nor the actual ability to organize "private associations" at will. Such organization as occurs must inevitably secure official sanction if it is to be formalized at all, and its activities must be kept within bounds of official approval.

It is therefore very difficult to secure comprehensive, reliable, and up-to-date information about the actual group basis of day-to-day Soviet politics. Perhaps the most familiar example of the kind of group politics that goes on in the Soviet Union is the persistent struggle between intellectuals and scholars seeking greater freedom from regulation and control and the government agencies and government-supporting scholars who oppose them. As the group strength and resources of the two forces have changed back and forth in the years since Stalin, so too have the rules and regulations that are at issue. In 1970, for example, a group including author Aleksandr Solzhenitsyn and a number of leading nuclear physicists apparently was able to secure the release of a Soviet geneticist, Dr. Zhores Medvedev, from a mental institution; he had been placed there for his agitation in favor of greater rights of free speech. There is evidence that plant managers of different enterprises compete in group fashion for scarce raw materials and scarce transport and that heads of local government in different cities or regions tend to compete for new factories or other benefits that can be conferred by governmental decision. While "interest group politics" in the Soviet Union is hardly comprehensible in the same terms as in Western democracies, it would be wrong to ignore groups that do constitute an important part of the raw materials of Soviet politics.

As the only political party permitted to exist, the Communist Party of the Soviet Union is even singled out in the constitution of the Soviet state as "the leading and guiding force of Soviet society, of all state and public organizations." The party was founded in the 1890s, and prior to its 1917 seizure of power was divided into two major factions—Bolsheviks and Mensheviks. Lenin, the determined leader of the Bolsheviks, insisted that the party should be relatively small, made up of dedicated and disciplined revolutionaries. Even after they had carried out the Revolution, Lenin and his comrades called their party the Russian Social Democratic Party (B), the "B" standing for Bolsheviks. It was not until the 1930s that the name Communist Party of the Soviet Union was adopted.

THE BOLSHEVIK CONCEPT OF PARTY

The Russian communists still adhere to the original Bolshevik concept of what the party ought to be. First, although it has grown to about 16.5 million members, the party is considered relatively small in that it includes only about 8 percent of the adult population. It was Lenin who set the standard when he said that the party should consist of a small group of dedicated revolutionaries. In his opinion, a large party would be unwieldy; numbers, he asserted, were not nearly so important as discipline and dedication.

Second, the Bolshevik concept of party also holds that the communists alone are all-wise. Therefore, to permit competing parties would be to introduce obstacles to the attainment of desired objectives; the Communist party must have a complete monopoly of power. More than that, the Communist party must speak with one voice; hence no factions within the party are permitted. Communists often speak of the party as being monolithic; in other words, it cannot be split into factions. Factions have nevertheless arisen, as we shall see, but they have been ruthlessly suppressed.

Third, the party is organized on the hierarchical principle. At the base of the party pyramid are some 300,000 primary organizations (once called cells). Above these are a number of levels of party organizations, each subordinate to the one above it. This means that there are local, area, and regional organizations, in addition to the party organizations at the republic and national levels.

AUTHORITY WITHIN THE PARTY

Theoretically, the party is governed according to the principle of "democratic centralism." Lesser party units elect members of higher units, which in turn elect others until the topmost level is reached. Hence the notion that all party bodies and party officers are democratically elected, and the corollary notion that lesser party units must obey the instructions of those above them.

In actual practice, democratic centralism has never worked this way, except perhaps at the beginning when there was some semblance of election of persons to party congresses and to the party's Central Committee. Since that time, those at the top have controlled the election of those below. Perhaps the only exceptions are party secretaries at the local level, who are chosen by secret ballot. But no one is "elected" to the highest governing bodies of the party except on the recommendation of those bodies themselves.

The supreme authority in the party is ostensibly the Congress, which is supposed to meet every five years. But Soviet leaders have been able to avoid convening the Congress for as long as a dozen years. Moreover, congresses are large and unwieldy affairs. Even when they meet, they are in session only a few days, most of which are consumed by speeches from the party leaders. There are no debates and no contested resolutions. The delegates are there to hear the leaders and to applaud their statements; the leaders are there to report on their achievements, to urge increased efforts on behalf of new or existing programs, and perhaps to signal new turns in the party line.

Much more important than the Congress is the Central Committee. It consists of 319 members (as of 1981) theoretically elected by the Congress and theoretically in charge of party affairs between congresses. In the early years of the Soviet regime, the Central Committee was small and met with reasonable frequency, and considerable discussion of party affairs took place. But because factions began developing, and because these could not be tolerated, meetings became less frequent and began to resemble those of the Congress in that no dissent occurred. During Stalin's reign, the Central Committee was not even called into session for long periods of time. Since his death, it has met with greater regularity, although there is little indication that it cannot be completely controlled by the top leaders.

The most important body in the party is the Politburo, or policy bureau of the Central Committee. Although its size has varied from time to time, most recently it has consisted of fourteen members and nine candidates. The Politburo is a self-perpetuating body. Although technically elected by the Central Committee, no one is ever proposed for membership except by the Politburo itself. Its members are the most important party members in the Soviet Union. From them emanate all important decisions and many lesser ones. As a general rule, there is a division of labor within the Politburo, each member being responsible for an important area or field of activity (e.g., agriculture, agitation and propaganda).

The implementation of Politburo decisions is left to the Secretariat, generally headed by from six to ten secretaries, several of them Politburo members. The most important person in the Secretariat, and hence in the Politburo, is the General Secretary (the title First Secretary was used between 1953 and 1966). While Nikita Khrushchev was only First Secretary, and not a one-man dictator in the Stalin pattern, he was generally conceded, in the words of George Orwell, to have been "more equal" than the other members of the Politburo. This was even more true of Leonid Brezhnev, whose title reverted to General Secretary.

Working under the supervision of the Secretariat is the party bureaucracy, consisting of some 200,000 *apparatchiki,* or full-time paid party officials. The figure is based on information supplied by Moscow to foreign communists, and may be too small; some Soviet defectors insist it should be larger. This body of party workers utilizes many part-time party volunteers, both as sources of information and as a means of conveying the party message. The bureaucrats' essential task is to see to it that party orders are transmitted all the way down the line and to report on their observations of how party and government agents are carrying out their assigned tasks.

Anyone who has reached age eighteen may be recruited for party membership, provided he or she is recommended by three party members who have
been in good standing for at least three years and who have known the applicant
professionally and socially for at least one year. Before full membership is
granted, however, the applicant must pass through a one-year probationary
period, referred to as "candidacy." The principal recruiting ground for party
membership is the Young Communist League (Komsomol). One becomes a
member of the Komsomol after progressing through other organizations designed for younger age groups; the most promising youngsters, numbering
close to 35 million, end up in the Komsomol, and from this elite organization are
chosen most of the future members of the party. As can readily be appreciated,
the various youth organizations constitute a long and careful screening process.

STRUGGLES FOR POWER WITHIN THE PARTY

According to communist theory, the party is a monolithic organization and is
therefore free from factional quarrels. In practice, all communist movements
have been beset with such conflicts. Because there are no democratic procedures for resolving them peacefully, they have been, in the main, resolved by
force.

In the initial years of the new regime, there were those who believed that
intraparty democracy (democratic centralism) could be a workable principle.
At first, a group calling themselves Democratic Centralists attempted to offer
opposition to the course being followed by the Leninist Central Committee.
Next another group, the Workers' Opposition, sought to exercise a voice in
party affairs. Both groups were silenced by Lenin, who had the party Congress
pass resolutions prohibiting activities contrary to the party line—a prohibition
extending even to top party leaders who might have disagreed with Lenin and
his close collaborators.

Although Lenin did not actually execute or imprison those colleagues
who disagreed with him, he removed them from positions of responsibility
and banished them to remote regions of the country. He thus paved the way
for the harsher actions of his successor, Stalin, who did not hesitate to imprison and execute even on the merest suspicion. Stalin's purge of the party reached
all ranks. Countless members of the Politburo and the Central Committee
were shot, often without any case being proved against them.

It was easy for Stalin to order the liquidation of lesser party figures. For
those of higher rank, however, he employed different tactics. At first he aligned
himself with one group, which carried the fight against certain deviationists
(left and right) from the party line; with these successfully removed, he aligned

himself with another group, which worked against the first. Thereafter, Stalin even adopted as his own the program of the latter group. He was thus able to discredit and remove all of Lenin's one-time colleagues, in the meantime securing the appointment of people loyal to him. As Secretary General of the party, he managed to control the election of delegates to party congresses, choosing candidates who would side with him in intraparty conflicts. In the end he made himself the unquestioned dictator of the party and therefore of the government.

The purging process continues, although under Khrushchev and Brezhnev it was not the bloody affair it had been under Stalin. Since Stalin's death, aside from the Stalinist head of the secret police, Lavrenti Beria, and a number of his alleged associates, no one reportedly has been tried and executed. Nevertheless, many party leaders have lost their posts or have been demoted; many have been criticized and have resigned. But there have been no reports of mass trials, confessions, and executions of the kind that occurred under Stalin. The purging process evidently has been tamed; Khrushchev's own ouster, for example, was achieved without bloodshed.

Political Institutions

Since, as we have seen, the Communist party is the decision-making body in the Soviet Union, the governmental apparatus operates as an adjunct of the party, carrying out its decisions. The result is a twin hierarchy of party and government. At all levels there are party and government bureaucrats, with the latter consulting party leaders at every step of the way. To a large degree the two hierarchies overlap; very often the top party leader in any given area is also the top government official in that area. Where this is not so, government officials expect, and get, advice and directions from appropriate party officials. In essence, therefore, the governmental structure may be viewed as the administrative instrument for carrying out party decisions.

THE FEDERAL PRINCIPLE

One of the most salient characteristics of Soviet society is the enormous ethnic diversity of its population. Only about one-half the total population of the USSR is Russian. Almost a fifth are Ukrainians; there are substantial numbers of White Russians (Byelorussians), Georgians, Uzbeks, Armenians, Kazakhs, and numerous smaller nationality groups. The Soviet federal system is designed primarily to recognize and keep within bounds the centrifugal forces exerted by the different nationality groups. Because of the bad tsarist record of treatment of minority nationalities, the Bolsheviks, who proclaimed their advocacy of self-determination and federalism, had some success in getting support from minority nationality groups in the early years of the regime. It was soon evident, however, that national autonomy would in large measure be meaningless. Nationality groups were told by Stalin, then Commissar for Nationalities, that autonomy could be national in form but that it had to be proletarian in content, and, as we have noted, the party leaders could not effectively be challenged on what was proletarian and what was not. In short, "national autonomy" could mean no more and no less than what the top party leaders said it meant.

Minority nationalities make up around one-half of the total population of some 263 million, and some of them are multiplying faster than the Russians. About 40 million are Moslems, which may have future implications, especially in view of the "awakening of Islam." At the same time, Soviet leaders in the early 1980s were aiming for linguistic uniformity. An unpublicized proposal in 1979 recommended that Russian be introduced in all non-Russian kindergartens and that teaching of Russian be intensified at all levels.

The organization of the Soviet Union does not meet the traditional tests of federalism, even in theory. The main component units—the fifteen republics—have no real substance of power. The Soviet constitution grants to the central government power so vast as to leave very little to the republics; furthermore, the constitution may be amended by the Supreme Soviet, and ratification by the republics is not required. In 1956, the Karelo-Finnish republic was even abolished altogether. But even if the theoretical requisites of federalism were met, the Soviet Union would still not be a federal state. A dictatorship can, and does, ignore constitutional requirements; and it does not tolerate independent or competing sources of power. It may employ the forms of federalism, but it does not endow them with substance.

GOVERNMENTAL STRUCTURE: LEGISLATURE

The top legislative body in the Soviet Union is theoretically the Supreme Soviet, composed of two chambers, the Soviet (or Council) of the Union and the Soviet of Nationalities. Both chambers are popularly elected for five-year terms, the former on the basis of one delegate for every 300,000 people, the latter on the basis of thirty-two delegates from each republic plus a smaller number of representatives from the various autonomous republics, autonomous regions, and national areas which exist within the fifteen union republics. Each of the two houses has about 750 members. There are no electoral contests since only one name appears for each office to be filled.

The Supreme Soviet is supposed to meet twice annually, although it has not always done so. Its sessions are brief, averaging no more than five or six days; many are joint sessions, taken up mostly with speeches from party leaders, who also present proposals to be voted upon. Voting is perfunctory; and there are no opposing speeches, conflicting amendments, or proposals for new legislation. Under the circumstances, the Supreme Soviet cannot be viewed as a true legislative body; it is rather the epitome of a rubber-stamp legislature.

Each of the union republics has a unicameral body called the Soviet, which in theory is the republic's legislature. There are also soviets at the regional and local levels. All are part of the administrative apparatus, charged with carrying out decisions and policies determined at the center.

Governmental Structure: The Executive

The Supreme Soviet elects a presidium, which acts as a formal collegial executive. It is composed of a chairman, vice-chairman, a secretary, fifteen vice-presidents (the presidents of the presidiums of the fifteen republics), and twenty-one members. Several top party leaders are always members. The presidium (through its chairman) receives the credentials of diplomatic representatives, confers titles of honor, awards decorations, and performs other functions associated with a chief of state. At the same time, as a permanent nucleus of the Supreme Soviet, it is authorized to perform most of the functions of the parent body when the latter is not in session.

The Supreme Soviet also elects the council of ministers, the directing body of the huge bureaucratic machine. The size of this bureaucratic giant can only be appreciated if one bears in mind that in addition to the normal governmental bureaucracy in a large industrialized nation, there are millions of people who operate the vast and far-flung network of government-owned economic enterprises. Following the pattern of development of Soviet governmental forms, which have so often been modified as a result of trial and error, the council of ministers, which is formally comparable to the cabinet in Western governmental systems, has been reorganized many times. It has varied in size; currently there are over 100 members. There is, however, a type of cabinet (presidium) of the council of ministers, numbering 14.

As might be expected, the council of ministers seeks to carry out party decisions. Although technically responsible to the Supreme Soviet, the ministers are in reality responsible to the party Politburo. No votes of confidence are ever taken in the Supreme Soviet, nor do its members propose motions of censure. Furthermore, several ministers are usually also members of the party Politburo, and hence are responsible to no one but themselves.

The Judiciary: Law, Courts, Political Freedoms

According to Marxist theory, in any given society the legal system is the instrument of the dominant class. Be that as it may, the Soviet leaders have made it clear that their system of law and their courts are the instruments of the party dictatorship. Soviet courts and judges are under no illusions on this point. It would be erroneous, therefore, to expect an independent judiciary in the Soviet Union, for the Soviet judiciary, like other governmental institutions, is but an arm of the administrative apparatus that seeks to implement party decisions. The job of the courts is to preserve the regime and facilitate the promotion of its programs, and conversely to strike down all those who would stand in the way.

Soviet law is code law, following in the Roman law tradition of the tsarist regime. Much has been added, however, because of the vast complexities of the Soviet system, particularly its rejection of the concept of private economic enterprise and the state's assumption of all responsibilities in the economic sphere; new categories of crimes (e.g., "economic" crimes) have been added to the code as a result. But the system operates much more along the lines of a Roman law system than do the American and British systems. The distinction between code law and common law systems was discussed in preceding chapters.

The Soviet court system consists of local, intermediate, and supreme courts in each of the fifteen republics, and a Supreme Court of the USSR. The lowest or local court, called the people's court, is presided over by a judge and two lay assessors; it has original jurisdiction in less important civil cases and minor criminal cases. The judge is supposed to have legal training and is popularly elected for a term of three years; the assessors are chosen for two-year terms by convocations of citizens at their place of residence or work (not at a regular ballot-box election). Decision is by majority vote; there are no juries.

The intermediate courts are based on the autonomous regions, areas, territories, and autonomous republics. They are presided over by five judges, elected by the soviets of the respective geographic units for five-year terms. They hear appeals from the local people's courts and exercise original jurisdiction in the more important civil and criminal cases. For the purpose of assisting a judge in the latter cases, there are panels of people's assessors.

The supreme court of each union republic has five judges and a panel of people's assessors, all elected by the supreme soviet of the republic for five-year terms. It has appellate jurisdiction, as well as original jurisdiction in civil and criminal cases of major importance; it also supervises the functions of the lower courts.

The Supreme Court of the USSR, elected by the Supreme Soviet for a term of five years, consists of a chairman, three deputy chairmen, and sixteen members. In addition, it has a panel of forty-five assessors. Its functions are said to be purely appellate, although the presence of the assessors would seem to suggest that there may be cases in which the Supreme Court exercises original jurisdiction—perhaps in those cases it may wish to remove from the dockets of the supreme courts of the republics. In addition, the constitution stipulates that the Supreme Court will supervise "the judicial activities of all judicial organs of the USSR and of the union republics," thus ensuring a uniform, centralized, and disciplined judiciary.

In addition to the regular courts, there are certain special courts that are not a part of the formal judicial hierarchy. The most widespread of these are the so-called comrades' courts, which are supervised by the local people's courts. They are to be found in such places as factories and apartment houses and handle minor offenses such as insults, petty theft, and small damage charges. They have the power to reprimand and to impose small fines. There are also military courts that deal with military offenders and violations of military regulations. Other special courts, now allegedly abolished, included transport and secret police courts.

In the late 1950s and the early 1960s extrajudicial law enforcement was broadened with the passage of antiparasite laws and the creation of a voluntary citizens' militia and children's commissions. Persons living on "unearned" income are considered parasites and subject to prison sentences or being sent to corrective labor camps. In addition, property not acquired by labor may be confiscated.

The members of the voluntary citizens' militia, sometimes referred to as "public-order squads," are supposed to patrol the streets during the evening hours for the purpose of combating drunkenness, rowdyism, and similar breaches of the peace. The members of these squads are recruited mainly from the communist youth organizations, and they operate under the guidance of party organizations and the police.

The children's commissions are of recent origin and are designed to handle lesser infractions or crimes committed by juveniles. For the most part these seem to involve thievery and group violence (malicious mischief, fist fights, joyriding), as well as drunkenness and running away from home. Apparently the majority of such infractions occur while the perpetrators are intoxicated. Among preventive measures that the authorities have experimented with is the imposition of evening curfews.

The prosecutor-general is given "supreme advisory power to ensure the strict observance of the law by all ministries and institutions subordinated to them, as well as by officials and citizens of the USSR generally"—which suggests far broader powers than are usually associated with the office of prosecutor in the Anglo-Saxon world. The prosecutor-general is chosen by the Supreme Soviet for a five-year term; he in turn appoints the prosecutors-general of the republics, regions, territories, and autonomous republics, who serve for five years. Prosecutors at the area, county, and city level are appointed for a like period by the prosecutors of the republics, subject to approval by the prosecutor-general of the USSR. In the performance of their duties, officials of the prosecutor-general's office are in no way subordinate to local organs of authority. There is some question, however, as to where the prosecutor-general's authority may be infringed upon by the secret police.

Soviet judicial practices have resulted in many innocent persons being punished. Although Khrushchev claimed that judicial reforms had put an end to such instances of injustice, the conduct of Soviet legal proceedings embodies practices that to any Western observer must appear incompatible with the impartial administration of justice. First, the Soviets employ the inquisitorial approach, in which the judge proceeds on the presumption that the accused is guilty, and so the latter has little or no opportunity for meaningful defense. Such an approach, which compels the accused to take the witness stand, is not necessarily bad; it is employed in all countries whose legal systems are derived from Roman law. But without a free press and a free legislature to act as guardians of justice, it may and does become a tool of tyranny. The accused may be browbeaten by the judge and has no opportunity for effective protest against the judge's actions.

Second, there is no right or privilege of habeas corpus in the Soviet system. This permits long pretrial incarceration — people being held for months, sometimes even years, with no formal charges being brought against them. Closely related to the absence of habeas corpus, and in part made possible by its absence, are forced confessions. During long periods of detainment a prisoner can be put through all sorts of torture to extract a confession, often being led to realize that such treatment will end only if he or she agrees to confess. Moreover, there is no protection against double jeopardy: A person may be tried any number of times for the same offense. And milder sentences may be appealed in favor of stiffer ones.

Other judicial practices, now allegedly abolished, should also be noted. One involved the sentencing of persons to work camps, for varying periods of time, by administrative authorities (generally the secret police). The usual charge was that they were "socially dangerous," although there was no legal definition of such an offense. Another practice was that of sentencing persons for acts not legally forbidden but analogous to forbidden acts (crime by analogy). Still another was that of holding members of a family responsible for acts of one of its members; such a charge was applied particularly to the families of soldiers who defected to the West.

Whatever gains may have been registered for the Soviet citizen in the sphere of the judicial system during the Khrushchev era were, to a significant degree, undone in the Brezhnev years. Old abuses have generally not been restored, but new ones have been inaugurated. For example, in the 1970s a number of dissidents were sent to psychiatric hospitals, a practice widely condemned by psychiatrists outside the Soviet Union. Moreover, persons applying for permission to leave the USSR have found themselves dismissed from their jobs, but exit visas have been denied them or they have been forced to wait several years before being able to leave. In addition, a number of intellectuals have been expelled, imprisoned, or exiled for "anti-Soviet activities" because they chose to monitor Soviet government violations of human rights, which the Moscow leaders had agreed to uphold when they signed the Helsinki Agreements in 1975.

Despite repression and the expulsion from the USSR of writers such as Aleksandr Solzhenitsyn and Andrei Amalrik (and others), and the exile of persons such as Andrei Sakharov, the dissident movement has not been destroyed. Certain underground publications (e.g., various *samizdat* pamphlets and the *Chronicle of Current Events)* continue to appear irregularly. An effort in 1979 by prominent literary personalities openly to publish new and largely apolitical periodicals was quashed by the government.

The constitution's bill of rights is one of the principal bases of the Soviet claim that theirs is a democratic constitution. But even in theory these rights are not guaranteed as they are in democratic countries. The article (50) dealing with these rights begins with the words "in conformity with the interests of the working people, and in order to strengthen the socialist system. . . ." Hence, the citizen is severely limited in advance as to the ends for which he or she may use the freedoms of speech and press. And the Communist party is the sole judge of what is in the interests of the working people and what will strengthen the socialist system.

In a similar vein, Article 51 states: "In conformity with the aims of building communism, citizens of the USSR are guaranteed the right to unite in public organizations. . . ." Among the public organizations mentioned are trade unions, youth associations, and other societies. The only political party mentioned is the Communist party, which is said to constitute "the leading and guiding force of Soviet society and the nucleus of its political system, of all state and public organizations." It seems evident, therefore, that the only organizational life that can exist in the Soviet Union, even in theory, is that which meets with party approval.

Other provisions of the bill of rights are subject to similar limitations. There is freedom for antireligious propaganda, but not for proreligious teachings. There is the right to work, but no right to strike. And there are a number of enumerated duties, such as military service and the duty to abide by the constitution, to observe the laws, and to maintain labor discipline. In sum, the constitution not only specifies the purposes for which "rights" may be employed but in addition insists that the furtherance of these purposes is among the primary duties of the citizen.

The 1977 constitution is very specific. Article 59 says: "The exercise of rights and freedoms shall be inseparable from the performance by citizens of their duties." Article 39 says: "The exercise by citizens of rights and freedoms must not injure the interests of society and the state. . . ." And Article 62 asserts: "The citizen of the USSR shall be obliged to safeguard the interests of the Soviet state, to contribute to the strength of its might and prestige."

The System in Action

The Soviet Union does not fit into the Marxist mold of social development, described earlier. First, Marx believed that proletarian revolutions would occur in highly developed capitalist states, where historical conditions would have produced a large, exploited working class and thus have prepared the way for revolution. Instead, Lenin and his comrades seized power in a predominantly peasant society. Second, the political system set up by them was not a dictatorship of the whole people or even of the proletariat, but a dictatorship of the Communist party. Finally, instead of being a transition stage toward a classless, stateless society, the Soviet dictatorship seems to have become permanent, a new ruling class.

The Soviet system, as a totalitarian dictatorship, is concerned with two broad classes of domestic problems. The first concerns the question of how to harness the people to the dictatorship, that is, how to get them to do the things that the wielders of power desire. The second concerns the organizational setup and management of the far-flung Soviet economic apparatus. While these two problems are intimately related, it is more convenient to treat them separately, beginning with problems of organization and administration.

THE ADMINISTRATIVE STATE

Before the Revolution, Lenin believed that administration could be a part-time affair. Anyone who knew the four rules of arithmetic, he said, could qualify as an administrator; and as the new society was built, the state would wither away. But Soviet reality came to bear little or no resemblance to this blueprint. The bureaucracy, instead of withering away, has grown. It is difficult to estimate its size, for in one way or another nearly everyone works for the government. Of course the very size of the country would require a large bureaucracy under any political system. Obviously a much larger apparatus is required by a dictatorship that sets out to remake society in its entirety and that believes complete control is necessary to achieve this. No wonder, therefore, that the Soviet system constitutes an administrative state *par excellence*.

The Soviet administrative apparatus is the instrument of the one-party state, with centralized control and direction. The Communist party issues a constant stream of directives, often changing with changes in the party line or simply as experience proves one solution to a political or administrative problem unworkable and dictates that another be tried. These latter directives indicate that the party is engaged in a constant effort to check on the performance of the bureaucracy.

The bureaucracy is recruited under the party's watchful eye. There is a civil service commission, but its task is not recruitment; rather, it is concerned with classification of personnel and with promoting efficiency and greater effort on the part of employees. Recruitment is more and more carried out on the basis of specifications put forth by individual ministries, which in many instances dictate the curriculum of institutions from which employees are to be recruited. At higher rungs of the administrative ladder, however, the party takes an increasing interest in the assignment of personnel. No important posts are filled without the knowledge and consent of the party Secretariat, perhaps including the General Secretary himself.

The bureaucracy, as we have seen, works under the direction of the council of ministers. In the council there are two kinds of ministries, all-union and union-republic. The former are vertically organized and operate through their own employees down to the lowest level; the latter are organized vertically and horizontally, but operate in the main through corresponding ministries in each one of the republics.[2] As has been noted, the number of ministries represented in the council has varied; at times it has been over 100.

But the present organization, which in general dates from 1957, does not mean that the administrative apparatus is withering away. The 105 regional economic councils that were then set up to supervise the activities of their respective regions were reduced in 1962 to 17. Supervision and direction were still to come from the center, though regional authorities exercised more discretion in the way they implemented Moscow's directives. This resulted in some particularism, with local interests emphasized at the expense of nation-

---

2. The term "vertical" is employed here to suggest a single, unified hierarchical organization. The term "horizontal" is employed to indicate two levels of organization, one national and the other republic. The internal organization of the latter, however, is hierarchical.

al; to remedy this situation, penalties were provided to punish regions that failed to deliver needed goods to other regions. By late 1965, Khrushchev's successors had abolished the regional councils. Thus, the trial-and-error principle was still operating.

The Soviet economy functions on the basis of plans. After they seized power in 1917, the Bolsheviks sought to have the government take over the entire economy. The result was chaos, so in 1921 Lenin launched the New Economic Policy (NEP). During the NEP period (1921-28) many capitalist managers were called back, and peasants were allowed to sell their produce at market prices. Economic recovery ensued, but also the emergence of some relatively well-to-do persons; therefore, in order to combat the reappearance of "capitalistic" features in the economy, the regime in 1928 launched a series of Five Year Plans, signifying its intent to establish rigid control in industry and agriculture. The general principle of the Five Year Plan has continued to be used, although some variation has taken place.

The basic goals of the plans are determined by the top party leaders; the means of achieving them are left to the State Planning Commission (Gosplan), which supervises a considerable bureaucratic apparatus. Ministers, statisticians, party secretaries, factory managers, engineers, technicians, and other experts are consulted with a view to producing plans that call for maximum effort all along the line as well as the best possible utilization of resources. Historically, the State Planning Commission had also exercised a great deal of authority in seeing to it that the plans were implemented. In late 1962, however, its functions were confined largely to long-range planning and coordination of annual economic plans. At the same time a new agency, the Council on National Economy, was created and given extensive authority to implement plans and to make prompt decisions on resource reallocation and other problems of day-to-day management.

The management of economic enterprises is characterized by two primary principles: the single-manager concept and capitalist patterns of reward. In the early years of the Soviet regime there was an attempt to run industries through trade-union committees, but it was largely unsuccessful, and by the 1930s the single-manager idea had won firm acceptance. Just at this point, however, the purges consumed many of the managers and created a fear of assuming managerial responsibility; virtually every decision was referred upward, so that Moscow found itself deciding minute details. In the past two decades, the freedom to manage has largely been restored, although primary decisions are still taken in Moscow. Managers are now less afraid to use their own discretion and imagination in implementing decisions.

Marx had said in the Manifesto that in a communist society each person would be expected to contribute according to his ability and would in turn be rewarded according to his need. Lenin, in the initial years of the Soviet regime, talked of paying everyone workingmen's wages. Stalin and other Soviet leaders soon learned, however, that the only way to increase production significantly was to introduce capitalist patterns of reward. Piece rates were introduced, with special bonuses to those who exceeded the established norms, and managers were accorded bonuses for overfulfillment of planned output. Engineering and technical personnel were rewarded at rates considerably above those of the average worker. The general result has been a wide disparity of reward, but there is no evidence of the development of a market economy, although some experimentation with certain market mechanisms (e.g., interest on money borrowed by enterprises, supply and demand) is now widespread.

In Soviet agriculture the dominant theme is collectivism. Although the Bolshevik slogan at the time of the Revolution was "all land to the peasants," they did not intend to foster private ownership of land. Following the NEP period, and in line with the Five Year Plan, the regime inaugurated collective farming. Organizationally, it took two forms: collective farms and state farms. In the latter, the government was the owner and manager; farmers were ordinary wage earners. In the former, the members of the collective held the land in common, not owning it but having its use in perpetuity. Management was by a board, theoretically elected by an assembly of all the members of the collective, which had to conform to basic governmental rules concerning the operation of collective farms in general.

Under the rules handed down by the government, collective farms sell their produce to the state at prices determined by bureaucrats. At the end of the year proceeds are distributed among the members of a collective. For several decades, there was no certainty as to what a collective farmer's income might be because production varied considerably from year to year. More recently, the government established a guaranteed annual minimum. In addition, members of collective farms are permitted small garden plots, whose produce is their own to sell at whatever price the market may bring. The same is true of a cow, chickens, and so forth that they may own. Because so many farmers were spending a disproportionate share of their efforts on the private plots, the government has from time to time initiated measures to discourage them, hence progressively diminishing the area of private initiative in agriculture. To ease shortages, however, the Soviet leaders have been forced to make additional concessions to the peasants' desire to produce privately.

Soviet agriculture is not efficient; a Soviet farmer produces food for only 7 persons compared to 46 by an American farmer. Moreover, private plots, which make up less than 4 percent of all arable land, produce 25 percent of the country's total agricultural product (much more if only vegetables and dairy produce are considered).

While the bulk of the land is in collective farms, events of the past few ✱ years seem to indicate that the regime was favoring state farms. For example, all of the area opened up in the 1950s, the so-called Virgin Lands, was organized into state farms. But present indications suggest that the collective farms will be preserved for some time to come.

In summary, then, it can be said that the Soviet administrative machine is large and growing. The very vastness of this machine, to say nothing of the many different efforts of the party to check on its performance, has resulted in confusion concerning responsibility. Too many people have their fingers in the administrative pie at too many places, making it difficult for even the party to assess responsibility. But someone must take the blame when things go wrong; consequently, many administrators have, in self-defense, entered into so- ✶ called protective alliances to help and protect each other. Evidence of bungling and inefficiency, together with party meddling, is ample — none of which makes for popular trust in the bureaucracy.

Finally, there has been a slowdown in the rate of economic growth. The ✱ Soviet economy suffers from too much of the gross national product going into the military. Despite its size and potential wealth, the Soviet Union has one of the lowest standards of living and suffers shortages of nearly everything except military weapons. Agriculture is in poor shape. Moreover, Soviet energy problems do not favor economic growth, and economic pressures in the 1980s are certain to be greater than those of the 1960s or '70s. Western specialists on the Soviet Union are reluctant to make predictions about the Soviet economy, except to reiterate that it will continue to have serious problems.

HARNESSING THE MASSES: REPRESSION
It was obvious from the beginning of the new regime that opposition would not be tolerated. To the Soviet authorities, whoever was not for them was against them, and real and imagined opponents were to feel the brutal repression of a systematic police regime. This repression took three primary forms: liquidation (summary execution), imprisonment, and surveillance by the secret police. All three came under the jurisdiction of the CHEKA, the secret police organization whose formal name was the Extraordinary Commission for Combating Counterrevolution, Espionage, and Dereliction of Duty. In subsequent years the name was changed several times. Today the secret police is under the Committee for State Security (KGB).

Those considered most dangerous to the Bolsheviks — chiefly former government officials and church and business leaders — were soon liquidated, many without the benefit of even a perfunctory trial. The bloodbath was extensive; no one, not even the communists, knows how many perished. The Bolsheviks took Lenin at his word that they should not be squeamish about spilling blood. In city after city, persons who had been prominent as judges, teachers, church officials, or administrators felt the terror.

Those who were considered slightly less dangerous, who were suspected of opposition but not marked for immediate liquidation, were thrown into prison. Some were put on trial and others simply sat in jail, uncharged. Some were sent off to labor camps and forgotten; many simply vanished without a trace. Often records were not kept, or were imperfectly kept. Those who were accidentally caught in the web suffered the same fate as those intentionally removed from circulation, for no one in authority really bothered or cared. Some people were fortunate enough to be released after a brief span of time, but this was due more to fortuitous circumstances than to any established judicial procedures.

In a third category were those who were suspect but not considered dangerous enough to warrant either liquidation or imprisonment. Literally millions in this category were subjected to secret police surveillance and the ever-present eye of the informer. Secret police tactics varied. In some cases there were brief periods of incarceration and questioning, accompanied perhaps by police brutality; in others, people were simply asked to report to a secret police office where they were questioned and released. Often the invitation was repeated, with the victim not knowing when it might mean a more permanent stay.

Secret police surveillance was a deliberate tactic, designed to intimidate all those who might think, however remotely, of working against the regime. The network of police informers, reaching into every office, apartment house, and group gathering, was designed to reach every possible dissident element. No one knew who the informers were, but all knew they existed. Often informer was pitted against informer as a means of cross-checking. Sometimes people were pressed into informing, and at other times they volunteered their services, perhaps in the hope that such voluntary activity might stand them in good stead in less fortunate circumstances.

✱   The secret police and the informers are still very much a part of Soviet society, but they are less openly in evidence than during Stalin's time. More important, the powers of the secret police have been curbed, and they are feared less. The Khrushchev decade (1953-64) witnessed a declining number of secret police repressions, a change that has led most experts on the Soviet Union to conclude that no present or future Soviet ruler could resort to the brutal rule so characteristic of the Stalin period. But repression in one form or another remains an integral part of the system.

HARNESSING THE MASSES: PERSUASION

In their efforts to get the people to do the regime's bidding, communist leaders have supplemented their techniques of force and fear with a massive attempt at persuasion. This persuasion takes several forms. First, the regime seeks to mobilize public opinion through ownership and control of the public opinion media. The extent of this control cannot be appreciated unless one realizes that in the Soviet Union there are no privately owned newspapers or publishing houses, no privately owned radio or television stations or privately produced programs, no privately owned theaters or privately made motion pictures. In the public opinion media field, the communists own and control everything.

In order to reach and involve every important segment of society, the party has created appropriate propaganda instruments, such as the *Literary Gazette*, a newspaper specifically created for writers and artists. Writers therefore cannot plead that they do not want to get into political polemics in the political organs of opinion, for the party has been particularly solicitous: It has created a special outlet just for them. How could they not show their gratitude by using it to extol the privilege of being writers in a communist paradise? Similarly, university professors cannot refuse to praise the virtues of science in a communist society because the party has created another special newspaper just for them. And if they should be busy, the party will find someone to write pieces for them.

Everyone who contributes to the propaganda output in the Soviet Union is provided with ample guidance by the agitation and propaganda section (Agitprop) of the party's Central Committee. Agitprop furnishes themes that should be stressed, slogans that need to be utilized, problems that need to be emphasized; and in many instances it provides texts of feature pieces or editorials. Those in the radio-television and newspaper fields receive a steady flow of materials to be utilized. Almost nothing is left to chance or to individual choice.

In addition to mobilizing and monopolizing the instruments of public opinion, the regime pursues its persuasion campaign through the so-called mass organizations. On a number of occasions these organizations have been described by Soviet leaders as "transmission belts" by means of which the party machine operates. Here the people are harnessed in a variety of ways to work for the regime's goals and programs. The most widespread of the mass organizations are the soviets. As local administrative bodies, the soviets, guided by a core of faithful communists, mobilize countless noncommunists to help in the pursuit of communist objectives. Soviet trade unions operate similarly. Rather than performing the tasks usually associated with labor unions, they are more concerned with promoting the regime's economic or other goals; in addition, they administer a large part of the social security program. Many other organizations serve similar functions. The Writers' Union, for example, is given the task of keeping writers in line. As the party's outpost among this important group, the Writers' Union sees to it that literary output conforms to what the party currently wants in literature. The same can be said for the association of artists.

Of special importance are the youth organizations. In some ways, the regime's major effort is concentrated on youth because it realizes that unless youth is won over, the outlook for communism will not be bright. Young children are organized into the Octobrists, where their first indoctrination begins. Next, they become Pioneers and are subjected to more subtle propaganda about Soviet leaders, the Soviet Union, and the outside world. The more promising among the Pioneers are selected for membership in the Young Communist League (Komsomol), which then becomes the principal recruiting ground for new party members. At every step of the way, through special newspapers, lectures, movies, and other means, the party seeks to inculcate the "right" attitude among the young, to steer them toward the communist way of life.

Third, the regime also pursues its persuasion campaign by regimenting the schools. The Western tradition of free inquiry is totally foreign to the Soviet educational system. Everything must fit into the concepts of the one and only true "science," the science of Marxism-Leninism. Moreover, there is great stress on science and technology, and little opportunity for liberal learning. Everything in education must point to specific goals and achievements, laid down by the party and supervised and directed by the ministries of education in each of the republics. Teaching materials and the teachers themselves are carefully screened by the ever-watchful party. All this is understandable, for the party views the schools as simply another instrument in the ultimate harnessing of the masses to do the regime's bidding.

Finally, the party seeks to neutralize or destroy all competing influences. The most important of these are religion and the home. In its campaign of repression, the party destroyed many churches or turned them to other uses, and countless clergymen were liquidated or imprisoned. At the same time, the party embarked on a systematic campaign, through ridicule, the establishment of "atheistic" museums, and the like, to minimize the effect of religious teachings. Subsequently, while continuing to heap scorn and ridicule on believers, the regime set about guiding and controlling the remaining clergy, in an effort to render them less harmful. And although the regime is in its seventh decade, there has been little letup in its antireligious campaign.

Similarly, the regime has conducted a systematic campaign to minimize the influence of the home. Initially it encouraged children to inform on their parents; now it seeks to combat home influence chiefly by taking children out of the home as much as possible and as early as possible. From the outset, women were encouraged to work and the government provided places for mothers to leave their young ones during the day. More recently, the regime has inaugurated week-care centers where children may be left on Monday morning and picked up Friday night or Saturday morning. In this way, the party can begin to shape the young generation at an early age, and with less competition from the home. All of this is in addition to the children's and youth organizations, to which reference has already been made. In short, the regime overlooks no opportunity in its efforts to produce the "new communist man." Article 66 of the 1977 constitution asserts that parents have an obligation to prepare children "for socially useful labor" and "to raise worthy members of society."

There is still considerable doubt that the effort to remake man by remaking society has accomplished results quite as revolutionary as intended. Undoubtedly the changes wrought in the society and economy since 1917 have been tremendous. But, then, vast changes have occurred in most other countries too since then. Undoubtedly the Soviet political system remains dictatorial and repressive in a form and degree unmatched in most other countries. But the tsarist regime before 1917, although less dictatorial and repressive, gave the Russian people little knowledge of, experience with, or preparation for, a truly democratic government. It is ironic that the Soviet system, which promised so much, has done even less in this respect.

Observers of the Soviet Union — scholars, politicans, journalists — are not in agreement as to (1) the long-run intentions of the Soviet leaders or (2) the prospects for change ideologically or structurally. In the opinion of this writer, the weight of the evidence concerning the first is that despite professions of a desire for détente (a lessening of tensions), the Soviet leaders feel uncomfortable and insecure with noncommunist centers of power, notably the United States, and will seek to lessen or destroy the vitality and integrity of such centers. Good examples of Soviet insecurity were their military actions in Hungary (1956), Czechoslovakia (1968), and Afghanistan (1979). The ideological compass by which the Moscow rulers have been steering makes it difficult for the Soviet Union as a communist power to stay within its boundaries indefinitely.

On the second point, despite some changes, the weight of the evidence seems to indicate that Soviet communism is incapable of changing in the direction of a democratic, parliamentary, pluralist system. It does not seem possible that the leaders could give up any of the supports (monopoly of force, monopoly of the economy, and the right to determine what people should think) of a social order that in its essence has been totalitarian. This is not to exclude the possibility that at some future date events such as strikes and demonstrations, although forbidden, might constitute at least a beginning toward significant modifications.

The regime's aging leaders must be greatly disturbed by the rising level of restlessness and discontent among the youth, who seem to be tuning them out. The new generation of young adults are bored by communist ideology, resentful of special privileges for the few, and impatient with the system's general shortcomings. These young people are mostly submissive, but also rebellious (mostly in attitude). They are not awed by the party, but for the time being they are confining their rebellion to trading in the black market and escaping into disco and other dance clubs. More serious signs are heavy drinking and a sharp increase in crime committed by the young. This legacy that the leaders are leaving behind would seem to be a sad commentary on a system whose promises led to great expectations but whose performances fall far short of meeting the basic daily needs of its citizens.

Variation on the Communist Model: Yugoslavia

The Yugoslav Communist party and its leader, Josip Broz Tito, utilized their control of a guerrilla movement in World War II to seize power in Yugoslavia. Tito received significant aid in weapons and other supplies from the Western Allies in the latter years of the war. The Soviet army provided critical help by taking the capital of the country (Belgrade) in October 1944 and turning it over to the Tito forces. A provisional government, which included a number of noncommunists, did not last long because the communists succeeded in their determination to force them out.

Once firmly in power, the communists copied the Soviet system lock, stock, and barrel. Their 1946 constitution was a veritable copy of the Stalin constitution of 1936. They set up a dictatorship of the proletariat with a federal structure (six republics) on paper, but in fact all significant power rested in the hands of the top party leaders. Nationalization and planning also followed the Soviet pattern, as did the harsh treatment of all opposition, real or imagined.

The Yugoslav Communist party's resistance to Soviet attempts at political and economic domination of the country led in 1948 to its excommunication from the association of Soviet-led communist parties (Communist Information Bureau, or Cominform). This action on the part of Stalin forced the Yugoslav leaders to reexamine their Stalinist model and to search for what they could call a real Marxist one.

The consequence was a 30-odd year search, with varied and sometimes dramatic modifications. The avowed goal was self-management, exemplified by the formation of workers' councils. The concept of self-management had political, economic, and other implications. In the economy, the Yugoslavs began increasingly to utilize the market mechanism, but its application was often nullified where party policy or the local interests of influential communists would be adversely affected. Competition was encouraged, but where this led to costly duplications of effort or where Yugoslav firms were undercutting each other in search for foreign markets, the party stepped in to establish control of the situation. Similarly, when workers councils' decisions were motivated by local or personal interests at the expense of the broader national interest, the party reasserted its power.

There were five economic reforms in the ten-year period from 1951 to 1961, indicative of a trial-and-error approach. Other reforms followed. Most of agriculture was de-collectivized and some concessions were made to private enterprise (family restaurants and bake shops, tailors, plumbers, electricians, repairmen). The overall consequence of these reforms was that Yugoslavia became a "consumerist society." The quantity, quality, and availability of consumer goods has far exceeded that of the Soviet Union or any other communist state. At the same time there was a price to pay—inflation, foreign exchange deficits, and unemployment. The last is not supposed to happen in a communist society. Fortunately for the Yugoslavs, several countries in Western Europe have provided employment for one million of them.

Politically, the principle of self-management produced widespread repercussions, especially in the 1960s. There were demands for democratization and decentralization, accompanied by the belief that the state should be less involved (de-etatization) and a desire for decreased political involvement (de-politicization) on the part of the people. In an effort to meet these demands, Tito and his comrades produced some drastic constitutional changes as well as deemphasizing the party's role as the source of commands. A series of far-reaching constitutional amendments in early 1971 gave the republics considerable political power, but when late in the year demonstrations in the republic of Croatia stressed nationalism and even separatism, Tito stepped in and purged the Communist party leaders there. Subsequently, he purged party leaders in the other republics, and in 1974 promulgated a new constitution—the world's longest—which again called attention to the importance of the dictatorship of the proletariat and to the party's guiding role.

Self-management is still highly touted, and is supposed to govern in all organizations except the military. The fundamental prerequisites for real self-management—freedom of speech, press, and association—do not exist in Yugoslavia. There is no right to advocate roads to socialism other than the official version of self-management. Decision making in governmental institutions, for example, is said to emerge from agreements among representatives of the six republics and two autonomous provinces. In the national parliament each republic has the same number of representatives, even though some republics are several times more populous than others. When difficulties arose and disagreements led to stalemate, the party, especially when Tito was alive, was able to resolve the issue. While the future may be uncertain, party members are instructed to be ever vigilant against developments that might go against party policy. Moreover, in the vast majority of cases the party decides who will be in self-management bodies and always retains a veto power.

There is some question as to how united the party may be, because in the liberalization period there were in effect six parties (eight if the two autonomous provinces are counted), suggesting division along nationality lines. In view of the fact that the nationality problem is far from solved, the potential for serious disagreement in party ranks needs to be kept in mind. This is especially true in the light of the country's severe economic problems.

The political liberalization of the late 1960s brought changes in the arts and literature, and in the media generally. No longer were party directives and party judgments the sole guides of what was good and appropriate. The result was considerable diversity and nonconformity. In 1972, hard on the heels of purges in the party, there began a purge of individuals in the communication media, accompanied by attacks on undesirable Western influences. While some remarkable and revealing items still appear in certain Yugoslav publications, a great deal of conformity has returned.

Several years before his death in 1980, Tito established a collective presidency designed to avoid power struggles. It is made up of one person from each republic and autonomous province, a total of eight. Each year they are to elect one of their number for president and one for vice-president, with an understanding that these positions would be rotated among the members.

Real political power is exercised by the Communist party's top body, the Presidium, consisting of twenty-three men. While members of this self-perpetuating body have echoed some of Tito's professions of democracy, the question whether a communist system can be democratized remains unanswered.

Variation on the Communist Model: China

The Chinese Communist party, under the leadership of Mao Zedong, forged a revolutionary movement in the years before World War II, justifying it as a way of opposing the Japanese conquest of Manchuria. Near the end of the Second World War and immediately after it, they employed their guerrilla forces to fight a revolution that brought them to power in 1949. Thereupon, they fashioned a political and economic system modeled on the Soviet one, in which the Communist party was all-powerful. Soviet-type repression of all opposition was rapidly inaugurated. China became a tightly regimented society. Moreover, the first decade of their rule was one of almost total dependence on the Soviet Union in economic and military affairs.

Following the denunciation by Khrushchev, in 1956 and after, of Stalin's methods in the Soviet Union, there was confusion among the Chinese leaders. Soon they began to see themselves as the only true followers of Marxism, and in a sense became more Stalinist than Stalin. In 1957 they launched the Great Leap Forward, an effort designed to achieve rapid breakthroughs in industry and agriculture by an intensive mobilization of China's great resource—human labor. Planning and experts were disregarded. The main results were severe economic dislocations, waste, and a sharp drop in industrial and agricultural production.

The collapse of the Great Leap Forward shook the country's confidence in its leaders and dashed all hopes for dramatic and rapid economic changes. Just as the more moderate elements in the bureaucracy were beginning to repair the damage, while for the most part paying lip service to the revolutionary values of Mao's thought, Mao launched the Great Proletarian Cultural Revolution.

Mao apparently believed that a "bourgeois stratum" (New Class) had developed—just as in the Soviet Union—that was sharply differentiated from workers and peasants by material privileges and high status. To him this was a form of capitalist restoration, a renouncing of the class struggle, and the establishment of elite concepts in all institutions of the society. Consequently, it was necessary to take measures to promote egalitarianism.

The Cultural Revolution was spearheaded by hundreds of thousands of high school and college students, organized as Red Guards, who were joined by adult "revolutionary rebels." A movement that began as a struggle against bourgeois influences in the cultural sphere soon escalated into attacks on party figures accused of protecting subversive artists, and subsequently spread to all segments of the society. Universities and libraries were shut down for several years; professors and bureaucrats were sent to perform physical labor and be "reeducated." Moreover, party officials were purged, with two-thirds of the membership of the Central Committee removed from power. The toll in human suffering was heavy, to say nothing of holding the country back in education, science, and technology. In the end, factional fighting became so severe in Red Guard ranks that the army stepped in to restore order. By 1969 the Cultural Revolution had come to an end, leaving China in considerable disarray.

In the early 1970s China experimented with varying forms of political organization, but really important changes came after Mao's death in 1976. These changes, including a new constitution and the rehabilitation (some posthumously) of many who were purged in the Cultural Revolution, have not challenged the power of the one-party dictatorship. The changes are largely policy-oriented. Past failures — in fact everything that went wrong after 1965 — were attributed to the Gang of Four, Mao's widow and three others (and by implication Mao himself). The Four and six others were brought to trial in late 1980, and in January 1981 were found guilty of a host of antirevolutionary crimes. Mao's widow, Jiang Qing, and one codefendant got death sentences, but these were suspended for two years, at which time they are to be reviewed.

Politically, although the dictatorship continues, there have been some interesting innovations and modifications. One of these permitted noncommunist candidates and voting by secret ballot, at least in some district elections. Another changed the judicial system, allegedly to provide legal protection to citizens, by requiring evidence other than confessions. The definition of "counterrevolutionary offenses," however, remains broad, and it is not clear if those sent to labor camps as a result of false accusations (officially admitted) have been released. Nevertheless, there seems to be a determination to replace the arbitrariness of the Mao era.

A 1978 Central Committee proclamation extolled democracy and basic rights: the right to speak out, the right to hold debates, the right to air views, and the right to write big-character posters. But within a year came a clampdown, partly because of a rising tide of dissent and crime, the extent of both having been seriously underestimated. More important, perhaps, is the fact that the Chinese communist leaders have never been comfortable with democracy and have tended to permit only limited and carefully controlled discussion. During their rule, the big four democratic freedoms have never been anything but instruments in ideological campaigns. During the trial of a dissident who was sentenced to fifteen years in prison in late 1979, the prosecutor asserted that democratic rights must be based on Marxism, the leadership of the Communist party, and the dictatorship of the proletariat.

On the other hand, there has been a seeming deemphasis of Marxist ideology. There has been a decline of slogans and banners, and much media output carries no Marxist message. There have been public declarations by top leaders that there is no longer a need for turbulent class struggle. Former puritanical attitudes toward dress and relations between the sexes have been dropped. There has been an open defense of intellectuals, most of whom suffered as a result of the Cultural Revolution. Mao's policies have been attacked, but he was spared personal responsibility until 1980.

The major changes of the late 1970s and early 1980s were most often described in terms of the goals of the Four Modernizations (in industry, agriculture, defense, and science and technology). In industry, the 1981-85 Five Year Plan placed emphasis on energy and building materials, with a corresponding deemphasis on steel production. Moreover, in some spheres new plants would be imported and foreign investments encouraged.

Like the Yugoslavs, the Chinese are experimenting with market socialism. The profit motive is designed to reduce waste and to cut costs. Wages will be higher in the more efficient enterprises. Moreover, workers are encouraged to establish cooperatives and produce and sell goods and services in short supply, with little or no control of profits from such ventures. Private street-side tailors and pedlars ply their trades, and apparently charge whatever the traffic will bear.

With the beginning of 1981, however, China's leaders admitted that liberalization was not easily overcoming the mistakes of the past. Consequently, the "period of readjustment" was going to be longer than expected, requiring the reimposition of some of the former controls. Liberalization had apparently contributed to increased spending, leading to an abrupt increase in the inflation rate. This could not be tolerated, said the leaders, asserting that the country must begin to live within its means. They hoped that the return to increased central controls would be temporary. Certainly, they did not want to nullify the new expectations that liberalization had created among urban workers and the youth. But whether they can overcome the paralyzing effects of a centralized bureaucracy remains to be seen.

Agriculture is to receive a high priority for the next several years. It is to receive larger budget allocations for investments, especially for irrigation and mechanization. Leaders in the agricultural sector are to have more leeway to make production and distribution decisions. Material incentives are to be increased, and private plots to be guaranteed. The importance of agriculture is underscored by the fact that China is 75 percent peasant, that 50 percent of the villages have no roads to connect them with the outside, and that agricultural production has been low. Therefore, it is likely to continue to be a major constraint on growth in the other sectors of the economy. Much of China still lives on the brink of hunger.

Education suffered severe setbacks during the Cultural Revolution. Universities were closed for several years, research institutes were stripped of their equipment, and science and technology lagged. Two years after Mao's death there began a determined effort to catch up. Some high school graduates are now allowed to go directly to the university. Rigorous entrance examinations for higher education have been reintroduced, class origins deemphasized, and the best students have been sent for advanced training to Japan, Western Europe, and the United States. Graduate institutes in history, religion, law, philosophy, and economics—which were closed in 1966—were reopened in 1978. Western books are reappearing in libraries.

The defense establishment is to be modernized, in large part through imports from the West. For the Chinese as they entered the 1980s, the Soviet Union constituted the main threat to world peace, and the Chinese leaders have implored the leaders of Western nations not to be complacent.

The Chinese leaders would no doubt like to change the world political map, but for the time being domestic problems will have priority at least for the near future. There is much consolidation needed because much confusion and foot-dragging resulted from abrupt changes such as the rehabilitation of persons earlier declared to be enemies. Moreover, some of the 12 million city young people sent to the countryside between 1968 and 1975, who have been coming home, have turned up among dissidents and criminals, alarming symptoms of disaffection. Adding to the leaders' woes was unemployment, which in 1980 stood between 10 million and 20 million. Finally, there is the problem of political socialization within the party so as to bring together the older members and the newer ones, because approximately half of the party members were admitted since the beginning of the Cultural Revolution. Party leaders must seek to make their decisions palatable to post-Mao members as well as to his one-time comrades.

Communist systems seem to require, first, that the Communist parties have complete and unchallengable political power. Second, they rest on collective (state) control of the economy, with tactical concessions to private enterprise here and there out of sheer necessity, accompanied by a hope and an expectation that such concessions will be temporary. Third, they depend on a far-flung police apparatus and its auxiliaries (such as informers). Fourth, they are supported by a carefully indoctrinated and controlled military. Finally, they rest on a well-organized and minutely orchestrated propaganda establishment, designed to reach everyone (perhaps in several contexts). At times tactical maneuvers may convey the impression that writers and artists enjoy considerable freedom, and sometimes they do, so long as their output is judged not to subvert the aims of the regime. And those who please the leaders are well rewarded.

In short, communist regimes do not rest on something as shaky as public opinion, but on the reliable instruments mentioned above. It would be difficult to predict, however, what would happen in times of serious crisis. It is possible that in such an eventuality the disoriented masses might grasp for ideas that would not be welcome by the leaders.

SUGGESTIONS FOR ADDITIONAL READING

On the Soviet Union

KELLEY, DONALD R. *Soviet Politics in the Brezhnev Era.* New York: Praeger, 1980.

KOLAKOWSKI, LESZEK. *Main Currents of Marxism.* 3 vols. New York: Oxford University Press, 1978.

MEDVEDEV, ROY A. *On Stalin and Stalinism.* New York: Oxford University Press, 1979.

OBSERVER. *Message from Moscow.* New York: Knopf, 1970.

RESHETAR, JOHN R., JR. *The Soviet Polity: Government and Politics in the USSR.* 2nd ed. New York: Harper & Row, 1978.

SAKHAROV, ANDREI D. *Alarm and Hope.* New York: Knopf, 1978.

SMITH, HEDRICK. *The Russians.* New York: Quadrangle/New York Times, 1976.

SOLZHENITSYN, ALEKSANDR I. *A World Split Apart.* New York: Harper & Row, 1978.

ULAM, ADAM. *The Bolsheviks: The Intellectual and Political History of the Triumph of Communism in Russia.* New York: Macmillan, 1965.

WESSON, ROBERT, ed. *The Soviet Union: Looking to the 1980s.* Stanford, Calif.: Hoover Institution Press, 1980.

On China

CHEN, JO-HSI. *The Execution of Mayor Yin and Other Short Stories.* Bloomington: Indiana University Press, 1978.

ECKSTEIN, ALEXANDER. *Chinese Economic Revolution.* New York: Cambridge University Press, 1977.

FROLIC, B. MICHAEL. *Mao's People.* Cambridge, Mass.: Harvard University Press, 1980.

LEYS, SIMON. *Chinese Shadows.* New York: Penguin, 1978.

MEISNER, MAURICE. *Mao's China: A History of the People's Republic.* New York: Free Press, 1979.

TERRILL, ROSS, ed. *The China Difference.* New York: Harper & Row, 1979.

WALLER, DEREK J. *The Government and Politics of the People's Republic of China.* London: Hutchinson University Library, 1981.

On Yugoslavia

COMISSO, ELLEN T. *Worker's Control under Plan and Market: Implications of Yugoslav Self-Management.* New Haven: Yale University Press, 1979.

DJILAS, MILOVAN. *The New Class: An Analysis of the Communist System.* New York: Praeger, 1957.

DODER, DUSKO. *The Yugoslavs.* New York: Random House, 1978.

RUSINOW, DENNISON. *The Yugoslav Experiment, 1948-1974.* Berkeley: University of California Press, 1977.

SIRC, LJUBO. *The Yugoslav Economy under Self-Management.* New York: St. Martin's, 1979.

STANKOVIC, SLOBODAN. *The End of the Tito Era: Yugoslavia's Dilemmas.* Stanford, Calif.: Hoover Institution Press, 1981.

STOJANOVIC, SVETOZAR. *In Search of Democracy in Socialism: History and Party Consciousness.* Buffalo, N.Y.: Prometheus, 1981.

4. The Japanese Political System

Until 1854, Japan lived in seclusion, geographically removed from the rest of the world, untouched by outside events, secure from external aggression, and sufficient unto herself. The age of Western colonial expansion slowly but steadily crept up to her perimeters. It was none other than the United States, seeking stopovers for its merchant ships engaged in trade with China, that intimidated the theretofore impermeable island nation with its "black ships" into opening its doors to foreign traders and diplomats. Suddenly and forcefully exposed to the threatening world dominated by expansionist and superior Western states, Japan, after a brief period of vacillation and confusion, began—from scratch, so to speak—an arduous, desperate, and perilous task of transforming her moribund, deeply fractured feudal society into a powerful modern state. Today, she is *sui generis*: the only advanced industrial as well as stable democratic nation in the underdeveloped, largely undemocratic non-Western world. Small, overcrowded, and bereft of natural resources as she is, Japan is the second largest economic power in the entire world, surpassing the massive Soviet Union, and virtually equal to the United States on a per capita basis. Her post-World War II democratic political system has demonstrated remarkable stability, with her people firmly committed to its maintenance. Notwithstanding her superior accomplishments, Japan still remains largely unfamiliar to Americans.

Constitutional Development

Throughout her feudal period, Japan was governed not by any constitution or a series of constitutions in the modern sense of the term but largely by custom and tradition. Her first modern constitution, promulgated by Emperor Meiji in 1889, was a response to the perceived requirements of the time. First and foremost, it was the product of an acute awareness by the nation's modernizing leaders that their nation was regarded by superior Western powers as backward and inferior, a quaint Oriental society outside the mainstream of history and progress. The principal reason for this view was Japan's lack of a modern constitution—a rule of law—which most of these powers had long developed as the most fundamental political feature of a modern state. The modernizing Japanese leaders therefore believed it incumbent upon them to establish a constitutional polity as the essential conditon for persuading those Western powers to begin dealing with their nation on an equal footing.

The Meiji Constitution was intended also to meet certain other requirements that the modernizing leaders considered crucial. Among these were the consolidation of these leaders' power in the new national government, the maintenance of sociopolitical discipline during the period of rapid national development through sacrifice and perseverance, and the promotion of national unity in order to withstand the danger posed by the Western powers. These requirements, among others, dictated the establishment of an authoritarian political system. Accordingly, the Meiji Constitution was based on the doctrine of Imperial sovereignty and governmental omnipotence. Democratic rights and liberties enumerated for the "loyal subjects" were not inherent; they were "gifts" from the benevolent Imperial Sovereign, to be exercised only "within the limits of the law," that is, within such limits as the Imperial government deemed appropriate. There was no independent judiciary to rule on the constitutionality of any of those limits. To the modernizing elite of the Meiji period, confronted by a task of unprecedented magnitude and urgency, the most fundamental precondition of national progress and viability was order, not liberty; and even for the most progressive among them, liberty could hope to grow only on the firm basis of order.

From an evolutionary developmental perspective, the Meiji Constitution, authoritarian as it was, should perhaps be considered appropriate to the spatial and historical context of a nation in perilous transition from tradition to modernity. And, however circumscribed those rights and liberties were, they nevertheless provided a general basis for the eventual growth of modern democratic practices and arrangements. Subsequent developments demonstrated that the constitution admitted of such evolutionary political progress. Party politics and electoral competition quickly emerged in response to the constitution's prescription for a popularly elected assembly. Moreover, even though the power of the assembly was significantly circumscribed, the Imperial cabinet soon found itself having to deal and work with it in order effectively to function as the nation's supreme governing institution. By the 1910s, the practice of "party government" had become well-nigh institutionalized, and in 1925 the political franchise was extended to all male adults. In the meantime, "oligarchs" of the Meiji period had one by one passed away, leaving the nation in the hands of younger generations of leaders more attuned to party politics and popular electoral competition.

Japan's incipient democracy was dealt an unexpected and fatal blow by the Great Depression, which also contributed to the destruction of many new democracies in Europe. Widespread economic dislocations and subsequent social unrest, and the prospects of political disorder, rendered the nation increasingly vulnerable to the demogoguery of antidemocratic forces that promised salvation through autocratic political order at home and imperialist expansion abroad. Consequently, the most illiberal elements of the Meiji Constitution were resurrected and distorted in practice; the nation, now led by the militarists and their antidemocratic civilian allies, marched down the path of increasing domestic repression and blatant external aggression toward the ultimate humiliation of 1945.

The constitution under which Japan is governed today came into being in 1947. Against the background of bitter national experiences of the 1930s and early 1940s, the new constitution was explicitly designed to institute and safeguard democracy. It is based on the doctrine of popular sovereignty, unambiguously guaranteeing civil liberties and political rights of the people, holding the government accountable to the electorate, and relegating the Emperor to the ceremonial symbol of national unity. The trauma of defeat caused by militarists also led the 1947 constitution to address the issue of war and peace and to renounce for the nation the right to wage war and use force for settling disputes with other nations. To ethnocentric Western democrats, it may appear surprising that such a quintessentially democratic constitution has proven so viable in an Eastern state with so recent a record of authoritarian practice and aggressive militarism. How can the "democratic transformation" of Japan be explained?

Democracy requires certain preconditions for its viability—widespread political literacy, social stability, and economic well-being or its promise. The Japanese in the late 1940s were among the best educated people in the world, not only in mere literacy, but also in some crucial political experiences. They had known the authoritarianism of the modernizing Meiji oligarchs, the incipient popular democracy of the late 1910s and '20s, and the repressive regimes of the late 1930s and early '40s. The shattering defeat of 1945 brought all these experiences under intense collective scrutiny. The virtually unanimous conclusion of the people was that democracy provided the only path to national restoration, progress, and well-being.

Japan is an extraordinarily homogeneous nation with little or no internal social hostility, despite economic differences among various strata of people and the traditional compartmentalization of groups. And patterns of interpersonal and social relations that evolved through the nation's long history of solitary existence, as we shall see, help obviate or minimize the kinds of social conflict that are common in other societies.

A third prerequisite for democracy is material well-being. It is axiomatic that democracy cannot survive in a society on the verge of starvation or without hope for a decent life for its people. In 1947 Japan was indeed at the depths of poverty and deprivation caused by war and defeat, but there was confidence among her people that they could restore their economy and promote its growth. Motivated by this confidence, they did indeed work with unflagging diligence and perseverance, and their government guided this collective national endeavor in achieving recovery and subsequent growth and expansion so rapidly that it astonished the world as an "economic miracle." The combination of popular confidence and its consistent vindication has reinforced the Japanese people's commitment to their postwar constitutional system.

Democracy in Japan shares a number of fundamental features with that in the United States and other practicing democracies. Nevertheless, no two democracies are altogether alike. Within the Western world we have seen variations in democratic practices. This is entirely natural, for the political system of any nation, however similar it may be to that of another, finds its stability in the tradition and the culture of the soil in which it thrives. It is this indigenous culture and tradition that at once adds to the system's viability and makes it distinctive. Japanese democracy is no exception. It is to these unique features of Japanese democracy—indeed the fabric of Japanese society—that we now turn.

Social Forces

Japan as a nation and a society evolved free from the force of events in and pressures from other parts of the world. She lived by herself, sufficient unto herself, adopting foreign cultural traits (mostly Chinese) only when it suited her, eclectically and selectively. This environmental autonomy and existential solitude prior to the mid-nineteenth century engendered an unusual degree of cultural homogeneity among the Japanese, a fact that later exerted significant influence upon the character of social relations and political interaction among groups and institutions in contemporary Japan. In discussing social forces in Japan, we believe that it is more illuminating to examine certain manifest behavioral features that are deeply rooted in culture and history than to describe social classes, ideological currents, or group dynamics.

Interpersonal and social relations came to be controlled and regulated by historically evolved, largely unwritten rules of conduct. In short, there evolved an extraordinarily potent sense of community at each level and context of those relations. This communitarian character of relations tends to avoid conflict and competition and instead to stress harmony and cooperation. Individualism as the Americans understand and value it is predicated on conflict and competition and is therefore incompatible with this character. In each context of social relations in Japan, therefore, there is a powerful inclination toward behavioral conformity and collective interest.

The central criterion of decision making in the United States is majoritarian democracy, in which decisions are made on the basis of numerical strength. It not only presupposes conflict and competition among participants in each decisional context but also views them as inherently beneficial for progress. It also signifies division between a victorious majority and a defeated minority. Since communitarian harmony is the most important collective interest in Japan, conflict and competition are eschewed in decision making. Generally speaking, substantive decision making is by consensus, not by a majority (although in a formal decisional arena such as the legislature, a vote is taken according to written rules). Decision making by the criterion of sheer relative strength of the larger number is viewed as inherently unfair to the minority. The interest of the minority, however small, should be scrupulously respected and judiciously accommodated, for otherwise internal harmony would be eroded. Thus, while decision making in the United States boils down to choosing one option among many, in Japan it is, as one analyst put it, "the coalescence of the only possible compromise out of all."

The principal requirement of communitarian harmony in Japanese culture imposes on the leader or leadership in each group or decisional context the kind of role that is vastly different from what is expected of leadership in the American context. To begin with, there is no Japanese word for "leadership." The person in a formal leadership position does not "lead" in the sense that his American counterpart does. He occupies the position, not because he is bright, most experienced, decisive, innovative, or otherwise endowed with the qualities Americans usually associate with leadership, but because of his relative seniority in the group or institution concerned and, particularly important, of his outstanding paternalistic qualities such as warmth, magnanimity, attentiveness to his subordinates' personal feelings and problems. Typically, his subordinates refer to him affectionately as "old man," "Pappy," and the like. An individual displaying an incisive mind, a forceful personality, or an aloof deportment is unlikely to become or be accepted as a leader, for the leader is not expected to overwhelm his subordinates by the superiority of his mind or position, or the decisiveness of his conduct, nor to dictate or impose his own preference on them, but rather to be the core of the human nexus that is the group, to be its father figure. In decision making, his role is one of a cooperative team player, a consensus builder, a compromise promoter among differing views and preferences. Decisional brilliance and dispatch are subordinate to decisional harmony.

Given the character of leadership in Japanese culture, the impetus for and the substance of decisions tend to flow from the bottom upward rather than from the top downward. Brilliance and imaginativeness are qualities valued in the subordinate, not in the leader, and it is the subordinate who is expected to provide the leader with ideas and options. The subordinate members within each group or decisional context discuss options freely among themselves, cultivate support for them, and integrate and accommodate differing views and preferences so as to ensure their acceptance by the group or institution when a decision has to be made formally. There is indeed an osmotic character to Japanese decision making. The leader adopts decisions thus arrived at and represents them.

As the reader may already suspect, consensualism is not very conducive to making hard decisions, for it is inclined to avoid a problem or issue that sharply divides the group concerned as long as possible or until it becomes palpably dangerous to do so. Internal disagreement is consciously repressed and its catalysis into decision is occasioned by an external input into the decision process. Consequently, consensualism as the principal criterion of decision making, when applied to the level of government, may seriously handicap the nation in coping effectively with its domestic as well as external environments. For, however preservative of internal harmony and order, it could critically deprive the nation of a vital capacity for decisive, expeditious, and responsive decision making that rapidly shifting circumstances may dictate.

Community and consensus generate a powerful tendency toward conformity, for they are incompatible with idiosyncrasy and personal self-interest, which cause annoyance and conflict. And this conformity renders each group, and ultimately the nation, unique in the minds of its members. Even a casual foreign observer in Japan would notice the sartorial uniformity of various classes of workers (e.g., white shirts and somber, more often than not gray, suits and matching ties for male white-collar workers; company-specific work clothes for blue-collar laborers). There are also company badges to be worn on the coat or jacket lapel. Persons find their own value only by being members of a group, the indispensable human nexus (community), and by partaking of its interest (consensus). American workers identify themselves by the profession or occupation they are in. ("I am an accountant" or "I am a civil servant," for example.) The Japanese do so by the group they belong to. ("I am with Toyota" and "I work for the Ministry of Finance.")

At the national level, too, this is largely true, albeit perhaps less compelling than at a lower level. The Japanese unself-consciously take it for granted that they are a unique people. For example, they assume their cultural exclusivity, while Americans believe in their culture's universality. Thus, the Japanese think that foreigners can never master their language nor really like such uniquely Japanese dishes as *sashimi* (raw fish) and are astonished when they do; the Americans assume everybody should speak English and love hamburgers, and are disappointed when they do not. This notion of exclusivity renders the Japanese highly ethnocentric in their external orientation and, conversely, communitarian and conformist in their internal outlook.

Community and consensus powerfully discincline the Japanese to engage in political dispute, which presupposes conflict. To the extent that there are groups with different interests conflict is inevitable. In the Japanese context, however, group conflict is mediated by the particular kind of relations obtaining among leadership strata of contending groups. Decisional interaction takes place at this leadership level, and here the rules of community and consensus obtain, albeit perhaps to a less psychologically compelling extent than within each group. Confrontation, which is the most acute form of political conflict, is eschewed; instead there is powerful pressure toward moderation, which can be maintained only through mutual accommodation and compromise and through avoidance of issues on which such accommodation and compromise seem unfeasible at the moment. This distinctly politophobic tendency inherent in community and consensus was powerfully reinforced by the disastrous experience of ultranationalist militarism of the prewar years, which had represented a radical form of confrontationist politics both at home and abroad. The political stability of postwar Japan is in no insignificant measure due to the conscious avoidance of such abrasive political behavior, especially on the part of the more salient sectors and strata of society and government.

Interest Groups

As an advanced industrial and democratic state, Japan contains a wide spectrum of interest groups ranging from farmers' cooperatives to business associations, from organized labor to professional organizations. More recently there have emerged an increasing number of single-issue pressure groups concerned with ecology, welfare, women's rights, taxes, smoking, and the like. Interest groups may be divided into two broad categories: those that are institutional clients of government ministries and agencies (e.g., farmers' cooperatives vis-à-vis the Ministry of Agriculture) and those that are not. A group belonging to the first category has an inside track, so to speak, and accordingly its political activity is discreet and directed to relevant ministry offices, administrators, as well as to members of the relevant policy committee of the ruling party. More often than not, there is a triangular personal relationship among senior ministry officials, influential members of the ruling party's committee, and leaders of the interest group. Many top leaders of the group are former high officials of the ministry or agency concerned, as are those influential members of the party committee. Higher civil servants, with the exception of the few who become deputy ministers and administrative vice ministers, by custom retire at or around age fifty, and many of them seek a second career as top officers of the very interests they once regulated and supervised. Some others seek elective offices, usually as Liberal Democratic party (LDP) candidates. This human bond facilitates mutually advantageous interaction among group, party, and bureaucracy. There is little need for public lobbying activities.

A group belonging to the second category is without such inside track or personal connections with party or with bureaucracy. As a consequence, it engages in open political and informational activities such as marches, demonstrations, rallies, pamphleteering, petitions to ministries and parliament, and electoral campaigns. Whether these activities bring benefits to the group concerned seems to depend on the extent to which they can generate popular sympathy and support.

Since our space is limited, we shall take a closer look at only the best-known group in each of the two categories suggested: big business and organized leftist labor.

Big business in Japan is organizationally represented by four associations: the Federation of Economic Organizations (*Keidanren*), the Japan Federation of Employers Association (*Nikkeiren*), the Japan Committee for Economic Development (*Keizai Doyukai*), and the Japan Chamber of Commerce and Industry (*Nissho*). They are collectively referred to as *zaikai* (literally, the high financial circle). *Zaikai* operates discreetly and unobstrusively. Many senior *zaikai* leaders are former high government officials, hence they share the career civil service human nexus with the incumbent senior bureaucrats as well as with influential members of the ruling party who are their former civil service colleagues. They can, therefore, informally make relevant inputs into government policy making. There is a very hazy line of demarcation between their personal and social relations, on the one hand, and their professional and political relations with bureaucracy and party, on the other. The informal pattern of interaction among *zaikai,* party, and bureaucracy is deeply institutionalized: Leaders of these three institutions meet at regular intervals over dinner, tea, or drinks in quiet restaurants and tea houses unencumbered by the probing eyes of the press and the public. The degree of influence *zaikai* exerts on policy making can only be guessed. It is frequently reported in Japan that a brief telephone call from *zaikai* leadership causes last-minute changes in legislative proposals and administrative directives. One veteran French Japan hand once remarked that *zaikai* leaders are the government behind the government.

Zaikai as a group has a penchant for discretion and seeks to avoid unnecessary abrasion with the public or its opponents, such as leftist parties and organized labor. While *zaikai* could mobilize any number of employees and workers of its member firms (corporations, their subsidiaries and subcontractors) for election campaign support for the conservative ruling party (LDP), it instead chooses to support the party through massive but largely secretive infusions of political funds into its campaign and other activities. Over 80 percent of the party's funds comes from *zaikai* sources. According to journalistic speculations that have never been refuted by *zaikai* or the party, this umbrella special-interest group in 1978 contributed in the neighborhood of $500 million to the party, a rather tidy sum by any standard. In any event, *zaikai* stays out of the political spotlight, for its principal objective is policy input into the government decision process, which can best be done through discreet informal contact and an equally discreet and informal political contribution to the ruling party.

The largest labor federation in Japan is the General Council of Trade Unions (*Sohyo* in Japanese abbreviation). Marxist in ideology, *Sohyo* consists mostly of politically militant public employees unions (total membership slightly over 4 million) such as the Japan Teachers Union, the National Railway Workers, the Japan Prefectural and Municipal Workers. It is closely allied with the Japan Socialist party, the largest parliamentary opposition group, which seeks to transform the nation by abolishing what it calls "monopoly capitalism." Inasmuch as it is the largest labor federation, consisting of tertiary-economic-sector unions whose strike or work stoppage could produce an immediate impact and repercussions of grave magnitude for government and society, *Sohyo* is enormously effective in promoting economic interests of its members, especially since their wages and fringe benefits ultimately come from public revenues, quite unlike in the private manufacturing sector where wages and benefits are subject to productivity and profit. The major avowed interest of *Sohyo*, however, is political, and thus far it has demonstrated its relative powerlessness.

Since it has no practical influence on the policy-making process controlled by the bureaucracy and the conservative ruling party, *Sohyo's* political activity is at once electoral and expressive. It engages in election campaign support for the Japan Socialist party, providing the party with political funds and organizational logistics through its affiliate unions and their members. The Socialist party, however, has never been able to threaten the conservative party's dominance. Consequently, *Sohyo,* like many permanently powerless groups in Japan and elsewhere, indulges itself in what is called "expressive politics," activities designed not so much to make practical political input into the nation's decision-making process as to express frustration with and opposition to it. Thus it engages in "struggles"—political strikes, demonstrations, marches, rallies—which are not intended seriously to influence the government but rather to reaffirm its own ideological commitment and to edify its own revolutionary self-image. In fact, this expressive dimension of *Sohyo* as an interest group seems more important than its electoral support for the socialists. As we shall see, *Sohyo's* relationship with the party has been such that it smacks of an attempt to turn the party into its expressive political instrument instead of strengthening the party's influence in the legislature, as a way of making a pragmatic policy input into the decision process. As a consequence, *Sohyo* as a political interest group remains stagnant, unable to exert the kind of influence it was organized to exert.

Political Parties

The history of Japan's political parties is as brief as her constitutional history. True, there were so-called parties and political associations during the early Meiji period before the promulgation of the 1889 Constitution, but they were all ineffectual, albeit often strident and pseudo-ideological, personal followings revolving around prominent and disgruntled out-of-power oligarchs vying for the first opportunity to get back into power. Viable parties and party competition for power began only after the coming of the Meiji Constitution. Competition for power was exclusively among conservative parties, which alone enjoyed the financial and political wherewithal; the leftist parties that eventually emerged with incipient democratization (such as socialist, peasant-based populist, communist) were intermittently suppressed and lacked both financial and organizational bases, as well as popular support.

Competition among conservatives was not so much over policy as power itself, for they represented essentially the same spectrum of interests, attitudes, and orientations, regardless of differences in public rhetoric and electoral posturing. With the coming of ultranationalist militarism in the 1930s, these parties, after a brief effort to maintain their political autonomy and institutional integrity, capitulated to the increasing power and intimidation of the potent coalition of militarists and their like-minded higher bureaucrats and merged into an umbrella national political association that helped promote war aims. As a consequence, most of the leaders of these parties were purged from politics and government during the American occupation after 1945.

The nation's defeat and subsequent introduction of democracy prompted a proliferation of parties, representing a wide political spectrum from timidly democratic conservative to communist. The requirement of a majority in the new parliamentary system eventually induced coalescences by the mid-1950s of numerous parties into a unified conservative (LDP) and a single Socialist party, leaving the communists at the periphery of the political arena. In subsequent years, opposition to the unified and dominant LDP became fragmented, enabling the latter to enjoy seemingly permanent supremacy in Japanese politics. At the outset of the 1980s, party division of parliamentary seats was as shown in table 1.

TABLE 1. PARLIAMENTARY SEATS BY PARTY, 1980

	House of Representatives		House of Councillors	
	Seats	% of Total	Seats	% of Total
Liberal Democratic party	284	55.6	135	53.6
Japan Socialist party	107	20.8	47	18.7
Clean Government party	33	6.5	28	11.1
Democratic Socialist party	32	6.3	12	4.8
Japan Communist party	29	5.7	12	4.8
New Liberal Club	12	2.3	2	0.8
Social Democratic League	3	0.6	2	0.8
Other Groups	0	0.0	2	0.8
Independents	11	2.2	13	5.1
Vacancy	0	0.0	1	0.4
TOTAL	511	100.0	252	100.0

The Liberal Democratic party. The ruling Liberal Democratic party (LDP) came into being in 1955 through a merger of the two conservative parties (Liberals and Democrats) that had fiercely competed for power throughout the preceding postwar years, and has since ruled the nation continuously. Its seemingly permanent dominance has rested on several ascertainable factors. One is the party's nonideological and pragmatic policy orientation. As a party, the LDP is without ideology, which is consistent with the politophobic tendency of Japanese society. Despite its "conservative" appellation, the LDP has by and large been flexible enough to accommodate the parliamentary opposition's demands and govern the nation in a manner that the people at large have found acceptable. Indeed, the party has been the political engine of the "economic miracle." In the process of promoting the nation's growth into international economic superstardom, it has also succeeded in noticeably reducing economic differences among groups and strata of the population. It has instituted an extensive national health program and consistently expanded welfare programs for those who were, for a variety of reasons, left out of the rising affluence and prosperity. In short, the LDP has been fairly reliable in meeting popular expectations for political stability and economic well-being.

A second reason for LDP supremacy is its electoral-organizational resilience. Its parliamentary membership consists of notables who are influential and respected in their districts by virtue of birth, status, and/or accomplishment, whom local residents call *sensei* (a term of great respect and affection, literally meaning "teacher" or "master"). Each of these MPs maintains an extensive network of grass-roots organizations called *koenkai* (supporters associations) formed to provide electoral support in the district. They are *personal* organizations, not the party's, although in most cases their members are registered as party members. Each *koenkai* is made up of friends, associates, allies, and their friends. Their loyalty to the MP is personal, not political or ideological, and the *koenkai* constitutes a human nexus of which the MP is the head. The purpose of *koenkai* members is to keep reelecting the MP, whose policy or that of the party is of little concern to them. The *koenkai* phenomenon is particularly strong in rural and semiurban districts where there remains a much stronger sense of community than in urban and metropolitan districts. Understandably, LDP electoral strength is more pronounced in the former than in the latter.

A third cause of LDP strength is its wherewithal. As the perennial ruling party, it has government revenue and patronage at its disposal, which it can manipulate to benefit specific groups or areas as rewards for their past support or inducements for future support. In addition, the party enjoys munificent financial backing from big business, which wants it to remain in power for obvious reasons. Laws governing political contributions are relatively lax, and there are many legitimate as well as illicit ways in which extraordinary sums can be transferred from *zaikai* and other well-heeled special interests to the party, its factions, and individual MPs. These funds are used by the party and its MPs to run well-oiled campaign activities as well as a gamut of other party functions, and by individual MPs to keep their respective *koenkai* happy and beholden to them. The MP sponsors cultural and athletic activities for the *koenkai* members and their families; sends them gifts on festive occasions; makes donations to charities, shrines, temples, and cultural and educational groups; and, through local lieutenants, throws parties and receptions for supporters and invites them to Tokyo for sightseeing tours.

Although pragmatic policy, extensive grass-roots organizations in the form of MPs' *koenkai,* and finance and patronage, among others, have enabled the LDP to retain its dominance in Japanese politics, the party is not without serious problems. By far the most critical and potentially fatal of them is fierce internal factionalism. LDP factionalism is personal, not ideological. A faction is an intraparty *koenkai*, whose objective is to increase its leader's influence in the party and thus attain the party presidency and (since the party is in power) the premiership and, in the process, obtain cabinet, party, and parliamentary posts (patronage) for its members.

Party leadership selection on the basis of factionalism is dangerously corruptive, for it invariably encourages the crassest kinds of political wheeling and dealing among competing factions (five major ones at this writing), involving almost unbelievable sums of largely illicit funds (popularly termed "black money") changing hands among factions and between faction leaders and their followers. The requirement of such large amounts of illicit funds (the 1972 party presidential election is said to have involved the circulation of anywhere between \$40,000 and \$80,000 per MP among factions) for leadership selection has deepened the financial ties between the party, on the one hand, and big business and other special interests, on the other, threatening the party's institutional integrity and organizational autonomy.

The winner in this kind of competitive bidding for (or auction of) factional support in leadership selection is the faction leader who has put together a more cohesive coalition of factions. This fierce and corruptive competition for power leads, ironically but inevitably, only to a sort of pyrrhic victory for the winner. The party presidency-premiership, because of the manner in which its incumbent is selected, is built on a stack of IOUs, and this critically inhibits the winner in the conduct of office.

Factionalism, which is increasingly abrasive, generates some serious impact on the LDP's decision-making capability, for it erodes the internal coherence of the party and undermines the flexibility necessary for a minimally imperative policy and consensus on personnel. The party is in danger of losing its capacity to govern by becoming internally stalemated and immobilized unless its factionalism is somehow moderated. It might lose its power to govern without losing it to an opposition party.

The Japan Socialist party. Two decades ago, the Socialists entertained the hope (and the conservatives feared) that, as the nation became more urbanized through economic growth, the party's electoral strength would grow and they would be able to capture power. The hope was not at all unfounded, for European socialist parties grew in strength with economic growth and concomitant urbanization and unseated conservative parties in Britain and Germany, for example. The Japan Socialist party (JSP), however, has failed to follow the path of its West European brethren because of its insistence on remaining the party of the revolutionary proletariat. The Japanese, as noted, are by and large nonideological. Moreover, with rapid economic growth and prosperity, members of the "proletariat" came increasingly to identify themselves as middle class (by 1970 over 90 percent of the Japanese viewed themselves as such). In contrast to its European counterparts, which deradicalized themselves as their nations became more urban and prosperous so as to broaden their bases of support into the middle and even upper-middle classes, the JSP persisted in its inflexible confrontational posture and dogmatic revolutionary polemic that were blatantly irrelevant to the political, economic, and social conditions of the nation as perceived by its people. As a result, popular suppport for the JSP has consistently declined even among the very groups that are the party's ideological clients, such as industrial labor, the young, and the educated, without any compensating growth in support elsewhere. As things stand at present, the party has no prospect of capturing power as its Western counterparts have done.

The JSP is not really a single party, it is two parties: the parliamentary JSP and the constituency JSP. The parliamentary JSP is actually quite moderate, for it consists of MPs who have been baptized in electoral politics and tempered by imperatives of practical legislative tasks. It makes no insignificant contribution to national legislation through informal negotiations with the ruling LDP to get its views accommodated, thus often improving the quality of final legislative products. Many of its members have close personal relations with LDP influentials. If it had control over the entire JSP so-called, as it once did, the political fortune of the party might not be nearly as depressing as it is.

The constituency JSP, consisting of the mass membership and party organizations, is radically leftist, incorrigibly doctrinaire, and determinedly confrontationist—in short, expressive in character. It is this JSP that has been penetrated by Marxist ideological groups, the largest of which is *Sohyo*. An overwhelming majority of party members are those militants of *Sohyo* unions and other leftist groups. Since the delegates to the all-important party convention are elected from each prefectural chapter by its radical mass members, the convention itself is doctrinaire, confrontationist, expressive. Party MPs had been automatic voting delegates to the convention by virtue of their parliamentary status and thus controlled the proceedings of the convention, but in the name of participatory democracy, the party in the early 1960s changed the relevant convention rules to require that every delegate be elected by his or her prefectural party chapter. And it is the convention that elects the party chairman, secretary general, and other members of the Central Executive Committee, which in turn speaks for the whole JSP.

As a result of this critical bifurcation of the party, JSP MPs and candidates are seriously handicapped in their electoral competition against the LDP and other opposition parties. The image their party (i.e., the Central Executive

Committee) imparts to the electorate is negative, consistent neither with the culture and tradition of society nor with the popular perception of economic and political realities of the nation. It more often than not turns off those voters (politically uncommitted or independent) who might otherwise be persuaded to vote for the party's candidates. Another serious handicap of Socialist candidates and MPs is that, as members of a party hopelessly out of power and feared or disliked by powerful and well-endowed special interests, they lack, and cannot hope to generate for themselves, sufficient wherewithal to attract and keep large numbers of local voters in their respective *koenkai.*

Other Opposition Parties. The Clean Government party (CGP) and the Democratic Socialist party (DSP) are middle-of-the-road parties, although in principle both are committed to moderate socialism. They are so close in policy direction to the more liberal sectors of the LDP that there is intermittent speculation about an imminent prospect of their merging with liberal LDP MPs to form a new centrist majority party.

The CGP is unique among the Japanese parties in that it is the only mass-based party; every other party began as a party of notables at the national level and developed whatever popular following it has only as a consequence. The mass movement out of whose womb the CGP sprang is the Value Creation Society (*Sokagakkai*), a militant religio-nationalist organization whose origin dates back to the prewar period. During the 1950s and well into the '60s, Society membership expanded rapidly among those segments of the population who had come to feel a moral anomie caused by rapid social, political, and cultural change and others who felt left out of the rising economic growth and prosperity. Less educated than most and often marginal in status as a consequence, Society members were politically and culturally conservative but populist in economic orientation. The CGP first emerged as the Society's political department in the mid-1950s and, after achieving some success in local electoral politics, entered national politics a decade later as a formal political party. Thanks to the mass organizational base it has through the Society (over 15 million members), the CGP, even though it has since severed its formal ties with the parent movement in order to broaden its popular appeal, has been assured of a certain level of electoral support, winning during the past ten years from 29 to 64 seats in the all-powerful House of Representatives.

The Democratic Socialist party was formed in 1959 by the more moderate members of the JSP and consciously patterned after West European social democratic parties, rejecting doctrinaire Marxism and the revolutionary rhetoric of the JSP. The distinction between it and the LDP in policy has become increasingly obscure because of the ruling party's successful cooptation of its

more progressive policy proposals. The DSP derives much of its organizational and electoral strength from its close alliance with the Japan Confederation
of Labor (*Domei*), the second largest labor federation (over 2 million members) in the nation, consisting of private-sector unions that are moderate in political orientation and in their relations with management. *Domei* unionists
predominate in the party's mass membership, and their unions provide much
of the party's political funds, campaign logistics, and electoral support. Many
DSP MPs are themselves former *Domei* leaders. The party appeals to pragmatic liberals who are tired of the faction-ridden LDP and has maintained
around 30 seats in the House of Representatives more or less consistently. Like
the CGP, it could become part of a new centrist party in case of a party realignment.

The Japan Communist party (JCP) today is much stronger than it could
have dreamed of becoming but two decades ago. It was then violently divided
into pro-Soviet and pro-Chinese factions and suffered from its traditional image of a conspiratorial subversive party with allegiance to an alien power or
powers. During the 1960s, the party purged both factions and, under new
leadership, began painstakingly to cultivate a new image of an open, democratic, "Japanese" political party, eschewing revolutionary jargon and polemic. It now professes allegiance to the constitution and favors the nationalization of only one industry — energy — focusing its activities on grass-roots issues
of pollution, congestion, high prices, and bureaucratic neglect of citizen grievances. As a result, its popularity grew significantly and, since the early 1970s,
it has maintained a parliamentary strength approximating that of the CGP or
the DSP. Nevertheless, its future growth appears limited. The term "communist" is still anathema to a great majority of the Japanese, conjuring up in their
minds the specter of the Soviet Union toward which they maintain visceral an-
tipathy and fear. They doubt that the party's current democratic protestations
are genuine. Its current electoral strength is the function of its well-disciplined
mass membership (around 400,000) and its grass-roots activities, as well as of
many protest votes against tedious LDP dominance. Moreover, the JCP is
likely to be left out of any party realignment precisely because it is communist.

The New Liberal Club (NLC) and the Social Democratic League (SDL)
are too small to be seriously reckoned with as parties. The NLC was formed in
1976 by several of the more progressive and younger LDP MPs, who had become frustrated by the ruling party's internal factionalism, corruption, and
complacency. Initially its novelty attracted some popular following, but the
bickering among its founders and its lack of sufficient policy distinction from
the LDP have since reduced the NLC to relative impotence and stagnation.
The SDL is a socialist equivalent of the NLC in that it was organized by a few

of the more moderate, pragmatically oriented members of the JSP who had been exasperated by the inflexible dogmatism and the politically debilitating leftist control of the major opposition party. Very much like the NLC, the SDL has been unable to carve out its own distinct position on the political spectrum and has remained even more insignificant than the NLC. Both the NLC and SDL lack organizational bases and financial support. Should there be a party realignment, however, they are both likely to join a new centrist party.

Japan's party system is not competitive, and this lack of competitiveness creates problems that could subtly affect the quality of democracy. The ruling LDP, since its position is secure, tends to be complacent and may be suspected of exerting itself less diligently than if it were constantly facing an effective opposition challenge. The opposition is so fragmented that it has no immediate prospect of unseating the LDP. Since the largest opposition party (JSP) cannot hope to be an alternative ruling party, it tends to be irresponsible. Power may corrupt, but in an important sense powerlessness corrupts also. A realignment of parties is needed if there is to be a more cohesive and dynamic ruling party as well as an opposition party with a capacity to replace it when its performance is less than satisfactory. It would be enormously difficult, however, to form a minimally viable consensus among the opposition parties. Nevertheless, the 1980s may prove to be crucial for postwar Japan's political and party history.

Governmental Institutions

A parliamentary democracy, Japan's political system consists of institutions and procedures familiar to Westerners. The monarchy is but the symbol of national unity. The highest organ of state power is the Diet (parliament), elected by and representing the people. The executive branch, headed by the Prime Minister and cabinet, oversees a professional civil service and is answerable to the Diet. The judiciary, presided over by the Supreme Court, is independent and has the power of judicial review. In its general contour and structure, the Japanese political system differs little from any other parliamentary system. There are some notable variations, however, in the operation and behavior of the various components of the system which reflect the nation's culture and tradition.

PRIME MINISTER AND CABINET

The Prime Minister is elected by the Diet from among its members, by custom from among the members of the all-powerful House of Representatives. Since

Diet seats are held by parties, the Prime Minister is the leader of the majority party, and has the power to appoint and dismiss cabinet ministers, provided that a majority of them are members of the Diet (in practice of the majority party). Each minister heads a ministry or one or more of the specialized agencies. The cabinet may contain a deputy prime minister. Since the Prime Minister's party controls a majority of the Diet seats, he is also in a position to decide, or at least significantly influence, the parliamentary agenda and conduct, the appointments of the presiding officer of each house as well as those of parliamentary committees. In a variety of ways, the Japanese chief executive's power appears extensive.

The actual power of the Prime Minister is quite circumscribed. Remember that the LDP leader is selected on a stack of IOUs to the rival factions. The formation of the cabinet is therefore affected in that the IOUs are paid off in patronage. The various factions receive cabinet posts (and subcabinet, party, and parliamentary posts as well), which must be carefully apportioned so as to obviate desertions. Such senior portfolios as foreign affairs, finance, international trade and industry usually go to the leaders of coalition factions or their top lieutenants. Other posts are distributed among those factions, including the Prime Minister's, according to the internal seniority of each. The rule of seniority is part of Japanese tradition. Sometimes, a few posts must be offered to the faction or factions that opposed the Prime Minister's selection. Cabinet formation is therefore a careful balancing act designed not so much to promote the competence and effectiveness of government as to guard the chief executive against actual or potential intraparty opposition. Thus, policy expertise, administrative competence, and political compatibility are secondary criteria in choosing cabinet members.

Factional alignment shifts almost constantly. Moreover, leaders of factions, in order to retain their positions, must satisfy their followers' desire for cabinet posts in order of seniority. Thus, the cabinet is reshuffled with great frequency, producing the so-called one-year ministers syndrome, some posts being held but for a few months. The particular criteria for appointment and the brevity of tenure cannot but reduce many, perhaps most, ministers to figureheads, and discourage seriousness on their part in the development of policy expertise and administrative competence required of ministerial responsibilities. This is indeed a very serious problem for the Japanese government.

THE DIET

The bicameral parliament consists of the House of Representatives and the House of Councillors. The former (the lower house) is all-powerful; in case of disagreement it prevails. The only exception is amendments to the constitution, which require a concurring vote of two-thirds of the members of each house. The upper house, however, has a longer and more secure tenure than the lower house. The 252 Councillors have a definite six-year term, with one-half of them being elected every three years; the 511 Representatives have four-year terms, which may be briefer should the Prime Minister dissolve their house and call for a new election. The Diet, as the highest organ of the state power, has the power of the purse; it can unseat the Prime Minister and the cabinet by passing a no-confidence resolution; impeach any member of the judiciary; and investigate the conduct of any segment of the executive branch. Each house has a range of subject-matter standing committees and special committees to deliberate legislative proposals and to investigate the manner in which they are implemented.

As the nation has become more modern (industrial and hence complex), however, the effective governing power has increasingly gravitated toward the executive branch and away from the legislative. The sheer size of the latter's membership and its division among competing parties make it increasingly difficult for the Japanese legislature to deal with the continuously expanding volume of problems with coherence and dispatch. Those problems have become increasingly complex, some even intractable, requiring greater technical sophistication. Most of the MPs are amateurs elected not for their policy expertise, technical competence, or political acumen but for their popularity in their districts. Moreover, much of their time is taken up in constituency business, party affairs, and, particularly in the case of LDP MPs, in factional maneuvering, wheeling and dealing. MPs are quite knowledgeable about issues that directly relate to their constituency interests, and some even have developed policy expertise in one or more specific issues of national importance such as taxation, environment, education. By and large, however, the effective power of policy initiation, deliberation, and formulation now resides in the executive branch. Even the Diet's power of the purse has become merely formal; the budget submitted by the cabinet (prepared by the bureaucracy and endorsed by the ruling party) for Diet approval is so mind-bogglingly complex that its parliamentary debate becomes little more than a ritual.

The culture of consensual democracy also affects the Diet's relationship to the executive branch even more than the fact that the cabinet is in the Diet, and strongly inclines parliamentary debate to be more ritualistic than substantive. There is little by way of an adversarial atmosphere between the legislative and executive branches. Every major legislative proposal is prepared by the executive branch and goes through informal negotiation among all parties concerned (i.e., the relevant agency or ministry, the finance ministry if it requires major expenditure or new revenue, the LDP committee or committees concerned, opposition parties). In other words, by the time it is presented to the Diet for deliberation and vote, it comes as the product of all possible compromises and accommodations. Opposition parties may still vote against it (the opposition must act like an opposition at least sometimes), but frequently it is just a matter of form.

THE BUREAUCRACY

The government bureaucracy—the civil service—is an enormously powerful institution in any modern society. Its power is the function of two major factors, among others: the imperviousness of bureaucrats to public opinion owing to their tenure, and their centralized control of information and expertise relevant to management of problems the government faces. Both the legislature and the cabinet depend on the bureaucracy for intelligence and skill in performing their respective functions. Moreover, the higher civil service is accorded enormous historical prestige. The government service as the most prestigious and honored career one could aspire to is rooted in East Asian tradition. In Japan, this tradition was greatly strengthened during the period of rapid modernization in the late nineteenth and early twentieth centuries. The first public university system, consisting of Imperial Universities, was established for the explicit purpose of educating future leaders of the nation, especially future public servants. The best and the brightest graduates of those Imperial Universities, especially Tokyo Imperial, were recruited into the government through rigorous examinations, and they were viewed by the multitude as models of intellectual excellence, moral probity, political impartiality, and selfless devotion to the public interest. As a consequence, the Japanese higher civil service not only was imbued with a vigorous esprit de corps but also assumed the role of guardian of the commonweal. Although this tradition has been somewhat diluted since 1945, the people still perceive the bureaucracy as more attentive to their common interest and well-being than either the Diet or the cabinet. In short, the higher civil service is still endowed with an aura of intrinsic authority and natural competence, and this reflects itself in its relationship with the party and the party cabinet.

One indication of the power of the higher civil service is the domination of party and cabinet by former higher civil servants. Senior bureaucrats, as we noted, retire relatively early in life, and the prestige they enjoy among the population encourages many of them to seek a second career in elective politics. Within the total LDP parliamentary membership, they are a minority, but they occupy positions of power and influence greater than that of their more numerous nonbureaucrat colleagues. Eight of fourteen postwar prime ministers were former bureaucrats, and they have occupied the office about 80 percent of the time. A majority of ministers of most cabinets have been ex-bureaucrats.

Another and more critical way in which the power and influence of the bureaucracy on the cabinet is manifest has to do with policy making. Since factionalism makes policy controversy dangerous (for any critical policy issue tends to be exploited for factional purposes, e.g., to weaken and even unseat the incumbent Prime Minster), the ruling party is not fertile soil for new policies and new policy directions. It can function as the ruling party on issues on which there already exists a wide consensus, but when a new problem or a difficult issue arises factionalism seriously inhibits consensus formation. The cabinet suffers from the same problem because it is a creature of the shifting factional alignment. Thus, in Japan's party government, a critical policy vacuum on any actual or potentially controversial problem or issue is often filled by the bureaucracy.

Sometimes the bureaucracy tends to postpone a difficult decision as long as possible, but the civil service as an institution is a much more cohesive human nexus than the party because its incumbents share common school ties and career experiences as well as a common elitist esprit de corps. Its internal competition is an objective clientele conflict, not a passion-generating competition for power or spoils. Thus, a new policy consensus is much less difficult within the civil service than within the ruling party or its cabinet. The latter can begin to operate as a decision-making institution only when the civil service, having formed a consensus of its own, makes a relevant input into it. Since the input comes from the impartial bureaucracy and not from a faction or a faction-tied MP or MPs, the intraparty consensus-building process now begins to function outside the context of factional competition. To a significant extent, it may be argued, the primary function of the ruling party and its cabinet is to legitimize decisions made by the bureaucracy.

THE JUDICIARY

The court of law does not occupy a prominent place in the popular consciousness in Japan, for the Japanese are uncommonly unlitigious. Because of the social forces we discussed earlier, the Japanese are not infatuated with formal rules, laws, and regulations in managing their affairs; they value unwritten codes of behavior instead. Invocation of formal laws or rules is likely to be viewed as admission of failure on the part of the party or parties invoking them in solving their problems informally, voluntarily, and discreetly in a spirit of civility and community. As a consequence, relatively few interpersonal and social problems are politicized or litigated, and where there is a conflict (and there are many conflicts and disagreements even in Japan), the natural in-

clination of the parties concerned is to seek informal mediation and settlement. Even problems that are taken to the court (unless they are criminal
cases) are more often than not settled out of court, which the judge himself encourages, to avoid the acrimony of public confrontation that would lead to
bitterness and animosity between the parties concerned. As a result, there are
not many lawyers in Japan, and the legal profession is not widely sought after
by college students.

Still, as a highly complex democratic state, Japan has an increasingly
wide range of political, social, and economic issues that do not lend themselves to traditional resolution or settlement and that therefore have to be formally adjudicated.

Under the prewar constitution, the judiciary was an arm of the executive
branch of government, directed by the ministry of justice. There was no recourse for grievances against acts of the government, and no power of judicial
review. The postwar constitution not only established an independent judiciary free from interference by other branches of government but vested in it the
power of judicial review. The only aspect of the judiciary on which the executive branch of government impinges is judicial appointment. The cabinet nom-
inates the chief justice of the Supreme Court (who then is formally appointed
by the Emperor) and appoints the other members of the same court, as well as
judges of inferior courts from lists submitted by the Supreme Court. Once appointed, these jurists effectively enjoy tenure until age seventy when, by custom, they are to resign. The Supreme Court justices need to seek popular approval of their tenure in a decennial referendum, but in practice this is a matter
of formality.

The way in which the power of judicial review has been exercised is interesting. A case involving the constitutionality of a law or an executive policy is
initially handled by a relevant district court, but the ruling may be appealed to
the Supreme Court. District courts have tended, in more controversial cases,
toward a literal interpretation of the constitution. The Supreme Court, in contrast, has usually reversed those lower-court rulings in a manner that clearly
suggested the presumption of constitutionality of the acts of government per-
taining to public order or national security (what has since come to be known
as a "political question"), that is, ruling in favor of the government rather than
the rights and liberties enumerated in the constitution. These cases were con-
tentious precisely because they involved issues that fell in the legal twilight
zone where rights and liberties of the people merge with the imperatives of the
state to maintain internal order and external security. Nevertheless, the difference in constitutional interpretation between the two levels of the judiciary
would seem primarily to be the function of the generational difference be-

tween Supreme Court justices and lower-court judges. Supreme Court justices are older, trained and matured in an authoritarian period when the interest of the state always superseded the rights of the individual. Lower-court judges are generally much younger, products of democratic postwar education and experience that stressed the rights of the individual and the citizen against government power. This does not necessarily mean that the Supreme Court will, over time, become more and more liberal.

The System in Action

Nations that are both industrial and democratic share a range of common problems — inflation, unemployment, deficit spending, education, welfare, pollution, labor relations — on whose handling governmental stability and party fortune depend. Japan has all these problems. At the same time each nation, by virtue of its particular cultural, historical, sociopolitical, and environmental conditions, has problems that are unique. One such problem in Japan is national defense. In most modern states, the defense capability of a nation to maintain its security and safeguard its territorial integrity is not a matter of partisan disagreement. Parties disagree over whether the nation's defense is adequate, whether this weapons system or that particular strategic option is appropriate; but there is no disagreement about the need for a strong defense capability. Not so in Japan. The manner in which this issue has been treated in the postwar period provides a good example of how Japan's political system works, for it has involved all the aspects of Japanese politics we have thus far discussed.

Article 9 (the so-called no-war clause) of the postwar constitution renounces "war as a sovereign right of the nation and the threat or use of force as means of settling international disputes" and declares that "land, sea, and air forces, as well as other war potential, will never be maintained." This is an astonishing declaration, with no parallel elsewhere, if taken literally. Precipitated by the aftermath of the traumatic defeat in war, the article immediately rendered Japan unique among nations. This pacifist "spirit of the constitution," in the eyes of a people who pride themselves in their uniqueness, indeed exclusivity, became a veritable badge of national distinction.

On the practical level, as threatening events began to emerge in the world, most of the Japanese were persuaded that the no-war clause does not prohibit the possession of means of self-defense. Consequently, shortly after the nation regained its independence early in the 1950s, the Self-Defense Forces (SDF) were established. The constitutionality of the SDF was affirmed by the Supreme Court in subsequent years, and it came eventually to be accepted by nearly 90 percent of the people.

Initially, the attitude of the Japanese was ambivalent toward the issue of national defense, and this ambivalence was significantly abetted by the United States. Recognizing Japan's inability quickly to establish a strong enough capability to deter or cope with aggression at the time when she was still engaged in the difficult task of economic recovery and growth, the United States concluded a security pact with Japan under which Japan would be effectively protected by American military might, including its nuclear capability. The SDF was to be expanded and upgraded as Japan's ability increased. This security arrangement with the United States made it possible for the Japanese to acknowledge the necessity of military defense of their country, and at the same time indulge in constant reaffirmation of their national uniqueness. Put a bit differently, the security provided by the United States gave free rein to the Japanese impulse for idealistic protestations of the spirit of the constitution, the very impulse that the parliamentary opposition, especially the JSP, exploited in frustrating the more security-minded ruling party.

This popular tendency forced the debate on national defense to be couched in a highly moralistic pacifist language, which would not even permit the identification of actual threats or potential adversaries. Instead it stressed the incontestable virtue of international concord and the incontrovertible superiority of peaceful diplomacy over a strong defense capability. The SDF was under constant suspicion of becoming a potentially aggressive instrument instead of scrupulously remaining "exclusively defensive." Indeed, candid and critical debate of the issue became a political taboo. The culture of consensual democracy avoided it, so long as the nation was assured of protection by the United States.

The general predilection to avoid the issue was never seriously challenged, even by the sector of society that might normally be viewed as favoring active rearmament (i.e., big business). *Zaikai* prospered in the postwar period in, or because of, the absence of heavy military spending. Behind the shield of American military power, Japan could engage in the single-minded pursuit of economic growth and prosperity (hence *zaikai* prosperity and aggrandizement) without the necessity of diverting her resources to military preparation. The depoliticization of the issue of national defense was thus eminently compatible with the interest of *zaikai,* particularly since few Japanese corporations had to depend on defense procurement for revenue and growth. Industries even marginally involved in defense contracts did form an association (called the Keidanren Defense Production Committee) to promote a strong military, but their activities had little discernible impact on the issue, in the absence of a sufficient consensus within *zaikai* at large.

Within the bureaucracy as well, avoidance of the issue of national defense soon came to be regarded as expedient. Defense expenditures during early years of the SDF were kept to a small fraction of the annual GNP—within 1 percent. This early budgetary practice, initially necessitated by economic circumstances, soon became popular with the various government sectors, especially the powerful "economic ministries" such as Finance, International Trade and Industry, Agriculture, Construction, Transportation, institutionally tied to growth-oriented client groups. As these sectors became more and more powerful and entrenched with the growth and expansion of the national economy, the 1 percent limit for defense spending came to be treated as virtually sacrosanct. The Defense Agency was vastly handicapped in interbureaucratic budget politics, for it was new and small, without full ministry status and without a powerful constituency.

In the meantime, the ruling party's political fortune also rested on continuing economic growth and expansion, which would best be promoted by minimizing defense spending. The party had a number of MPs, including very influential leaders, who were deeply concerned about what they viewed as the dangerously low level of SDF capability. Their concern, however, was constantly overridden by fears of political disputes with the opposition parties, which would invariably be exploited by intraparty factions competing for party leadership. To a considerable extent, the issue of national defense was a political taboo even within the ruling party, to be avoided as long as possible.

Until the latter part of the 1970s, the issue remained dormant within the decisional process. And even though the SDF budget continued to rise with the growth in the nation's GNP, the SDF effectively remained what one critic called a "parapolice force," with its capability remaining unchanged or, as some analysts argued, declining relative to the external environment.

As we have noted more than once, Japan's consensual decisional process begins to deal with a difficult issue only when it has become impossible or palpably dangerous not to do so, or when there is a powerful input into it from without. In the latter part of the 1970s, there indeed was a growing recognition in the more salient sectors of the decisional process that the nation's safety was increasingly threatened and that it would be dangerous to continue to avoid the issue. This recognition was precipitated by a number of worrisome developments, among them the following: (1) a radical change in the military balance in East Asia caused by the withdrawal of the United States from the Indochina peninsula and the general lowering of America's politico-military posture in the Western Pacific in general, together with the Soviet Union's vast expansion of its air and naval forces in the region; (2) post-Vietnam political and military developments in Indochina, the crises in Afghanistan and the Persian Gulf region, and the potential danger they singly and cumulatively posed to Japan's lifelines; and (3) an increasingly apparent likelihood that the United

States, whose military capability was stretched thin, might, in the event of a serious contingency in Europe or the Middle East, abandon temporarily the defense of Japan.

Almost simultaneously there was a relevant external input, and that was America's unprecedentedly persistent demand that Japan increase her own defense efforts to the level commensurate with her economic power and security responsibility. Washington had frequently complained that Japan was not doing the best she could for her own defense, but its complaint had never been forceful and persistent enough to force Tokyo to begin seriously coping with the issue. Now Washington's demand became far more intense and persistent, greatly bolstered by the destabilizing developments just mentioned.

As a consequence, unprecedented phenomena began to appear one after another in Japan relating to the issue of national defense, especially since late 1977. In a loosely chronological order, they included the following: (1) a sudden upsurge in the number of articles and books discussing the issue of national defense from a sharply more realistic perspective than had ever been the case; (2) the Prime Minister's annual policy address to the Diet, devoting a separate section to the issue of national defense; (3) the director general of the Defense Agency calling the nation's attention to the inadequacy of the SDF; (4) a Defense White Paper explicitly referring to the "danger" posed by the Soviet military expansion in East Asia; (5) LDP and some centrist opposition MPs urging the establishment of a Diet committee on national security; (6) the decline in moralistic pacifist attacks on the SDF by leftist opposition and in its stead the rise of a more critical and inquisitive tone of questioning; (7) SDF leaders publicly expressing their views and concerns about the nation's defense posture and capability; (8) *zaikai* leaders publicly speaking up for a rapid increase in defense expenditure and organized labor in the private sector urging expanded defense efforts; (9) the cabinet announcing a plan to establish a cabinet council on national security; (10) the Foreign Ministry openly siding with the Defense Agency in urging a large increase in the SDF budget; and (11) the Prime Minister publicly acknowledging the inadequacy of the nation's defense efforts. These developments would have been unthinkable several years earlier. The issue of national defense finally came out of the closet of political taboos.

These unprecedented events in Japan suggested that the process of forming a relevant and more critical consensus on the issue of national defense was activated. Consensus formation, especially given the character of leadership in Japanese culture, may take time. At this writing, a consensus has not been reached fully, for considerable disagreement remains within each of the salient sectors of the decisional structure as well as among them. Disagreement, however, is no longer constitutional or ideological; it now is essentially fiscal and technical. That the nation must strengthen its defense capability is no longer a matter of fundamental dispute.

This is not to say that everything that is happening to the issue of national defense is desirable, however necessary the emergence of a critical consensus may be. The recognition of the destabilizing external environment and America's unusually intense and persistent demand that Japan increase her defense efforts more or less coincided with the growth of gloom in Japan over the nation's economic condition, worsened by the effect, among others, of OPEC petropolitics and consequent downward economic trends in industrial nations at large. The conjunction of these two separate sets of developments gave rise, within *zaikai* and certain sectors of labor, to an expanding demand for increased defense efforts. This demand was motivated at least in part by the self-interests of these groups to seek economic recovery through massive infusion of defense contracts. There is little doubt that their newly perceived self-interests contributed to the ongoing process of a new consensus formation. There is, therefore, a potential danger that they, together with the Defense Agency and their new allies in the party and the bureaucracy and elsewhere, might exceed the hazy boundary of probity and lead to the emergence of a self-aggrandizing military-industrial complex. This fear may not be entirely unwarranted, for consensus, once aimed in a given direction, tends to feed on itself.

No political system operates uniformly and invariably over time or throughout its many dimensions, for no system is totally static in the criteria and parameters of its operation nor definitive in the pattern of behavior of its various components. Every system is evolving, however indiscernibly. The Japanese political system is no exception. What we have seen in this chapter, therefore, is nothing more than what a student of comparative politics should know at the first instance of exposure to the only advanced industrial democracy outside the Western world.

SUGGESTIONS FOR ADDITIONAL READING

AUSTIN, LEWIS. *Saints and Samurai: The Political Culture of the American and Japanese Elites.* New Haven: Yale University Press, 1975.

BAERWALD, HANS H. *Japan's Parliament: An Introduction.* New York: Cambridge University Press, 1974.

BURKS, ARDATH W. *Japan: Profile of a Postindustrial Power.* Boulder, Colo.: Westview Press, 1981.

CURTIS, GERALD L. *Election Campaigning Japanese Style.* New York: Columbia University Press, 1971.

GIBNEY, FRANK. *Japan: The Fragile Superpower.* New York: Norton, 1975.

IKE, NOBUTAKA. *A Theory of Japanese Democracy.* Boulder, Colo.: Westview Press, 1978.

NAKANE, CHIE. *Japanese Society.* Berkeley: University of California Press, 1970.

REISCHAUER, EDWIN O. *The Japanese.* Cambridge, Mass.: Harvard University Press, 1977.

STOCKWIN, J.A.A. *Japan: Divided Politics in a Growth Economy.* New York: Norton, 1975.

TSURUTANI, TAKETSUGU. *Political Change in Japan: Response to Postindustrial Challenge.* New York: McKay, 1977.

WARD, ROBERT. *Japan's Political System.* Englewood Cliffs, N.J.: Prentice-Hall, 1978.

5. Political Systems of the Third World

The term Third World gained some currency in the 1960s and '70s as a convenient label for all the countries left over after counting those of the "First" and "Second" worlds.[1] The first two chapters of this book surveyed several political systems of the First World. These, West European and North American, were among the first to undergo the political and economic changes associated with the Renaissance, the Enlightenment, and the Industrial Revolution. From feudalism through monarchy and mercantilism emerged a few national societies whose political systems came to be called "democratic" and whose economic systems came to be called "capitalist." Widespread political beliefs in each of them came to emphasize some version of "popular sovereignty" or "rule by the people," and of national independence or "self-determination." Their governments included elected civilian chief executives and / or legislatures, and their customs and laws provided some measure of civil rights and liberties. Their economies were based on private (individual or corporate) ownership of land, businesses, and factories, and on beliefs about markets and competition as mechanisms for setting wages and prices and as the arbiters of economic success or failure. The changes that brought these politico-economic systems into being were accompanied by a great deal of civil strife, violence, and international warfare. Japan, although non-Western, also belongs in the First World, by virtue of her high level of economic development and democratic political institutions.

We have seen in chapter 3 how the "Second World" of socialist or communist nations came into being with the Bolshevik phase of the Russian Revolution of 1917. After the Second World War a number of both "old" and "new" nations were added to the list of communist political systems. In them, factories, businesses, and land were to varying degrees nationalized, or made the

1. See, for example, Irving Louis Horowitz, *Three Worlds of Political Development* (New York: Oxford University Press, 1966). Other frequently used designations are "developing nations," "emerging nations," and "LDCs" (less developed countries). According to Horowitz, the phrase "third world" was first used by Frantz Fanon, an Algerian, in *The Wretched of the Earth* (New York: Grove Press, 1965), which is a translation of Fanon's *Les damnes de la terre* (Paris: Francois Maspero, editeur, 1961).

property of the state in the name of the "proletariat"—the working class. All economic activity was coordinated by central planning organs of government. Government thus became the primary instrument for speeding economic development, especially by industrializing the economy. In each country one party, the Communist, claiming to represent workers and peasants, monopolized political and economic power. Other parties were either eliminated or, in some instances, were tolerated only if they were very small and did not challenge the ruling party's ideology and control of the politico-economic system. Thus did the Second World embark on its own path to economic and political transformation, seeking to "catch up" economically with the First World.

During the same period, and continuing into the present, an even larger number of countries (many thinking of themselves as "new nations," mainly erstwhile colonies of First World nations and located in the Middle East, Africa, and Asia, but also including older countries, mainly in Latin America) came to be referred to as countries of the "Third World." Although they varied considerably among themselves in size, resources, culture, and historical background, these countries embodied the "third wave" of modernization, especially in their aspirations and efforts to "develop" economically. They represent a third zone of concerns in world politics; their emergence is still transforming the dyad of Western and Soviet-bloc tensions into a triad including North-South tensions. Many Third World governments have sought to avoid emulation of or close entanglement with either of the superpowers who dominate East-West relations. But the First and Second Worlds continue to be the principal if not the only sources of capital and technologies so desperately needed for Third World development. The Third World does possess raw materials and natural resources, some of which are needed by the industries of the other two. In addition, First World countries are interested in existing and potential markets for both capital investment and manufactured goods in the Third World. The United States and the USSR also provide contrasting "models" of the economic development desired by Third World countries. Moreover, if the East is interested in exporting communism, so is the West interested in preserving and extending the conditions in which capitalism can grow and function. Inextricably interwoven with these economic factors are the political considerations deriving from strategic security concerns of both First and Second World governments. Thus many Third World countries find themselves related in significant and often tension-filled ways to First or Second World countries.

The nomenclature of this three-part classification is far from satisfactory. Portugal, for example, nominally a First World nation because of the nature of its economy, imperialist history, and more recent democratic government, is quite poor and much in need of further economic development. The People's Republic of China, the Democratic People's Republic of Korea, and the Socialist Republic of Vietnam are likewise very poor, but because of their ruling parties, official ideologies, and international alliances, they are usually counted among Second World countries. And metropolitan regions of some Latin American, Middle Eastern, and Asian countries are comparable in some ways to many First World metropolitan regions.

Moreover, while within each of these three "worlds" there is recognition of important shared interests in international relations, none of them, and least of all the Third, acts as a unit in relation to the other two. True, the NATO alliance links many of the Western nations, the Warsaw Pact alliance includes most East European communist nations, and about eight dozen Third World government leaders meet periodically in conferences of "nonaligned" nations. But NATO does not include Austria, Finland, Ireland, Spain, Sweden, and Switzerland in Western Europe, and does include Turkey in the Middle East. France has withdrawn militarily from the alliance and Greece is expected to do so. The Second World is split by the deep antagonism between the USSR and China, while Yugoslavia, initially in the Soviet orbit and still communist-ruled, has been one of the leaders of the nonaligned nations. Some Third World countries, such as Egypt and Panama, Cuba and Ethiopia, are clearly "aligned" with the United States or the USSR. Other Third World governments, although "nonaligned," notably India, consider themselves socialist; while some others reject the labels associated with the other two, proclaiming that they follow a third way that avoids the perceived excesses and defects of both.

Despite these anomalies, the terminology does provide a convenient way to designate, even if imprecisely, the countries and political systems with which we are concerned in this chapter. Where greater precision is called for, it will be provided by the context or by specification.

Why should we be concerned with these Third World countries? They come to the attention of most of us, at least momentarily, when the news media report natural or other disasters, or abrupt (to us) changes in leadership, and crises, often violent, in their governments and politics. But there are so many such countries—well over 100—how can we possibly hope to make any sense of the fleeting news images of military takeovers, assassinations, urban riots, and guerrilla warfare? Surely we cannot be expected, even as informed and conscientious citizens, to know enough of individual countries to understand the causes and meanings of the 1980 riots in India, the war begun in 1980 between Iraq and Iran, the 1980 military *coup d'etat* in Liberia, or the assassination of Anwar Sadat in 1981. (By the time these words appear in print, any reader of newspaper front pages or viewer of network television newscasts will be able to update this list with comparable events.) Besides, there are so many baffling differences in culture; in political, economic, and social systems; and in relevance to our own concerns. Small wonder, then, that many people — even among the presumably "educated" — tend to treat most such events, and the news reporting them, as peripheral, as not important enough to warrant sustained attention, much less serious "backgound" study.

Sometimes, however, dramatic events, such as the capture and holding for more than a year of the U.S. diplomatic hostages in Iran and the U.S. involvement in the recent war in Vietnam, can not only grip our attention but can have direct and keenly felt impact on our daily lives and our political processes. Yet it is no exaggeration to say that both of these painfully dramatic episodes in faraway lands resulted, in significant measure, from prior ignorance. It was ignorance not only on the part of the vast public but also on the part of many of those at the highest levels of government, both civil and military. Lack of adequate knowledge and the resulting use of inappropriate assumptions in the analysis of events and trends led to tragic chains of miscalculations and policy decisions. Both might have been avoided if sufficient knowledge and understanding had been available to and used by U.S. Presidents and their most important foreign policy and military advisers, or perhaps even to sufficient numbers of U.S. citizens.

There are additional reasons for trying to learn more about the politics and governments of the Third World. Three-fourths of the world's population are Asian, African, or Latin American; their net population growth rates are well above those in European, North American, and other industrialized parts of the world. Large proportions of the world's supply of various natural resources essential to the survival of industrial societies come from Third World countries. Petroleum is one of which we have become acutely conscious. But there are others such as bauxite and aluminum, chromium, cobalt, and zinc, to mention a few.

To the extent that we ignore what is happening in the Third World, to the extent that we "screen out" these nations and people from our attention, we contribute to conditions in which our government (and other important First World representatives in the Third, such as giant multinational corporations) can more easily make the kind of mistakes that will increase the tensions, hostilities, and restiveness already apparent in relations among the First, Second, and Third Worlds. This could have calamitous consequences for us, our children, and our grandchildren.

Just as important in the long run, although less obvious, is one essential kind of knowledge we can acquire by directing our attention to the Third

World. Political change, interacting with economic and social change, is under way there at a very rapid rate. Cultural distance—as well as geographic —makes it possible for us to observe the complexities of such change much more objectively than we can in our own society. The more we understand political change in the varying conditions of the Third World, the better we can understand it at home, for the common denominator everywhere is the human species, with its potentials as well as its limitations. The knowledge we gain can be crucial to our hope of bringing politics and government within range of our aspirations for our own society.

We cannot go into much detail or depth about individual countries here. But we can try to specify some of the salient general considerations that can provide a context and framework for understanding the political systems of many Third World countries. With this in mind, it should at least be possible to ask the most relevant questions when, for whatever reason, we want to be able to interpret and assess Third World political events when they are reported in the media of mass communication.

Great Variety—Common Problems

Given their geographic distribution around the world and their individual histories, it is hardly surprising that there is extraordinary variety among Third World countries. They range in population size from a few tens of thousands (Dominica, Seychelles) to hundreds of millions (India). Ethnic groups speaking all the major languages and between 2,500 and 5,000 other languages (depending on how "language" is defined) can be found, usually several and sometimes many per country. All imaginable races and racial mixtures, all the major religions and many more other religions than most of us have even heard of, some based on combinations of elements of others, some ancient and some new, flourish in profusion. Differing languages, racial characteristics, and religious identifications are often related in complex ways to class, caste, and social status, and are also often important factors in political conflict. But some examples of relatively harmonious coexistence among such diverse groups can be found, as new and old nationalisms seek some form of political unity and recognition.

Other aspects of cultural variety among Third World countries are also important for understanding their politics. In some there is a long and rich heritage of sophisticated artistic expression, including literature, music, sculpture, and architecture. Much of this, just as in the history of Western art, expresses or is inspired by religious themes. In others, art mainly takes the form of handicrafts, body decoration, story telling, and folk music and dance. In both instances, some political activists and leaders find a wealth of symbols to draw upon to mobilize popular sentiments for political purposes. This may be related to movements of awakening national consciousness, or of opposition to foreign (Western) technology and life styles, which are depicted as threats to traditional values, or to both. Mahatma Gandhi chose the spinning wheel to symbolize both his opposition to foreign colonial rule and his desire to resist the erosion of village institutions by industrial technology. At the same time he and his followers promoted far-reaching social reforms in the name of justice, such as the abolition of caste oppression of "untouchables."

Some traditional cultures emphasize a division of labor in which women do the agricultural work as well as the housework, in addition to bearing and raising children. Men are responsible for hunting, animal husbandry, fishing, village or tribal politics and religious ritual, and fighting to defend village or tribe or to acquire booty, including wives. In other cultures both men and women share the agricultural and other heavy work and divide other tasks and activities according to different patterns. Values associated with some cultural patterns, such as handicraft production and trade as well as agriculture, are more receptive to technological change than are other values rooted in differing cultures. These factors are of obvious relevance to governmental programs of economic development which are under way almost universally in the Third World.

Among all the kaleidoscopic diversity within and between these countries, we can nevertheless point out a few similarities that are crucial for any approach to understanding their politics. Later we shall look more closely at four of these: ambivalence and frustration related to certain aspects of modernization; internal cleavages based on linguistic, ethnic, class, and other subnational loyalties; relative political instability; and the prominence in politics of armed forces. First, however, let us begin to examine one fundamental problem that conditions most of the others in Third World countries: poverty.

To envisage entire societies as poor may not be easy for those who have never lived in such a society, or who have never themselves experienced real poverty. Yet we must try, for poverty and its consequences pervade so much of the life of most Third World countries that, unless we can begin to comprehend it, we will find it next to impossible to see clearly their governments and politics.

Imagine, first, that your chances are small to live much beyond the age of forty or fifty. Imagine that you have had no more than three or four years of schooling—or none at all. This you may not see as a deprivation, for the same is true of all of your family and friends. And perhaps, given the life ahead of you, you may not even be able to conceive of any use for more formal education; certainly it will not make you rich, for everyone knows that the few who have any wealth got it because they were lucky enough to be born into families that already had it. What would your life be like if you had never read a book? Imagine also that your mother or father is very ill and that there is no medicine, no doctor, no hospital. While the illness lasts, you and your brothers and sisters may have to reduce the amount of your already insufficient food to contribute to the nourishment of the sick parent, and you will have to do his or her work in addition to your own. Imagine that one or two of your brothers or sisters died as infants—and that such is the normal experience in all the families you know. Imagine having had to work in the fields since the age of six. Imagine not being able to imagine doing much else for the rest of your life.

These examples are but an effort to gain a few glimpses into the lives of the great majority of the people in most Third World countries. They are intended here to convey some of the meaning of the statistics that follow. To begin, contemplate this: *More than one-half of the world's over 4 billion people live in 70 countries whose average per capita income is less than the equivalent of $600 a year.* The comparable figure for the United States is $8,612.[2]

As important politically and economically as such widespread poverty is, we should not allow it to obscure the differences in the degree of poverty within and between Third World countries. First, in each country there is a small elite of wealthy or privileged people. Its size in relation to the total population, although very small, varies; but their homes, automobiles, clothing, clubs, banks, and the restaurants and other retail businesses they support are in stark contrast to the masses of the poor in the cities. The contrast is all the greater with rural peasants, who typically make up the largest proportion of the total population. In the cities, one can also see middle-class people. Many are civil servants—functionaries of the government. Others work in or own small shops, or are professional people: lawyers, doctors, engineers, and so on. But such middle classes as exist are proportionally much smaller than the comparable classes in the United States, Canada, or Western Europe.

Second, there are significant differences in the degree of poverty among Third World countries. To show these, a few elementary statistical measures are needed.

2. These and other interesting data are available in a number of published sources, some easily accessible. To illustrate this ease of access, the figures used here were compiled from *The World Almanac and Book of Facts,* 1981, published annually by Newspaper Enterprise Association, New York. See pp. 513-98. This and other similar annual publications are sold in bookstores and at magazine racks in other kinds of stores. A more extensive source is C. L. Taylor, *World Handbook of Political and Social Indicators* (3rd ed.; New Haven: Yale University Press, 1981).

There are several methods by which poverty, or its opposite, wealth, can be estimated for a country. One that we made use of above is average per capita income (PCI), which is arrived at by dividing the total income of a country by its total population. These figures, of course, are subject to error, but this is not a serious shortcoming when we are comparing nations or sets of nations between which differences are clearly fairly great. What per capita income figures do *not* take into account are, first, total wealth, of which income is a periodically measured component; second, the distribution of income within a country (small fractions of the population may receive disproportionately large proportions of the country's total income); and third, in poor countries a large proportion of the rural population subsists on what they grow and make themselves, having very limited monetary means of selling or buying anything. The second and third of these are particularly important in Third World countries, for in almost all of them, as alluded to above, we find a small minority of wealthy families and individuals whose income is high even by First World standards. In most of them, much of the rural population live at or barely above the level of subsistence. But if we keep these things in mind, per capita income figures can be suggestive of relative levels of poverty in Third World countries.

Another measure, supplementing the one just used, reflects some of the consequences of low per capita income. It is the Physical Quality of Life Index (PQLI).[3] This index combines three elemental statistics: infant mortality, life expectancy of those who survive to age one, and literacy. In a rudimentary and revealing way, this index, ranging from o to 100, measures the degree to which three basic benefits of modernized society—life chances, health services, and educational opportunities—have become available to the populations of different countries.

These two measures, PCI and PQLI, are given for each country in the *World Almanac* and are incorporated in table 2.

Even after recognizing that population and income figures are estimates, and are thus subject to error, the differences revealed by the figures in the table are striking. The 16 First World countries, with only 13 percent of the earth's population, receive 60 percent of total per capita income. One hundred and three countries, with 70 percent of the world's population, are classified here as "very poor," with average incomes of less than a dollar a day, and physical quality of life indices of only 56. These figures reflect a reality that underlies—and often shapes—politics in all such countries. Many in the West, who worry

3. The source for the PQLI, cited in the *World Almanac, 1981,* p. 513, is Martin M. McLaughlin and the Staff of the Overseas Development Council, *The United States and World Development, 1980* (New York: Praeger, 1980).

TABLE 2. DATA ON 153 COUNTRIES

	First World[a]	Second World	Third World (1st Wld. oriented)	Third World (2nd Wld. oriented)	"Nonaligned"	Totals or Weighted Averages
Very Rich ($6,000 or more)						
No. of countries	16	0	4	1	0	21
Pct. of world pop.	13[c]	0	.3	.003	0	13
Pct. of world income	60	0	2	.2	0	62
(Weighted av. PCI)[d]	(8,257)	0	(6,406)	(6,335)	0	(8,209)
(Weighted av. PQLI)	(96)	0	(35)	(49)	0	(95)
Rich ($3,000–$5,999)						
No. of countries	6	2	1	0	0	9
Pct. of world pop.	4	.7	.0006	0	0	5
Pct. of world income	6	2	.03	0	0	8
(Weighted av. PCI)	(3,867)	(3,993)	(3,725)	0	0	(3,887)
(Weighted av. PQLI)	(94)	(93)	(21)	0	0	(94)
Poor ($1,500–$2,999)						
No. of countries	4	6	8	1	1	20
Pct. of world pop.	.3	8	3	.3	.9	13
Pct. of world income	.4	10	3	.3	1	15
(Weighted av. PCI)	(1,838)	(2,496)	(1,675)	(1,561)	(1,986)	(2,218)
(Weighted av. PQLI)	(84)	(91)	(71)	(45)	(52)	(82)
Very Poor ($1,499 or less)						
No. of countries	0	8	76	11	8	103
Pct. of world pop.	0	25	23	3	19	70
Pct. of world income	0	6	7	.5	2	16
(Weighted av. PCI)	0	(240)	(609)	(312)	(144)	(341)
(Weighted av. PQLI)	0	(70)	(55)	(28)	(43)	(56)
Totals: No. of countries	26	16	89	13	9	
Pct. of world pop.	17	34	26	3	20	
Pct. of world income	66	18	12	1	3	
(Weighted av. PCI)	(7,136)	(864)	(798)	(585)	(224)	
(Weighted av. PQLI)	(95)	(76)	(57)	(31)	(43)	

SOURCE: All figures from, or computed from, *The World Almanac and Book of Facts 1981* (New York: Newspaper Enterprise Association, 1981). The figures are dated 1975–79. [a]Notes for this and other terms in table are included in the addendum to this chapter (see pp. 193–94).

that a particular country is "going communist," overlook matters that are usually of greater importance to most people in that country: food, shelter, and clothing.

Explanations of Third World Problems

To identify a problem is, for many people in modern societies, to set in motion a search for its causes. There is an almost automatic assumption that there must be one or more causes that "explain" the situation we define as a problem. Once found, the causes may turn out to be (or can be made) susceptible to human intervention. By dealing with the causes, we can hope to eliminate, reduce, or otherwise change the problem so as to make it more tolerable. At least we may discover a way of getting around the problem or avoiding contact with it. This applies as much to economic and social problems as to those of the "natural" physical world. All this is but common sense, we would say if asked.

It was not always so in what are today modern societies. And it is not always merely "common sense" in many other societies today. For the overwhelmingly greater part of human existence, traditional views of life explained, as ordained by "nature" or by divine power, many kinds of events and conditions that we regard today as avoidable, changeable, or fixable by human action. Conservative traditional beliefs counseled resignation to natural disasters such as devastating storms, floods, droughts, and earthquakes. The social order, no matter how grotesquely unjust, harmful, or inefficient, was also a part of "nature," divinely sanctioned, or both. The path of wisdom was therefore to accept them. If we look about us we can see surviving influences and remnants of such beliefs in contemporary society. Many, for example, conceive of economic competition in a capitalist system of private ownership—quite apart from its virtues of technological innovation and productivity—as somehow more "natural" than other economic systems. Such a view overlooks the man-made changes and innovations that created property law, market systems, the legal invention of the corporation, and the like. Or, for divine sanction, consider the claims made by the major organized religions (and probably most of the minor ones) with regard to the institution of marriage, or rituals following death. (These examples, needless to say, are not offered so much to illustrate the earlier statement concerning injustice, harm, or inefficiency as for their relevance to that concerning beliefs about nature and divinity. But we note in passing that neither has escaped serious criticism from thinkers concerned with the three values mentioned.)

In looking for general explanations of patterns of politics in Third World countries, we need to go beyond the immediate historical causes, such as the interrelated events that resulted in the overthrow of the shah of Iran and the replacement of his government by one dominated by Islamic religious leaders. To understand such events we must interpret them in a framework of ideas about trends and causes that are applicable to other instances of political change. To the extent that our general explanations are applicable to more than one such instance, we can save much time and effort in understanding each individual case. We do this anyway, consciously or not; for example, we project our beliefs about human nature, or morality and immorality, into our explanations. The problem facing the analyst is to find concepts that can be used without allowing personal preferences to prejudge the means and outcomes under consideration.

Here we will use the concepts "traditional society" and "modernization" to organize our explanations. In doing so we must avoid the implication that one is good or bad, and the other is therefore bad or good. This is difficult, for we do assume that modern society (of which the United States is an example) is more consistent than traditional society with such things as science, industrial technology, and rational bases of law, much of which we consider good. We need to keep in mind that change related to these has been and still is accompanied by violent conflict, exploitation, and misery and that incorporating modern ideas and ways into society by no means guarantees an end to such scourges.

We have already touched on several characteristics of "traditional" society. In addition to varying cultural patterns, beliefs fostering acceptance of the status quo, and relative poverty, the economies of such societies are predominantly agricultural. The bulk of the population is rural, typically living in many small villages. There is little mobility, social or geographic. Families tend to be large, and family obligations (e.g., taking care of the aged and the ill, defending family honor, and treating relatives more favorably than others) are stressed. Very few people are literate, and those few are often priests or officials—members of a privileged class. Infant mortality is high, and life spans are generally short. Custom, tradition, and ritual govern most aspects of life.

Towns and cities may exist as centers of religious worship, government, and trade. But their size is limited by the agricultural production of surrounding areas, or of other areas with which trade is carried on, for such urban centers depend on the availability of an agricultural surplus for their survival. A tiny minority of relatively wealthy landowning families often constitutes a ruling class, access to which is closed for most of the population. Trade, commerce, and military conquest may permit growth of such cities to considerable size, and in some the arts may flourish.

Government maintains the social order in relative internal peace by supporting the prevalent religion, often leading the performance of important rituals; by settling disputes; by punishing transgressors; and by maintaining armed forces. It sometimes constructs temples, monuments, roads, dikes, canals, and other kinds of what we would call public works. For all these, as well as to provide a privileged and comfortable if not luxurious way of life for rulers and officials, it collects taxes or tribute. When needed, it drafts labor for construction work and manpower for military service. Often, religious, economic, and political beliefs and institutions are blended and combined, or at least are not clearly separated.

Such societies may eventually support civilizations, as in ancient Egypt or Babylonia, Mohenjo-Daro and Harappa, Shang China, or the Olmecs in what is now Mexico. Classical Greece and Rome are examples closer to us in time and culture as sources of Western civilization. But of most such civilizations, most of us are aware mainly of the lives and achievements of the elite, rather than of the much more numerous rural populations supporting the elite. Traditional society need not be restricted to earlier "civlizations." More generally, the concept can, with allowance for variations of degree, be usefully applied to most preindustrial societies, including those whose basic organization is tribal.

What we call "modernization" began with technological innovations in Western Europe only a few centuries ago, in association with the Renaissance, the Enlightenment, and the Industrial Revolution. Mining, manufacturing, construction, travel, and trade began to transform societies as economic production and productivity increased far beyond the limits imposed by traditional technologies. Such changes rested upon and went hand in hand with the increase of scientific knowledge. Much of the old order was swept away, often to the accompaniment of wars and revolutions. What remained of it had to adapt and accommodate itself to new and continually changing patterns of living and thinking.

We can single out three components of this fateful transformation. Ancient beliefs and attitudes gave way to new ways of viewing the world, nature, and the role and destiny of humankind. A "new psychology" began to spread in England and on the Continent. Many things, it was learned, could be brought under human control and rearranged to a much greater degree than traditional beliefs had conceived. A better life on earth could be achieved by knowledge and action. If traditional culture included such ideas, they were relegated to the realms of magic and the supernatural.

A second component of modernization is the physical or material. Application of new knowledge, which gradually was organized into the sciences, led to more and more complex and powerful technologies. Machines increased economic production. Disease control lowered mortality rates and prolonged life. Construction and travel were revolutionized. New sources of energy and new methods of converting it to human uses vastly increased human control of the natural environment—and the potential for human freedom. New material standards and styles of living became possible. These had the effect of greatly increasing the range of choices open to individuals and societies. This led to the third component: the social and political. New forms of human organization became possible. Among them were huge factories, far-flung business firms, cities of millions of people, and governments of vast complexity and power. New forms of social control as well as new forces of social disruption appeared. Both greater democratization of government and greater concentrations of governmental power were made possible.

While these changes in Western thought, technology, and society were under way, their consequences began to be projected around the globe. European exploration, trade, religious missions, and military and political expeditions established and expanded colonial empires. A few Western nation-states extended their influence, control, and exploitation to traditional societies on distant continents. But inevitably, the revolutionary ideas and technologies of the imperial powers sowed the seeds of destruction, not only of non-Western traditional societies, but of the colonial empires themselves.

Nevertheless—and here we can begin to understand some of the problems of Third World countries today—the various processes of modernization do not proceed at the same rates, and certainly not in harmonious patterns. They produce dislocations, disorganization, and conflict in all aspects of political, economic, and social life. These processes have themselves contributed powerfully to the extent of human poverty and misery. A leading example is modern medicine and public health technologies. These have brought many diseases under control and have reduced infant mortality. The result is more people, living longer lives. But birthrates in Third World countries continue at high levels, contributing a major share of the world's population growth. From A.D. 1 to A.D. 1800 the world's population tripled, growing from about 300 million to a little over 900 million. In the 180 years since A.D. 1800, it has more than quadrupled, passing the 4 billion mark in the mid-1970s. By the year 2000 it will be about 7 billion if present trends continue. Population growth is rapidly outrunning technology's ability to expand and distribute the food production required for the survival of so many people.

Also, modern means of transportation and communication have disseminated ideas and images from the more modernized societies to the less modernized part of the world. This has fed and intensified the aspirations and expectations of hundreds of millions of people whose traditional institutions are increasingly unable to satisfy their needs and hopes. But the spread of images of modern life was begun well before the economic, technological, and political means were available that might allow the realization of such aspirations. As aspirations for a better life are reduced by population growth to a basic struggle for mere survival, and as traditional beliefs and order-maintaining social structures are weakened, little imagination is needed to foresee mounting political pressures and problems. Thus we can see that it is not poverty as such that causes the political problems of the present world, but poverty in conditions of weakened traditional beliefs and structures, where awareness of possibilities of a better life are widespread.

Let us look more closely at some of the clusters of political problems confronting many Third World countries. As traditional beliefs about the bases of legitimate government, such as divinely sanctioned hereditary monarchy, have eroded, more modern beliefs such as the consent and representation of the governed have not been widely accepted beyond the educated few. In many countries elites with Western-style educations reveal ambivalent attitudes, seeking to conserve valued elements and aspects of traditional culture while adopting much of modern knowledge, technology, and ways of living. In some instances, such as Pakistan, Iran, and Saudi Arabia, many of the educated few seek a viable way of retaining and strengthening the religious basis of governmental authority. This may be accompanied by both resentment of the West and reluctance to give up positions of influence and privilege as economic and social change spreads through society. Or some of the elite may share the frustration and sense of injustice of the less advantaged at the inability to break the grip of poverty on the country. Whatever the individual reaction to the experience of socialization by two different cultures, traditional and Western, problems of self-identity and ambivalence toward goals often prove difficult to handle. Their effects on behavior render the latter more difficult to understand by observers who have not had such experience. It is in some ways analogous to the experience of racial minorities in a society such as the United States, except that in the Third World it is the favored elites who have experienced this "double socialization."

Another constellation of problems aggravated by modernization processes in many Third World countries has to do with cleavages based on ethnic, regional, and class differences. The problem discussed above is one manifestation of this kind of cleavage, in which socioeconomic class differences are reinforced by a foreign-style education of many in the elite. This usually includes the learning of a foreign language, the lack of which may effectively bar many from possible channels of upward social mobility such as governmental employment at levels other than the lowest and most menial and it has often caused suspicions about the true loyalties of members of the elite. But on a larger scale, loyalties to groups such as tribes or to those speaking different languages, particularly when such groups are identified with particular regions, may result in extremely difficult problems of integration and assimilation into a "nation-state."

For the "new" nations, especially in Africa, boundaries are a legacy of colonialism, drawn by colonial powers. Such boundaries were often the results of conflict and treaties among colonial powers; thus they sometimes grouped traditionally hostile people within a colony while splitting previously unified people and their lands on both sides of a colonial boundary. Postindependence political leaders have had to get diverse people to accept a common and newfangled national identity so that a government of all can acquire enough legitimacy to function. This has never been easy, and in some instances brutal civil wars have been fought, as in Nigeria. Such situations have provided regional leverage for foreign involvement, as in Zaire (then the Congo) just after independence. Given its many different languages and internal ethnic antagonisms, which erupt into violence not infrequently, one of India's principal accomplishments has been sheer survival without breaking into pieces along ethnic lines. It is significant that the common language of governmental administration has continued to be English. The imposition of the official language, Hindi, is still resisted in non-Hindi-speaking states.

Given the presence to some degree of divisive factors such as these, many Third World countries lack sufficiently widespread acceptance of basic rules to govern political conflict. Political leaders often cannot assume that their opponents will refrain from violence and are therefore ready to use it themselves. Significantly, this has become true of older Third World nations as well as of newer ones, as the unsettling forces of modernization have spread. Latin American politics, perhaps more clearly than African, are often riven by conflicts along socioeconomic class lines, as in Argentina, Brazil, Bolivia, Chile, Nicaragua, and El Salvador in recent years. In such conflicts the military forces of the government are often the decisive factor. Nicaragua is a recent exception—as was Cuba over two decades ago. In these two, the government's armies were not able to resist guerrilla forces.

A major part of the explanation in Cuba and Nicaragua was corruption and repression on the part of the government and the military, which destroyed the government's legitimacy in the eyes of much of the population, especially rural peasants and many of the middle- as well as lower-class urban people. On the other hand, one of the frequently used justifications for military forces' turning on their civilian masters, overthrowing their government, and setting up a military dictatorship is the corruption and incompetence of civilian government.

To summarize, we can often find a few important, underlying, explanatory factors in the seemingly unpredictable processes of political conflict and change in Third World countries. One of these is poverty, which has often become more acute and more politically explosive as a consequence of partial modernization of traditional societies. Such partial modernization has weakened or undermined traditional institutions and values, and has disseminated images of and aspirations for a better life for millions. But the means for realizing such aims are insufficient or absent. Elites, partly modernized, find themselves ambivalent, or refuse to risk their privileged positions, which many see threatened by the modernizing changes occurring throughout their societies. Internal cleavages hinder the development of national consciousness in many countries. Without sufficiently institutionalized rules for the nonviolent resolution of political conflict, the military forces are often involved in the maintenance of order by repression of rebellions. The outcome is often military dictatorship, which is at present the most characteristic form of government in the Third World.

With these general considerations in mind, let us now survey several specific political institutions and processes in the Third World.

Political Institutions and Processes

In relatively stable political systems it is possible to identify fairly well defined institutions of government. Through the activities of officials who hold office in them, legitimate and authoritative decisions are made or ratified: laws, decrees, and so forth, which establish government policies and spell out rules that affect the people subject to that government. Specific governmental institutions are authorized to enforce or carry out the decisions made. Other political processes, involving individuals, parties, interest groups, and nongovernmental institutions, go on in relation to the governmental decision-making processes, seeking to influence them. The general reason for seeking such influence is that the outcomes of governmental decisions affect the distribution of burdens and benefits throughout society: who pays how much in taxes, whose activities are regulated and in what ways, who receives what services, subsidies, authorizations, exemptions, and so on. Although the threat of coercion by police or military forces is never absent in enforcing such decisions, rules, and policies, it is normally used only in maintaining public order and apprehending and punishing criminals.

The organization, processes, and functions of these governmental institutions can be examined on the assumption that one is dealing with matters directly relevant to the question of how that society is governed. This is so even if one discovers that other individuals, groups, institutions, or classes of people, not a part of the formal governmental institutions, and contrary to official doctrine and public symbolism, exercise great influence, even to the point of controlling the decisions made by the government.

But in many Third World countries, the situation of some governmental institutions is not as clear-cut as just described. In some, change may be occurring so rapidly, or may have occurred so recently, that both participants and observers may be uncertain as to who is doing what, or who is supposed to be doing what. Some government organizations may be at a standstill, doing little or nothing, or engaging in activities that result in things not expected, to judge by their titles or their place in the structure. Other organizations and activities may exist only on paper. Officials may be giving attention and deference to persons or organizations whose place and role in the political process are far from obvious, even if detectable. In short, both image and reality may be unclear and inconsistent with each other, or related in such complex or indirect ways that even participants may be uncertain about some of them.

The consequence of this is that formal governmental structure, often designed according to a First World (or Western) model, may not be the best place to start looking for evidence as to how a Third World country is governed. One may find offices such as President or Prime Minister, or organizations labeled "Legislature," "Senate," "Assembly," or "High Court of Justice." But until we discover just what the officials in these offices and organizations do, and with what consequences, it is not safe to assume that the functions associated with such names in governments of modernized countries are those actually carried out.

This is not to suggest that in First World countries there is an exact one-to-one fit between the formal structure and image of government and the actual structure of power and influence. Inevitably discrepancies exist. For example, it is commonly recognized in the U.S. government that the office of the Presidency exerts much more influence over lawmaking than a reading of the Constitution might suggest. But the office itself, and its relations with Congress and the courts, are sufficiently institutionalized that a fairly elaborate and intricate set of understandings and expectations exist for any incumbent. This is often not the case in offices of the chief executive of the government of Third World countries.

Here we need to be more specific about the concept of "institution" and the process of "institutionalization." When we say that certain organized activities are institutionalized, we mean that they have become habitual and normal and that they endure because they are *valued* by participants and by others affected by or related to them in beneficial ways. A criminal justice system composed of police, courts, and jails becomes institutionalized because both the people employed by them and the public at large value them. This support is enough to outweigh the lack of support by those who are punished by the system. Similarly, other organizations set up to perform governmental functions by exercising legitimate power ("authority") can become infused with value and can endure as long as they are so valued. To say that an institution is valued means more than that it is wanted or desired. It means that those valuing it share some degree of consensus that it *should* or *ought* to exist, as a matter of what is "right" or "proper."

Three further points must be noted about institutions. It takes *time* for a structure of activities to be institutionalized to the degree that it will be supported and maintained beyond the time that particular individuals occupy and perform roles in them. Second, to endure, institutions have to change so as to *adapt* to changes in their *environment*. At the same time, and third, they do not merely react passively to such changes. They usually seem and are able to *influence* or *control* significant parts of their environment so as to ensure their survival.

From these comments we can gain some understanding of why some governmental organizations in Third World countries seem not to be doing what one would expect, or why they seem to lack permanence and strength. Let us take the example of a body set up as a legislature. Leaders of many newly independent nations came to power, over the last thirty-five years or so, promising to set up democratic governments. Many tried this by drafting and promulgating written constitutions modeled on those of more modernized countries of the First World. To be democratic, it was assumed, a government should have, among other things, an elected legislature. Thus the new constitutions provided for one. But two problems had to be faced. One was that many in the population had little or no understanding of elections or legislative bodies. Their conception of government may have been limited to experience with colonial officials, or to traditional chieftains or kings often supported (and manipulated) by colonial officials. This problem was not fatal; it was possible for the new government to mount a campaign of public information and propaganda and to have its supporters get large numbers of the population to turn out and vote.

The other problem was more serious. Before and at the time of independence, there may have been other contenders—rivals—for leadership. Some or all of these might be regarded by leaders currently in control, not merely as rivals, but as traitors to the national cause. Could one actually risk being defeated in an election by such people? Of course not. They could not even be allowed on the ballot. Or if, for whatever reason, they could not be excluded that way, there were other ways to assure that one's opponents would not win. (Along with other modern ideas, Third World political leaders have also learned something of the fine art of rigging elections.)

The trouble with such methods of electing legislative bodies was that people—even uneducated rural peasants—were not so stupid so as to fail to see through the charade. If they did not see through it immediately, the rivals and their supporters made every effort to ensure that they did see through it. Thus the legislative body eventually elected did not stand much chance of becoming a working, effective institution. Even supporters of the leaders who organized such elections were hardly unaware of how they had won, and so could not give unadulterated respect to this new symbol of democracy. Most of the time they adjusted to the reality that their legislative activity had to occur within limits acceptable to those wielding effective executive powers—often those assuming the title of president, sometimes military leaders. Meanwhile the opponents, seeing their path to legitimate power blocked in such a way, were sometimes persuaded that their only chance was to foment revolt aimed at overturning the new government. Not a very good start for a government whose leaders may have been sincere in their desire to institute democracy.

Not all new nations, or older nations undergoing modernization, followed paths similar to that just outlined. India and Sri Lanka, Columbia, Costa Rica, Mexico, Venezuela, Barbados, Jamaica, Cameroon, Gambia, Ivory Coast, and Senegal are examples of Third World countries that appear to have made successful beginnings toward the institutionalization of elected governments and moderately democratic politics. Several of these have experienced crises and setbacks, however, and all continue to be faced with very severe economic problems. In these countries, and all the more in other Third World countries where the form of an elected legislative body is maintained despite an almost complete lack of substance, such governmental structures have to be viewed as symbolic. Their presence may express an aspiration for popular representation in lawmaking and in checking possible excesses of executive power. Additionally, and often primarily, a docile and compliant legislature is useful as a means of legitimating decisions made by chief executives, regardless of the intentions of the latter with regard to the eventual democratization of the political system. In this sense, and whether deliberate or not, the appropriate models are the political systems of the Second World.

The importance and the power of chief executives in governments around the world reveals that such prominence is not a uniquely Third World phenomenon. What is more characteristic of Third World politics is that such powerful political leaders came into office by military *coup d'etat*, and many leave office the same way. Some of the reasons for and circumstances surrounding such military intervention have already been suggested. Here we need to inquire into variations in this pattern.

First, however, we should note that there are about a dozen hereditary monarchies or royalist governments in the Third World, in which the military are influential but subordinate to the rulers. These include such nations as Jordan, Saudi Arabia, Morocco, and Nepal. In Thailand the monarchy has been retained, but the military control the government. Such governments, generally conservative, seek to keep the disruptive forces of modernization under control through authoritarian government, some adaptation, and the guidance of economic development so as to preserve the existing socioeconomic structure.

In another twenty or so Third World countries, ranging from Mongolia, North Korea, and Vietnam in Asia, through such African countries as Angola, Benin, Ethiopia, Guinea, and Mozambique, and Algeria, Libya, and South Yemen in North Africa and the Middle East, to Cuba in the Western hemisphere, Marxist regimes led by or closely supported by military forces have won power after *coups d'etat* or guerrilla wars. Leaders of most such governments have sought to organize single parties to mobilize and control popular support. They usually receive military and economic aid from the USSR and allied East European governments. At the present stage, however, it is clear that the military forces are more important than the official parties in many such political systems, especially those in Africa. The probability of evolution toward democratic politics under such leadership was never high, and seems even slighter today.

Other military-dominated political systems of the Third World range from South Korea, Taiwan, Bangladesh, and Indonesia in Asia, through Iraq and Yemen in the Middle East and Somalia, Sudan, Uganda, and Zaire in Africa, to most Latin American countries. (In Ghana and Nigeria in Africa and Ecuador and Peru in South America, military regimes have recently handed control of government back to civilians after years of military rule.) In most of these, chief executives have relied more on armies than on political parties to sustain their rule—some have outlawed all political parties.

Some military regimes in Latin America are of particular interest; they seized power in the 1960s and '70s in countries where constitutional governments with reasonably fair and competitive elections, and effective civilian chief executives and legislative bodies, seemed to be well along toward institutionalization—although economic problems were causing instability in politics. Notable among these were Brazil, Chile, and Uruguay. In Brazil and Chile, elections had produced governments and policies that, to conservative and not so democratically disposed generals and admirals with the support of much of the upper and middle classes, appeared dangerously radical and leftist. Specifically, the position and interests of landowning, business, and financial elites were threatened. The military officers seized power in *coups d'etat* and instituted purges that included the use of uncharacteristically brutal torture of suspected leftist opponents. Many suspected opponents were killed, or simply disappeared.

In the case of Uruguay, the military intervened in a situation of a deteriorating economy, aggravated by the inability of the civilian government to suppress an urban guerrilla movement. The military regime, employing stringent measures, replaced the civilian president and eventually stamped out the guerrillas and terrorists.

These examples underline the fragility of democratic institutions where modernization has created expectations and demands that threaten the interests of well-entrenched economic elites and that in any event could probably not be satisfied through democratic processes. This creates a painful dilemma for those who see the undeniable need for fundamental economic and social change in the interest of elemental justice, but who are dedicated to orderly and legal processes for effecting change. The actions of military governments in these circumstances contribute to intensified hatreds that, in the absence of significant improvement in the socioeconomic conditions of large majorities in such countries, portend even more future violence.

Where chief executives have been or are military men, there has been at least the appearance that the person holding the office is the most powerful individual in the political system. In reality, such persons are often significantly dependent on a council of officers, whether or not such an arrangement is formalized. Moreover, the formal title of president does not provide immunity from being forcibly overthrown by a fellow officer, or by a group of them. Such has occurred both as a consequence of policy disagreements and because of the ambition of other officers. Politicizing the upper levels of the armed forces can greatly weaken the discipline of military command. To the degree that an army has become professionalized, generals often discover that the aptitudes, skills, and knowledge required for a successful military career are not the same as those required for successful political leadership. Leaders of guerrilla forces, on the other hand, are more likely to understand political leadership and can more easily function as leaders of governments. Nevertheless, nothing guarantees that either kind of leader will have much understanding of the complexities of economic policy. For this they often have to turn to people in the one set of structures that are likely to be fairly well institutionalized in Third World political systems—the civil bureaucracies.

The bureaucracies, or administrative components of government, are employers of a fairly large proportion of the professional and technically trained people in many Third World countries. Whether the product of colonial administration or of long-standing independent government, these agencies are indispensable instruments for the exercise of governmental authority. If the decisions and policies of political leaders are to be carried out, if the programs launched are to have any effect, it is the administrators who will do it.

Political leaders learn that their commands are not alone sufficient to ensure that these things will be done. They also find that they are dependent on administrators for much of the information they need for governing. Such information may be in the form of reports on the status and effects of programs. It may be in the form of technical knowledge required to plan and design such programs in the first place. The political leaders also discover that their orders and instructions are subject to much interpretation and reinterpretation as they pass downward and outward through the bureaucratic hierarchy. For all these reasons, it is often difficult for governmental leaders to accomplish what they intend. The administrative structure, in appearance nothing more than a tool for doing the government's work, is in reality a baffling network of power, resistant to change and often full of obstacles to action.

Whether political leaders seek to stimulate modernization or to channel it in desired directions, they often discover that the kind of attitudes, knowledge, and skills required is scarce in the bureaucracy. Officials experienced in collecting revenues, issuing licenses and permits, drafting regulations, and keeping voluminous files of records may find it impossible to think of innovative ways of instituting and managing developmental programs. They may lack initiative or be unwilling to take responsibility for decision making when situations require flexibility and quick decisions.

Such shortcomings as these are frequently compounded by long-standing practices of petty bribery and the exchange of favors among administrative officials as a means of getting things done. Employment by and advancement in administrative agencies may depend on complex networks of patronage and nepotism. On a larger scale, the complexity of regulations and procedures makes it possible for some administrators, who understand them from years of experience, to delay or block action—or to conceal the embezzlement of funds or engage in smuggling of contraband materials. In other words, corruption of various degrees of magnitude may be embedded in the bureaucracy. Some political leaders may wish to profit from it themselves. Others may close their eyes to it, realizing that serious efforts to root it out will drain time and energies needed for trying to bring about desired or mandated results in governmental action.

Paradoxically, conditions such as these—and they are not unusual—present problems that are the opposite of those discussed previously with reference to modernization. Bureaucracies often suffer from an excess of institutionalization. This is often linked to traditional cultural patterns and other elements of society, such as the family. Thus bureaucracies cannot be easily reoriented, nor can they be purged and repopulated by new officials because there are not enough such new people with the necessary skills and experience.

Courts of law in Third World countries, in contrast, are often more vulnerable to the political changes related to modernization. This is because, as organized structures, they are smaller in size than the complex of bureaucratic institutions. More importantly, the locus of judicial decision making is more visible. A judge, or a small panel of judges, presides at trials and renders decisions, or hears appeals from lower courts and renders decisions. Judges may delay, but eventually they must decide. Thus when political struggles break the molds of institutionalized government and become matters of sheer power and coercion, the very survival of judges and judicial institutions usually requires a keen awareness on their part of the goals and wishes of those wielding the greatest power. This can result in judicial decisions ranging from a general bias in favor of the dominant leaders and their supporters to the outright politicization of courts. In the latter event, harassment and persecution of the regime's opponents and dissidents can be given an aura of judicial legitimacy. (The politicization of courts of law is not a Third World invention. First and Second World models are provided by Nazi Germany, Fascist Italy, and the USSR. It is now standard practice for revolutionary regimes, once in control of government, to set up "revolutionary tribunals" to convict and often execute captured leaders and followers of the overthrown regime.)

The emphasis thus far given to some of the consequences of modernization should not be allowed to imply that political turmoil is constant in Third World countries. Between crises, changes of leaders, and outbreaks of civil disorder, individual countries may experience years of relative calm. During such periods, patterns of politics and governmental action proceed normally — but "normal" is of course shaped by the kinds of factors that have been discussed, and by memories of the kinds of events that have been mentioned. Depending on time and place, political discussions are often carried on with a semi-conspiratorial air, with words chosen carefully and many indirect allusions. Or, if a foreigner joins the group, the subject may be quickly changed. During such periods, the public press often provides little guidance to politically important events, and its commentary is typically supportive of the regime, for the mass media often operate under government supervision. Tourists passing through may get a few insights into the workings of the political system. If the regime is authoritarian, the tourists usually see little evidence of it.

Political parties do exist (where they are not prohibited altogether) and to varying degrees go about their work of trying to mobilize and extend their support. If there is but one party, the official one, its posters carrying pictures, symbols, and slogans are much in evidence. Many of its activities may be carried out by government employees, and the distinction between party and government may be blurred. If there are several competing parties, they are often small, with relatively little formal organization and few full-time workers. Some may be little more than loose networks of friends and relatives, inactive except at times of elections.

The country's political elite is small, and most of its members know one another personally. It includes, in addition to the top officials of the regime, high-level bureaucrats and military officers; members of wealthy business and landowning families (unless the regime happens to be Marxist), partly in but not of the elite; resident foreign business people; and cultural and intellectual figures such as editors, artists, and prominent professors. There may be leaders of important interest groups, such as importers and exporters, producers of and dealers in raw materials and export crops, or students. But interest groups are not as numerous as in more economically developed and modernized countries, and the number of distinct interests is relatively small. In the capital city, much of the social life may revolve around the embassies of foreign governments, which give frequent receptions and formal dinners.

Despite its relatively small size, the elite is not a homogeneous group of people with identical political views. A frequently found difference is that between pronationalist and proforeign groups. In time of crisis this can become bitter. Another line often distinguishes those with modern scientific, technical, and professional educations from those with more traditional educations, such as law or the liberal arts.

Usually, the urgency and critical nature of political, economic, and social problems facing the country are not much in evidence in the daily lives and the official assemblies and ceremonies or social gatherings of the elite. It is politics and business as usual—until the next crisis begins to build or the next outbreak of open struggle or public disorder. It may be tomorrow. Or it may be next year.

Futures in the Third World

The changes of modernization in the First World have had several centuries to transform traditional into predominantly modern societies. Even so, these transformations produced revolutions, civil wars, wars of independence, and great international wars, not to mention hardships forced upon the rural and urban poor. Third World political systems are having to undergo the transition — or its beginning phases — in a much briefer period. The destabilizing and exploitative effects of early modernization create revolutionary situations in which both indigenous rebels and foreign powers can seek to shape the direction of political change.

This basic problem of acceleration is intensified by three ominous trends. The first is rapid population growth, which exceeds many societies' ability to increase food production. The prospect is more famines and epidemics as population pressure on resources increases. These have already begun in the poorest Third World countries of Africa.

Second, the entire globe's natural resources, needed to sustain the First (and increasingly, the Second) World's "high technology" societies, are being depleted at dizzying rates. International struggles for access to and control of such resources by the industrial powers are likely to intensify. The Persian Gulf crisis may be repeated in other regions, with reference to other natural resources. Weaker Third World countries may well become increasingly dependent clients and pawns of the major world powers.

Third, this voracious consumption of resources is producing changes, some of them irreversible, in the earth's land surface and water. This includes the depletion of agricultural topsoil, the destruction of oxygen-producing foliage, the increased need for poisonous herbicides and insecticides, and the need for increasingly expensive (in energy conversion terms) fertilizers. Ground water levels are being lowered in industrialized regions; acid rain has become a cause of international dispute; and rivers, lakes, and even the oceans are showing serious consequences of continuing industrial pollution. In the earth's atmosphere, long-term temperature changes may already be under way as a result of smoke with chemical and particulate pollution, and solar radiation may become more dangerous because of such things as damage to ozone.

All of this leads to a pessimistic prognosis, particularly for the Third World. Much of it will never "catch up" economically with the present industrialized countries. Beyond "neocolonialism," it is conceivable that some will come again under more direct political and/or military control of rival industrial nations. But much more probable than that conjecture are the wrenching changes that face the First and Second Worlds, for they cannot escape the consequences of resource depletion and environmental damage.

Is there no basis for hope in this gloomy situation? If there is, it will have to depend on three human capacities. One is, ironically, manifested most clearly in many parts of the Third World today. It is the simple ability to continue to hope when prospects are darkest. If the hopes of Third World people for a better life can help inspire new hope in the often jaded and pessimistic

First and Second World peoples, and if all such hopes can be channeled into motivations to focus intellectual and other resources on realistic analysis of the problems we all must share, the second capacity may be more widely invigorated. It is creative ingenuity. Science and technology have helped us into this dangerous impasse; we have little else to use to find a way out. But for such ingenuity to be fruitful, the human race will have to rely on a third, still underdeveloped capacity. We will have to develop greater wisdom in managing our collective affairs than has been apparent in our history.

This will require coping with the vast, degrading, and dangerous differences in wealth between the rich and the poor nations. The benefits as well as the burdens of modern life will have to be shared more equitably. Not equally — it would not be realistic to aim at that. But more equitably is perhaps a realistic goal. It will also require both rich and poor nations to learn to do much better in conserving the resources that remain. This may call for more sacrifice, and greater changes in the way they live, on the part of the rich — and resource-consuming — nations. Insofar as science and technology offer ways out, they will have to be a more advanced science and a more humane technology. To achieve the latter will require not so much ingenuity as wisdom. For somehow, our many political systems and the people they select to guide them and support them must transcend the dangerous conflicts of power and ideology in today's world. Awareness of common problems, and efforts to identify and make meaningful the commonalities of higher goals of contending ideologies may, after millennia of recorded conflict among people, seem rather utopian. It would be indeed — if the alternative already visible were not so calamitous. For modernization has not only forced the Third World into a race with time. Inexorably, it has forced us all into the same race. The higher expressions of the human spirit — hope, creativity, and wisdom — have never faced a race so deadly. Politics as usual will no longer do.

Addendum

Notes for table 2, p. 175:

a. Classification of countries into First, Second, and Third Worlds, and within the latter, into First or Second World-oriented, or nonaligned, was guided by three criteria: (1) the claims or pronouncements of their governments; (2) the economic system in relation to government, the party system, especially whether a single communist party effectively monopolizes control of government; and (3) external trade and foreign aid relationships and/or military alliances. In some instances these indicators are mixed or unclear, and the author's not infallible judgment influenced the classification. These considerations produced the following lists:

First World: Australia, Austria, Belgium, Canada, Cyprus, Denmark, Finland, France, Germany (Federal Republic), Greece, Iceland, Ireland, Israel, Italy, Japan, Luxembourg, Malta, Netherlands, New Zealand, Norway, Portugal, Spain, Sweden, Switzerland, United Kingdom, and United States.

Second World: Albania, Bulgaria, Cambodia, China, Cuba, Czechoslovakia, Germany (Democratic Republic), Hungary, Korea (Democratic People's Republic), Laos, Mongolia, Poland, Romania, Union of Soviet Socialist Republics, Vietnam, Yugoslavia.

Third World (with First World orientation): Argentina, Bahamas, Bahrain, Barbados, Bolivia, Botswana, Brazil, Burundi, Cameroon, Cape Verde, Central African Republic, Chad, Chile, China (Republic), Colombia, Comoros, Costa Rica, Djibouti, Dominican Republic, Ecuador, Egypt, El Salvador, Equatorial Guinea, Fiji, Gabon, Gambia, Ghana, Guatemala, Guinea-Bissau, Guyana, Haiti, Honduras, Indonesia, Ivory Coast, Jamaica, Jordan, Kenya, Korea (Republic), Kuwait, Lebanon, Lesotho, Liberia, Madagascar, Malawi, Malaysia, Maldives, Mali, Mauritius, Mexico, Morocco, Nicaragua, Niger, Nigeria, Oman, Pakistan, Panama, Papua New Guinea, Paraguay, Peru, Philippines, Qatar, Rwanda, St. Lucia, St. Vincent and the Grenadines, Samoa, Saudi Arabia, Senegal, Sierra Leone, Singapore, Solomon Islands, Somalia, South Africa, Sudan, Suriname, Swaziland, Tanzania, Thailand, Togo, Trinidad and Tobago, Tunisia, Turkey, Uganda, United Arab Emirates, Upper Volta, Uruguay, Venezuela, Yemen, Zaire, Zimbabwe.

Third World (with Second World orientation): Afghanistan, Algeria, Angola, Benin, Congo, Ethiopia, Grenada, Guinea, Iraq, Libya, Mozambique, South Yemen, Syria.

Third World (nonaligned): Bangladesh, Bhutan, Burma, India, Iran, Mauretania, Nepal, Sri Lanka, Zambia.

Twelve "minicountries," each with a population of less than 100,000 (and a combined population of less than 500,000) are not included in this analysis. They are Andorra, Dominica, Kiribati, Liechtenstein, Monaco, Nauru, San Marino, São Tomé and Principe, Seychelles, Tonga, Tuvalu, and the Vatican.

b. The four categories (very rich, rich, poor, and very poor) are based on per capita income as indicated by the figures in parentheses after each such label. Distortion is greatest in the "very poor" category where no less than 58 countries have per capita incomes of less than $500. Also, 6 Third World countries are classified as very rich or rich only because oil revenues give them high per capita incomes. These are Gabon, Kuwait, Libya, Qatar, Saudi Arabia, and the United Arab Emirates. However, their combined and weighted PQLI is only 37, indicating that these new riches have not yet been transformed into much improvement in living conditions for the bulk of their populations. For example, the PCI of Qatar is $12,500 (highest in the world; the United States is $8,612); but Qatar's PQLI is 32, while that of the United States is 95.

c. All percentages and averages are rounded to the nearest whole number, except for those less than 1.

d. Averages for each category are weighted by the population of each country in that category so that the figures given reflect numbers of people rather than numbers of countries.

SUGGESTIONS FOR ADDITIONAL READING

APTER, DAVID E. *The Politics of Modernization.* Chicago: University of Chicago Press, 1965.

BINDER, LEONARD, ET AL. *Crises and Sequences in Political Development.* Princeton: Princeton University Press, 1971.

BLACK, C. E. *The Dynamics of Modernization.* New York: Harper & Row, 1967.

FANON, FRANTZ. *The Wretched of the Earth.* New York: Grove Press, 1956.

HOROWITZ, IRVING LOUIS. *Three Worlds of Development.* New York: Oxford University Press, 1966.

HUNTINGTON, SAMUEL P. *Political Order in Changing Societies.* New Haven: Yale University Press, 1968.

INKELES, ALEX, and SMITH, DAVID H. *Becoming Modern.* Cambridge, Mass.: Harvard University Press, 1974.

MESAROVIC, MIHAJLO, and PESTEL, EDUARD. *Mankind at the Turning Point.* New York: Dutton/Reader's Digest, 1974.

RIGGS, FRED W. *Administration in Developing Countries.* Boston: Houghton Mifflin, 1964.

TAYLOR, C.L., and HUDSON, M.C. *World Handbook of Political and Social Indicators.* 3rd ed. New Haven: Yale University Press, 1981.

WARD, BARBARA. *The Rich Nations and the Poor Nations.* New York: Norton, 1962.

Index

About the Authors

ALEX N. DRAGNICH received his bachelor's degree from the University of Washington and his master's and doctor's degrees from the University of California at Berkeley. He taught at Western Reserve University before going to Vanderbilt University in 1950 where he was professor of political science and for four years chairman of the department. In 1978 he became professor emeritus and for three years thereafter he was with the Hoover Institution at Stanford University. He is the author of *Tito's Promised Land, Major European Governments, Serbia, Nikola Pasic, and Yugoslavia,* and *The Development of Parliamentary Government in Serbia.*

JOHN T. DORSEY, JR. received his undergraduate and graduate degrees from the University of Alabama and also studied as a Fulbright scholar at the University of Paris. From 1953 to 1961 he taught at Michigan State University and in 1961 he went to Vanderbilt University where he is now a professor of political science. He has been a visiting professor at the Fundação Escola de Sociologia e Politica de São Paulo in Brazil. Professor Dorsey has contributed chapters to several books, including *Government and Politics,* and is the author of articles in American and foreign journals.

TAKETSUGU TSURUTANI received his doctorate from the University of Wisconsin in Madison in 1966. Prior to joining Washington State University in Pullman in 1969, where he is now a professor of political science, he taught at the University of Maine in Orono and the University of Nevada at Las Vegas. In 1979-80 he was a Rockefeller Foundation Fellow in International Relations and wrote *Japanese Policy and East Asian Security.* He is also the author of *Politics of National Development: Political Leadership in Transitional Societies* and *Political Change in Japan: Response to Postindustrial Challenge.*